ENVIRONMENTAL COOPERATION IN EUROPE

IN EUROPE

The Political Dimension

edited by OTMAR HÖLL

Westview Press

Boulder • San Francisco • Oxford

Austrian Institute for International Affairs Series

Published in 1994 in the United States of America by Westview Press, Inc., 5500 Central Avenue, Boulder, Colorado 80301-2877, and in the United Kingdom by Westview Press, 36 Lonsdale Road, Summertown, Oxford OX2 7EW

Library of Congress Cataloging-in-Publication Data
Environmental cooperation in Europe : the political dimension / edited by Otmar Höll.
    p.   cm. — (Austrian Institute for International Affairs series)
    Includes bibliographical references.
    ISBN 0-8133-8622-5
    1. Environmental policy—Eastern Economic Community countries—Congresses.   2. Environmental policy—Europe—Congresses.
3. Environmental policy—International cooperation—Congresses.
4. Environmental law—European Economic Community countries—Congresses.   5. Environmental law—Europe—Congresses.
6. Regionalism—Europe—Congresses.   I. Höll, Otmar.   II. Series.
HC240.9.E5E59   1994
363.7'0094—dc20   94-33962
                                                                         CIP

This book was typeset by Susanna Mai, AIIA.

Printed and bound in the United States of America

⊗   The paper used in this publication meets the requirements
    of the American National Standard for Permanence of Paper
    for Printed Library Materials Z39.48-1984.

10   9   8   7   6   5   4   3   2   1

Contents

Acknowledgments

This volume is the product of a two-day conference on the political dimension of environmental cooperation in Europe, held in Vienna in November 1991. The authors — scientists and ecological experts from various European countries — represent a great variety of knowledge and experience. In light of the discussions at the conference they have revised and updated their papers.

Thanks are due to the Ministry of Science and Research, the Ministry for Environment, Youth, and Family, and the Austrian Federal Chancellery for their financial support and the housing of the conference. I also want to thank Monika Stepanovsky and Hanspeter Neuhold for their help in organizing the conference and finalizing the volume, Wendy Caron and Edith Wegscheider for linguistic and editorial work, and, last but not least, Susanna Mai, whose strength and patience in processing the manuscripts was indispensable for the publication of this book.

Otmar Höll

Abbreviations and Acronyms

A	Austria
ACE	Action for the Environment Program
AOSIS	Alliance of Small Island States
ARGE	Arbeitsgemeinschaft (working community)
AS	Austrian schilling
ASCEND 21	Agenda of Science for Environment and Development into the 21st Century
B	Belgium
BAT	best available technology
CCMS	Committee on the Challenges of Modern Society
CEDAR	Central European Data Request Facility
CEI	Central European Initiative
CEN	European Committee for Standardization
CFC	chlorofluorocarbon
CH	Switzerland
CIS	Commonwealth of Independent States
CMEA/ COMECON	Council of Mutual Economic Assistance
CITES	Convention on International Trade in Endangered Species of Wild Fauna and Flora
CS	Czechoslovakia
CSCE	Conference on Security and Cooperation in Europe
CSD	Commission on Sustainable Development
CSFR	Czech and Slovak Federative Republic
D	Deutschland (Germany)
DESD	Department of Social and Economic Development
DM	Deutsche mark
DNA	desoxyribonucleic acid

E	España (Spain)
EBRD	European Bank of Reconstruction and Development
EC	European Community
ECE	Economic Commission for Europe
ECOSOC	Economic and Social Committee
ECU	European Currency Unit
EEC	European Economic Community
EFTA	European Free Trade Association
EIA	Environmental Impact Assessment
EIB	European Investment Bank
EIS	Europe Environment Information Service
EMEP	European Monitoring and Evaluation Program
F	France
FAO	Food and Agriculture Organization
FF	French franc
FPÖ	Freiheitliche Partei Österreichs (Freedom Party)
FRG	Federal Republic of Germany
GATT	General Agreement on Tariffs and Trade
GB	Great Britain
GDP	gross domestic product
GDR	German Democratic Republic
GEF	Global Environment Facility
GNB	Gabcikovo-Nagymaros barrage system
GNP	gross national product
G-7	Group of 7
G-77	Group of 77
H	Hungary
HELCOM	Helsinki Commission
HELCOM PITF	Helsinki Commission Program Implementation Task Force
I	Italy
IADB	Inter-American Development Bank
IAEA	International Atomic Energy Agency
ICCR	Interdisciplinary Centre for Comparative Research in the Social Sciences
ICSU	International Council of Scientific Unions
IDA	International Development Association

IEEP	Institute for European Environmental Policy
IEW	International Energy Workshop
IIASA	International Institute for Applied Systems Analysis
ILO	International Labor Organization
IMF	International Monetary Fund
IMO	International Maritime Organization
IPCC	Intergovernmental Panel on Climatic Change
ISO	International Standards Organization
LDC	least developed countries
LIFE	community financial instrument for the environment
LRTAP	Long-Range Transboundary Air Pollution
MEDSPA	Mediterranean Special Program of Action
METAP	Mediterranean Technical Assistance Program
NATO	North Atlantic Treaty Organization
NDC	newly democratizing country
NEFCO	Nordic Countries' Environmental Fund
NGO	nongovernmental organization
NIEO	New International Economic Order
NL	Netherlands
NSA	National Security Agency
NORSPA	North Sea Special Program of Action
ODA	Official Development Assistance
OECD	Organization of Economic Co-operation and Development
ÖNORM	Österreichische Norm
ÖVP	Österreichische Volkspartei (Austrian People's Party)
PE	population equivalent
PHARE	Pologne-Hongrie Actions pour la Reconversion Economique
PL	Poland
R	Rumania
RAINS	Regional Acidification Information and Simulation
REC	Regional Environmental Center for Central and Eastern Europe
SCAR	Scientific Committee on Antarctic Research of the International Council of Scientific Unions
SEA	Single European Act

SEK	Swedish krona
SOP	Society for the Protection of Nature
SPÖ	Sozialdemokratische Partei Österreichs (Social Democratic Party of Austria)
TACIS	Technical Assistance for the CIS
TEMPUS	Trans-European Mobility Scheme for University Studies
UN	United Nations
UNCED	United Nations Conference on Environment and Development
UNCTAD	United Nations Conference on Trade and Development
UNDP	United Nations Development Program
UNEP	United Nations Environment Program
UNCED	United Nations Conference on Environment and Development
USSR	Union of Soviet Socialist Republics
US$	US dollar
VOC	volatile organic compounds
WRI	World Resources Institute
WMO	World Meteorological Organization
WWF	World Wide Fund for Nature
YU	Yugoslavia

Introduction

Otmar Höll

The international dimension of environmental problems has long been apparent, whether transboundary emissions stemming from industrial pollution, the degrading water quality of shared rivers, or the pollution of oceans. Most of today's environmental degradation of the environment can be traced back to centuries before, when the degree of pollution was, in local contexts, even higher. There was more dirt and soot in the air and almost unrestrained waste disposal into the water of industrial cities in the 19th century. Thus, a higher proportion of intestinal diseases was evident at that time. But normally these problems had no or only little impact on regional or even global ecosystems. Pollution of the global environment gradually became an enduring concern in the second half of the 20th century.

Since the beginning of the 1960s interest has been growing among scholars, concerned citizens' groups, and policy makers in environmental theories and alternative economic and political strategies. Yet, the scale and extent of environmental problems have increased dramatically since then as a result of rapidly growing industrial production processes, an increasing amount of fossil-fuel consumption, and — especially in the South — as a consequence of poverty and population growth. It is a well-known fact that in this century up to now the global consumption of fossil fuels has grown by a factor of thirty and industrial production by a factor of fifty. Most of that growth, about four-fifths, has occurred since 1950. Taking into account the tremendous differences in economic and social development between individual countries and between the various regions of the world, the industrialized countries of the North represent not only more than two-thirds of the total world gross domestic product (GDP) and two-thirds of world trade, but this region also accounts for more than three-quarters of the world's pollution and is the heaviest consumer of natural resources, above all, energy. This has placed a heavy responsibility on the industrialized countries for environmental protection, the efficient use of natural resources both in a regional context and with regard to their technological and financial capabilities, and the solution of global environmental problems.

The tremendous increase in the extent of manufactured environmental degradation, together with an inadequate understanding of ecological processes, makes it clear that nature and the environment must no longer be seen as an *external* or *free* factor of economic development. Pollution has become a threat to human health *and* the whole biosphere. Interaction between economic production, social consumption, and complex ecosystems has become a major issue on the international agenda because of its transboundary character.

At the 1972 United Nations Conference on Human Environment (UNCHE) in Stockholm the *environment* was considered for the very first time a "global issue" by a broad international public. The subsequent creation of the United Nations Environment Program (UNEP) established environmental protection as an internationally accepted issue. This conference[1] was the first in a series of United Nations (UN) meetings throughout the 1970s that set out to challenge the postwar era perception of the world as an open space without charge, where societies and nations individually strive to maximize their material welfare standard. At that time the comprehension of an interdependent world system, operating under a number of common constraints, took hold.

Since then, several regional and international environmental treaties have come into force and considerable attention has been given to identifying the causes of the growing degradation of the environment, to analyzing long-term consequences, and to developing response strategies. However, taking into account the increasing concern for environmental problems expressed at scientific meetings and international conferences and by the mass media, and considering the growing concern from politicians, comparatively little has been achieved so far. In fact, since the early 1970s new major threats have arisen.

Keeping this poor record in mind, the prospects for effective international environmental cooperation are modest indeed. The dichotomy between the ever-increasing economic and ecological interdependence of states and soci-

---

1. The background philosophy of the conference can be found in a book published by Barbara Ward and René Dubos, *Only One Earth: The Care and Maintenance of a Small Planet*, New York (1972). The perception of the problem at that time was more or less anthropocentric, nature being understood as a resource for human use. The value attributed to ecosystems was that which can be defined by humans. At the same time an alternative school of thought gained prominence, in which nature is seen as a superior whole with inalienable rights and humans are but a component of the biosphere who must accept ecological constraints in order to ensure continuation of the whole system.

eties, on the one hand, and the fragmentation of the international system of more or less sovereign states, on the other hand, is the reason for the lack of real improvement. The anarchical structure of the international system and the special character of environmental problems that make them difficult for politicians to deal with,[2] fuel a vicious spiral of insecurity and mistrust that seems to make cooperation among nations all but impossible. In this sense environmental issues cut across all categories of political and/or private realms, another reason that makes them difficult for the political sector to handle properly.

This is especially true at the international level. Despite major changes and the increasing importance of international organizations, the structure of the international political system continues to rest primarily upon the independent and autonomous stance of states and therefore on a broad spectrum of different socioeconomic capacities and interests which this entails. The internationalization of environmental problems seems to be the most striking characteristic of the 1980s debate. The depletion of the ozone layer, the warming up of the atmosphere by greenhouse gases, and the rapid loss of biological diversity do not respect national boundaries or welfare societies: these are global threats that cannot be overcome by any single nation.

The publication of the Brundtland Report in 1987 and the United Nations Conference on Environment and Development (UNCED) 1992 in Rio brought a change in the global ecosystems' approach. The report announced the necessity to integrate development and concern for the environment. This change of perspective is best captured by the introduction of the term *sustainable development*, which quickly became the catchphrase of the late 1980s. Sustainable development, described in the Brundtland report as a "development which corresponds to the needs of the present generation without jeopardizing the options for the later generations of satisfying their own needs and choosing their life style," was regarded as endangered because of the unsustainable industrial production in the North and the poverty of the "underdeveloped" societies of the South. Deforestation of rain forests and desertification processes in the South quickly identified the "developing world" as the main agent of global destruction. The claim to abolish poverty, however, did not find its equivalent in removing the ever-increasing industrial production of the North; but, on the contrary, the global environment could only be protected through a new era of *sustainable growth*. Without going

---

2. The atypical character of environmental issues is that environmental stresses often do not touch people's lives for a rather long period of time. Their impact may be hard to pinpoint and their causes hard to trace. Multiple causes may result in major and unpredictable degradation.

into detail about the outcomes of UNCED[3] the conference itself must be characterized as an ambivalent undertaking. From the side of the industrialized countries, the conference was regarded as an environmental conference; from the side of the developing countries, the expectations were more on improving development. The "marriage" of environment and development was never really on the table in Rio.

There is good reason to believe that better results could be achieved, if nations tried to cooperate first at the regional level.[4] And that is what this publication is about. Europe, being one of the world's most industrialized regions with a high level of population density, is confronted with a constantly increasing degradation of its natural environment. Since the breakdown of Communist regimes in Eastern Europe it has become obvious that the extent of environmental degradation in the region had been highly underestimated. In addition, environmental awareness has been growing, especially in Western Europe, and has become an increasingly important political factor. Considering the unity of Europe's ecological environment, national policies and international cooperation must be analyzed.

It is the aim of the authors of this volume to take stock of the present state of environmental degradation from theoretical (Mayer-Tasch, v. Prittwitz, Sand) and empirical point of views (Döös, Freudenschuss). Particular emphasis is given to Europe in the respective fields in which action is very urgent. Particular attention has been given to international organizations and institutions in Europe that deal with ecological problems (Hull, Bongaerts)

---

3. A short analytical summary of the outcomes of the Rio Conference and texts of the three documents that emerged from the UNCED process and the two conventions presented for signature on the occasion of the Rio meeting, have been published in Stanley B. Johnson (ed.), *The Earth Summit: The United Nations Conference on Environment and Development*, London/Dordrecht/-Boston (1993). Cf. also the contribution of Irene Freudenschuss (Chapter 3 in this book).

4. The meeting of European Environmental Ministers in Lucerne (Switzerland), on April 28-30, 1993, that led to the agreement on a strategy for an "Environmental Action Program for Central and Eastern Europe" was a follow-up to the first "Environment for Europe" Conference held in Dobris (former Czechoslovakia) in 1991. The meeting concluded with a ministerial declaration that calls on central and eastern European governments to undertake essential policy and institutional reforms and provide resources for actions and investment, while western governments, the EC and others should intensify their support for (environmentally sound) reforms. One important outcome, e.g., was the consensus among delegations on using taxation as a measure to reduce CO_2 emissions. The next ministerial conference on "Environment for Europe" will be held in Sofia (Bulgaria) in 1995.

and case studies on regional environmental cooperation such as the Baltic region (Kohonen, Amann), the Nordic Council (Ågren), and Central Europe (Potyka, Hardi, Vargha) were integrated. The special features of specific environmental negotiating processes and their results are also described (Lang, Sjöstedt). Two contributions focus on the characteristics of international environmental law and the adequacy of the normative solutions provided by it (Bothe, Hafner). Finally, national political processes are presented in a comparative perspective (Lauber, Berrini, Höll). In their contributions the authors try to find some answers, taking into account relevant socioeconomic factors in national environmental policies.

Opening Remarks

Franz Vranitzky

If one analyzes public opinion it will become clear that within the last years people's fears and expectations with regard to their security have fundamentally changed. People are, for instance, much less afraid of *outside military* aggression. They have become concerned about *internal* conflicts or ethnic problems that escalate to violent confrontation — the situation in Yugoslavia offers a good example in this respect. But mainly their fears take a different direction, and the fear of environmental devastation and its immediate effects on peoples' lives rank very high on the list of concerns.

States and governments are therefore faced with new demands in this sphere and also with demands for new forms of international cooperation to cope with them. Thus, within a relatively short time, in parallel to this growing concern about the environment, we also find a growing consciousness that the international community has to *respond* to this concern and develop a framework to deal with these problems.

Many institutions and organizations have already taken up the issue, and I am glad that the Austrian Institute for International Affairs has brought together so many distinguished experts to discuss the future possibilities for environmental cooperation. As President of the Institute, as well as on the behalf of the Austrian government, I bid you welcome to this conference.

I have intentionally chosen "security" as my starting point because I am fully convinced that our concern for the environment and for environmental protection can only be met successfully, if one takes a very comprehensive view of the issue. In my view, sound environmental policies are thus an integral part of security policy. They are part of the overall quality of life, of the general well-being of a society. They cannot be separated from sound and *economic* policies, and we have to regard the environment as an economic resource and to pay attention to the new demands on and obligations to our economies in this respect.

Modern economies are basically about the fact that they produce *more with less,* that they achieve *higher productivity* and higher output by using always *less* resources, with less physical labor, by using all options of recycling, and the like. It is only a flourishing and well-developed economy that will be able to meet the sometimes very costly demands of environmentally acceptable production methods. On the other hand, in a market-oriented system, economies produce what people want, and people today do want and do care about a cleaner environment. One of the many aspects of the disastrous economic development in the former Communist countries is that they have not learned this lesson — that they tried to maintain capital-intensive, labor-intensive, and resource-intensive industries, which were economically as well as environmentally damaging.

On the other side, we cannot accept a development in which a clean environment becomes the privilege or the luxury of the wealthy. We cannot ignore the fact that the greatest environmental problems exist in the countries of the Third World where they block further development and become an additional and very real threat to the already damaged situations of these countries. Environmental and development policies, therefore, have to go hand in hand. It is a good indicator for the international awareness of this link that the World Bank, for instance, now demands an environmental impact statement for every major investment. On the same basis, Austria attached great importance to the UNCED held in June 1992 in Rio de Janeiro.

Upon my initiative a group of distinguished scientists and experts drafted a proposal for an International Environmental Charter which consists of three parts. Part one deals with the biosphere in general, its selfregulatory capabilities and the limits thus set for human activities. Part two contains basic objectives and guiding principles on environmental management, and part three sets out priority areas of action. I presented this proposal for the first time in October 1990 to a conference of the Parliamentary Assembly of the European Council dealing with environmental protection in the East-West context.

I also submitted this proposal to the Secretary General of UNCED '92, Mr. Maurice F. Strong, expressing my hope that it may serve as a major input to the Earth Charter/Rio-Declaration on Environment and Development. I am pleased that the Austrian proposal has been well received and that some major aspects have been incorporated in the Rio-Declaration on Environment and Development.

Nongovernmental contributions to UNCED '92 proved also to be extremely important. Austria promoted Non Governmental Organization (NGO) participation in the preparatory process and therefore hosted the International Council of Scientific Unions' (ICSU) preparatory conference on an "Agenda of Science for Environment and Development into the 21st Century" (ASCEND 21) in Vienna. This conference brought together renowned scientists from North and South, East and West, from various disciplines and backgrounds. The results of this conference served as the input of the scientific community to UNCED '92.

Of course I am aware of the problem that despite serious and intensive preparations UNCED '92 did not meet all expectations. We were all moving on new and unchartered ground. We are at the beginning of creating a cooperative framework, a kind of environmental law that will regulate the activities and the obligations of states. This demands a lot of new thinking, and also calls on the cooperation of countries that are not themselves immediately affected by environmental damage. It is in the nature of global challenges that each and everyone has to contribute to possible solutions. Austria is thus committed to play an active role in the follow-up process of UNCED '92.

On the other side, the international community has always been resourceful and creative in responding to new demands; think, for instance, of the relatively quick development of space law to accompany the progress made in space research and in technological capabilities. I am thus confident that we will also find the appropriate answer for what is truly one of the most pressing global problems of our time.

PART ONE

The Globalization of
Environmental Problems

1

Europe and the Atlantic Community in the Context of an Ecological World Order

Peter Cornelius Mayer-Tasch

1. Introduction

On September 13 and 14 in the year 1515, the armies of Francis I of France and the Swiss Confederation were locked in combat over the Duchy of Milan not far from the little Lombard town of Marignano. When the Swiss generals became aware that they would prove no match for the superior power of the French, they called mass ranks and sounded the retreat.[1] If historical accounts are to be trusted, this retreat became an act of greatness; taking not only the wounded, but also the flags and weapons they had captured, the Swiss left the battlefield in a rectangular formation — closed without and open within, heads held high and *mit werhaftiger handt* (hands raised to parry).[2] This was an "orderly retreat" par excellence, which simultaneously proclaimed the orderly retreat of the confederation from the European scene of might, night, and fight and heralded a policy of neutrality, which is soon to mark its half millennium, and which has shielded this people from much damage and destruction.

---

1. For a detailed account of the history of Marignano see Hans-Rudolf Kurz, *Schweizerschlachten,* Berne (1962), pp. 196 ff.; and Georg Thürer, *Die Wende von Marignano,* Zurich (1965), pp. 32 ff.

2. Cf. the chronicle of Ludwig Schwinkhart covering the period from 1506–1521 (1539), edited by Hans von Greyerz by order of the Historical Society of the Canton of Berne, Berne (1941/1942), p. 179.

If this episode of legendary greatness, captured in a colorful fresco 400 years later by Ferdinand Hodler,[3] remains in my memory, it is because Marignano seems to offer a meaningful paradigm of what is facing the nations of the world today, above all the industrialized nations with their multidimensional dominance (with the Atlantic alliance once more to the fore, still calling the tune). This paradigm is evident at a time of the free market economy's worldwide triumph over planned economy and of the disintegration of the Eastern bloc, at a time of increasing convergence within Europe and a show of power in the Middle East in a world helplessly dependent on oil; all the signs appear to point to nothing less than retreat. The popular slogan coined with reference to Germany's highways, "Free roads for free citizens," seems to have turned into a kind of global motto of the dynamics of civilization. However, that invisible hand, which promised in Adam Smith's hopeful vision to bring "the arbitrariness of the one" into accord with "the arbitrariness of the other, according to a universal law of freedom" (Immanuel Kant),[4] evidently has more important things to do; it is untiring in carving new signs into the palace walls of our neo-Babylonian global society founded on socio-political, socio-economic and socio-ecological exploitation. There are, as we all know, unmistakable signs of disaster. Even before the threshold of the third millennium, the modern *Homo faber's* thousand-year battle to conquer an earthly, *more geometrica* paradise appears to have been lost once and for all. Whether this is true, whether salvation and good can still be expected from the retreat of the combatants of progress from their brand of civilization, or whether all that remains is to take up position in Utopia's curio cabinet, these are the topics which receive attention in the following sections.

2. The Lost Battle: Is There a Future?

The modern struggle over a progressive technological and economic paradise seems to have been lost for all members of global society — for the upper class in North America, Europe, and Japan; for the middle class in Asia; and for the lower class in Africa and Latin America. Lost, what is more, under mutually reinforcing economic, ecological, and (power) political condi-

---

3. The fresco *The Retreat of Marignano,* painted in 1990, can be seen in the armory of the Swiss National Museum in Zurich.

4. Immanuel Kant, *Metaphysik der Sitten: Einleitung in die Rechtslehre,* Chapter C, margin numbers 38–40.

tions. An initial outline of the foreseeable anabasis of our dynamics of civilization — scene: the world — may be drawn by examining the Atlantic Treaty partners (Western) Europe and the United States.

2.1 The Wealth Paradox

Considering first the economic aspect, it may sound strange to speak of a lost battle at a time when the average material standard of living in the industrialized nations is higher than ever before in the known history of humanity, and all countries with developing industries or with none at all aspire to reach this road to success. It is not necessary to be reminded that cycles are at the heart of the most ancient of human wisdom — as described, for example, in the Chinese *Book of Changes* (I Ching),[5] the oldest book of wisdom in the world whose underlying structure, according to the latest scientific findings,[6] corresponds to that of Desoxyribonucleic Acid (DNA). The facts supported by "common sense" speak for themselves:

In the first few centuries of that intense struggle of modern science and technology to extend the human power of life — *scientia et potentia*, as Francis Bacon wrote in his *Novum Organum*[7] — and thus also the struggle to raise the material standard of living, all efforts bore only modest fruit in Europe. The wealth of the few (approximately 10 percent) was countered by the poverty of the many (about 90 percent). It is true that between the mid-15th and mid-19th centuries a number of labor-saving and productivity-increasing machines were invented and put to use. The twofold yoke of dwindling resources and population growth — both caused partly by this situation, which in its turn was the inspiration for technological innovation — turned this development into a race between the tortoise and the hare.[8] Only at the tail end of the Industrial Revolution during the 18th and 19th centuries, made possible not least of all by energy, did the material prosperity of a middle class spreading slowly in Europe and faster in the USA, begin to show continuous growth. Europe, the USA, and Japan, with growth rates of between 2.5 per-

---

5. The most convincing German translation is given by Friedrich Wilhelm, Cologne and Düsseldorf (1956).

6. Cf. Frank Fiedler, *Die Wende, Ansatz einer genetischen Anthropologie nach dem System des I Ging,* Berlin (1976), and recently; Katya Walter, *Chaosforschung, 3-Ging und genetischer Code: Das Tao des Chaos,* Munich (1992).

7. "Scientia et potentia in idem coincidunt," *Novum Organum,* Book 1, I, 3.

8. Cf. among others Marvin Harris, *Cannibals and Kings. The Origins of Cultures,* New York (1978), pp. 249 ff.

cent and 5 percent, are today's high priests of progress moving on the platform of the economic sun pyramid.

It is a well-known fact that upon the sun pyramid sharp knives were flashed, and that the sacrificers found it easier to advance than those they sacrificed.[9] Thus the economic success story of Europe (and, to a lesser extent, the USA, owing to its larger quantities of natural resources) is a story concerning the provision, sacrifice and utilization of victims. The account of this rapid advance, which took some 150 years, was also an account of the military rule and economic exploitation of most of the rest of the world by the high priests of progress and their countless assistants — basking first in the vindicating glow of Christianity, then in that of progress. Recently, this advance seems to have become more difficult, and in the future it will probably become even more so, if not impossible. If it retains its widespread success, the sacrificers will be driven to suicide on their own sacrificial altars.

The present-day wealth of the rich is created not least by the exchange of logistics (high-tech), machinery, weapons, and chemicals for raw materials and (luxury) foodstuffs from the poorer and poorest countries. The economies of the poorer and the poorest, opened up during colonial times with the use of armed force and cunning and now largely adapted to the export and import needs of the rich, and the economies of the rich, specifically adapted to this exchange, are the scene of a gigantic matériel battle; this battle has been described in the headline as "world economic system."[10] That the battle is lost and that the world economic system as it stands today "has no future" (to quote the poet Ludwig Fels[11]), has two main causes which influence and permeate each other. Firstly, economic actors on the world stage are exposed to increasing competition from new arrivals who dispute their right to a place in the sun. Secondly, as a side effect of their definition of the fairness of exchange, the current economic actors' wherewithal with which to continue practicing such a right — economic, and thus in the end economic and political-power wherewithal — is fast disappearing.

As far as the question of competition goes, from a European point of view the USA was the first to emancipate itself and, later, to take part in the game. From the viewpoint of the Atlantic alliance Japan was upstart number

---

9. Cf. also Marvin Harris, op. cit. (footnote 8), pp. 99 ff.

10. Cf. particularly Bernd M. Malunat, *Weltnatur und Staatenwelt: Gefahren unter dem Gesetz der Ökonomie,* Osnabrück (1988), pp. 69 ff. passim; and Peter J. Opitz (ed.), *Weltprobleme,* 3rd. edition, Bonn (1990), pp. 145 ff. (article by Wesel), pp. 179 ff. (article by Nida-Rümelin), pp. 201 ff. (article by von Pilgrim), pp. 231 ff. (article by Franzmeyer), and pp. 269 ff. (article by Büttner).

11. Thus in the (unpublished) poem *Fall.* Cf. on this Peter C. Mayer-Tasch (ed.), *Im Gewitter der Geraden: Deutsche Ökolyrik,* Munich (1980), p. 25.

two. Nowadays not only the so-called four little tiger states — South Korea, Taiwan, Hong Kong and Singapore — but also Indonesia, Malaysia and Thailand are hard on their heels. And others will follow, including the painfully developing market economies in Eastern Europe, which as planned economies had played the game too clumsily and thus were forced to leave the biggest piece of pie to the "capitalists." In any case, a common characteristic of the developing countries as they make future appearances on the world market will be that they will no longer agree to exchange modalities of the past; they will put their faith in extensive self-sufficiency, mainly in vital sectors such as agriculture. The economic scope of the old rich will thus become increasingly limited — a development which will also be expressed in their increasingly ruthless competition among themselves. The USA's fear of competition from Japan and from the European Community with Germany as its "economic head of steam" is well known. The National Security Agency (NSA), the Pentagon's subordinate, is said to have recently stepped up its activities in economic espionage, among other areas of interest.

However, all these efforts will provide only limited long-term help for the industrial countries. Not only is there an ever-increasing number of competitors, not only will a growing number of markets previously maltreated during the neo-colonial period restructure themselves, but the continuation of present economic practices, with all their ecological side effects, will pile a burden of reparation and compensation onto the industrial nations far exceeding their capacity to pay. This upper class of the community of states represents approximately 25 percent of the world's population, but uses about 75 percent of the energy produced in the world — and uses it in frequently outrageous relations. In the USA, for example, which has the highest per capita energy consumption in the world, David Pimentel of Cornell University has worked out that the production of 100 grams of beef, with a caloric value of 270, requires the expenditure of 22,000 calories; the production of a can of corn, also containing 270 calories, requires only 2,790 calories.[12] That such a profligate society can have no future is evident not only in the USA's nose-diving balance of trade, but also in the research calculations which have assessed that all the world's oil reserves known today would be exhausted within 10 years or so if the rest of the world decided to adopt the energy consumption typical of present-day American agriculture.

There is another reason why this kind of energy-based society has no future; energy consumption is also a measure of effects on ecology, and in the future the remedies needed to rectify such effects will be financially beyond reach (quite apart from the effects being only partly remediable and from

12. Cf. "Expert Says Only Hope to Feed World Is with Food Production Unlike That in US" *NY Times,* December 8, 1976.

their further implications). The situation in Germany, aspiring with all its might to emulate America in terms of energy consumption, may throw some light on this situation. According to the calculations of the Institute for Environmental Research and Prognoses in Heidelberg, presented in late 1990, the socio-ecological costs — that is, ecological damage plus the social effects of that damage — for the then Federal Republic of Germany in 1989 totalled some DM 475 billion, compared with an annual budget of between DM 260 billion and DM 280 billion.[13] That these figures, so deeply in the red, are not a sign of immediate economic bankruptcy is solely because nature is still carrying our debts for us — that she has granted us a reprieve before the (even more inevitable) collapse. Then economic and ecological bankruptcy will coincide.

2.2 The Necessity to Change

This hopeless viewpoint has brought me to the ecological aspect of the battle astrology ahead. I have already emphasized that this aspect has enormous economic implications; however, its existential implications are even more momentous. As everyone must know by now, the matter at stake is not merely the chance of a good life,[14] declared by Aristotle to be the goal of all politics, but plainly and simply the chance of survival. Striving and living go hand-in-hand, a truism which is overlooked perhaps precisely because it is so evident. Anyone whose eyes are fixed only on the goal and not on the path is bound to stumble. In our quest for a good life we are in the process of forfeiting life itself.

Mobility and stability, growth and stagnation are mysteriously related. Our very existence depends on movement, yet we find again and again that our inability to stop at the right moment endangers — or could endanger — our existence. The old saying *festina lente* ("more haste, less speed") gives this dialectic principle a new status as a rule of human behavior; it has been well documented in biology in the laws of survival of ecosystems. This wisdom admittedly has no place in growth rates and growth targets, and especially not in those of the industrial nations. For example, at the annual economic growth rate of 4 percent partly attained and partly aspired to in the Federal Republic of Germany (FRG), the country's gross national product

---

13. Cf. Umwelt- und Prognose-Institut Heidelberg e.V., *Ökologische und soziale Kosten der Umweltbelastung in der Bundesrepublik Deutschland im Jahre 1989*, (UPI-Report No. 20), Heidelberg (1991), p. 78 and passim.

14. Cf. Aristotle, *Politics*, Book 1.

would attain the level of the gross national product of the world within one human lifetime. As economic growth stands in direct relation to energy input, it does not require much imagination to picture what the ecological consequences would be if the FRG (whose growth rate is considerably exceeded not only by Japan, but also by the average Asian growth rate) were to become the gauge of the Atlantic alliance — let alone the whole world, which nonetheless averaged an economic growth rate of 3 percent in 1989.[15] Even now plant, animal, and human life is under immediate threat from the side-effects of our prodigal doings and dealings — the greenhouse effect, the hole in the ozone layer, the dying forests and the ever-increasing pollution of water, soil and air.[16] Speeding up this global process of devitalization, or even merely continuing it, will certainly make life on this planet more and more arduous and finally terminate it altogether — just as bacteria in a test tube filled with nutrient solution will develop and reproduce to the point of self-destruction.

Apart from the fact that lack of insight and willpower makes it probable that the ominous course of our civilization will continue despite all the portents, this course is additionally gathering a special momentum. Large areas of this Earth are becoming unusable (these areas include not only lands in the Third World stricken by famine and poverty and prey to exploitation by elements from home and abroad, but also infertile agricultural Promised Lands, like the American corn belt, that have been created by harmful farming techniques[17]); in addition, apparently unstoppable population increases are taking place in poverty stricken areas.[18] For these two reasons both latent and overt population migrations will take place, causing both direct and indirect conflicts over raw materials, energy, and the environment. Given the present advanced state of arms technology, this situation can but

---

15. Cf. IMF, *World Economic Outlook,* October 1989 and October 1990 (reprinted in Barbara A. Fliess, Zur Weltwirtschaftsstellung der USA, in the supplement B/49/90 November 30, 1990 of the weekly "Das Parlament," p. 19). The study finds an average growth rate of 5 percent in Asia and 4.9 percent in Japan.

16. Cf. among others Peter C. Mayer-Tasch in cooperation with F. Kohout, B.M. Malunat, and K.P. Merk, *Die verseuchte Landkarte: Das grenzenlose Versagen der internationalen Umweltpolitik,* Munich (1987), passim; Ken A. Gourlay, *Poisoners of the Sea,* London (1988); Paul J. Crutzer and Michael Müller, *Das Ende des blauen Planeten: Der Klima-Kollaps, Gefahren und Auswege,* Munich (1989).

17. Cf. Werner Schädle, "Wüsten wachsen," in Peter J. Opitz (ed.), op. cit. (footnote 10), pp. 53 ff.

18. Cf. Josef Schmid, "Bevölkerungswachstum und Entwicklungsprozeß in der Dritten Welt," in Peter J. Opitz (ed.), op. cit. (footnote 10), pp. 25–51.

only increase the speed of our ecological descent into hell, a foretaste of which is the oil slick in the Persian Gulf.

2.3   The Direction of Change

The last-mentioned perspective clearly reveals the powerful political dimensions of these problems. It refers to a chapter of events which can be written, in one form or another, for every advanced civilization known to man.

In Francis Bacon's writings — at the beginning of the modern faith in science — there had been frank talk of *scientia propter potentiam*; nowadays, at the pinnacle of our faith in growth, people no less frankly profess their faith in the belief *crescentia propter potentiam*. For the beneficiaries of this growth, economic growth results first in social and political power, and is sought not least for this reason. But this growth only results in an increase in power as long as it does not devour its own ecological — and thus at the end, also its economic — environment. From this critical point onward economic growth is counterproductive in power politics too; power turns into impotence, doings and dealings become death and destruction.

Much, if not everything, speaks for the idea that this critical point has long been exceeded in most of the industrial nations caught up in the euphoria of growth, even if this has not been made clear, or not sufficiently, by their governors and governments. The effort made by the Atlantic industrialized nations — in particular, to maintain or further their position in the worldwide struggle for economic, political and military power — eclipses everything previously experienced. In particular, it implies an enormous and constantly increasing energy input — and thus energy requirement. To meet this requirement, massive and ever-increasing amounts of energy must be consumed at a time when world resources are steadily decreasing. Anyone wanting a clearer picture of this consumption pattern may study national figures for energy consumption growth rates over the past decades and calculate the increase in securing, generation and production costs for the most common forms of energy. If the cost of politically or even militarily securing (for example, the Gulf War) free access to the most important energy sources is included, this consumption rockets into uncalculated — and uncalculable — heights. Now as always, it has become the pacemaker of the dynamics of disintegration of our civilization.

The implications and consequences already mentioned of securing, producing and consuming energy and other natural resources lead to a weakening of the Earth's regenerative powers as an ecosystem; this in turn leads to a decline in economic power and in the lifeforce and will to achieve in the individual nations. To avoid this dilemma, nations engage in ever-shifting conflicts over extension, assertion, or evasion in their struggles over land, energy, and resources, from which they emerge further weakened and finally crumble in exhaustion. Where is the glory of Babylon, whose zealous irrigation led to the salination and desertification of its land of twin rivers.[19] Where is Rome's power of pacification, once obliged to extend far beyond the Mediterranean area to cover its requirements of energy — slaves, in other words — and other resources? What did Spain, formerly a mighty power and promised half the world by Alexander VI in the Treaty of Tordesillas (1494), have, once its oak forests — smashed into planking (again) in 1566 by storms in the Channel — had been felled?

All these historical examples — which can be extended more or less ad infinitum — seem fairly harmless in today's view, since their socio-political and socio-ecological dynamics of self-destruction only affected individual regions. Modern science and technology, however, has magnified man's power to titanic dimensions — as great a challenge to the gods as in mythological times.[20] In consequence of this magnification, the world has become "small," and we can and must experience the world, whose horizons were once limitless, increasingly as the "one world" so frequently cited. Crises which at first appear only in isolated regions can rapidly turn into global crises, because they are generally only an expression of global developments. Thus the hunger of the industrialized nations for energy, resources, and growth is satisfied not least of all at the expense of underdeveloped countries with colonial structures. And the inhabitants' own exploitation of nature in these countries, in addition to that already imposed by outsiders or caused by it, has in its turn economic and ecological consequences for the industrial nations. As the pre-Socratic Anaximander observed, "Things exact penance and revenge according to the extent of their injustice."[21]

Whichever point of view we choose as our vantage point to regard this one small world, the great battle of technologically and economically based civilization for progress and happiness seems to have been lost on all fronts. And even the Atlantic partners who still seem on the way to victory — that is, Europe, especially Germany, and the USA, are not exempt from this scenario of destruction in the twilight of civilization. Thus there is more than

---

19. Cf. Petra Eisele, *Babylon: Pforte der Götter und große Hure,* Berne and Munich (1980), pp. 145 ff.

20. Cf. the narrative in Karl Kereny, *Die Mythologie der Griechen,* Munich (1981), vol. 1, pp. 26 f.

21. The fragment quoted is published in *Natur denken: Eine Genealogie der Politischen Ökologie,* Peter C. Mayer-Tasch (ed.) in cooperation with Armin Adam and Hans-Martin Schönherr, Frankfurt (1991), vol. 1, p. 31.

sufficient reason for reconsidering how it might still be possible to avert or at
least moderate the coming disaster.

3. The Orderly Retreat:
What Is Necessary?

The *Homo faber et oeconomicus* still loves to parade in the glittering
garment of the Citizen of the World, which resembles more and more the
shirt of Nessus. The way things are, however, the only medium- and long-
term solution is to sound the retreat from the race of progress, which has degenerated into an inglorious matériel battle and cannot be won with civilization's powers of logic and logistics in their present state. Only man's retreat
can offer some prospect of attaining global socio-economic, socio-ecological,
and socio-political equilibrium.

If this retreat is to be an orderly one, it first requires the massing of all
forces involved in the battle. This massing of forces is twofold. As an intellectual process it implies comprehension of the futility of continuing battle —
that is, comprehension of "that which has no future" (Ludwig Feld) — as well
as a decision to cease battle and to aim for safe ground — in other words, to
do what is necessary. As a socio-political process it implies the transmutation
of this comprehension and decision into social reality. I would like to exam-
ine both aspects.

If the retreat of Marignano was able to become an act of legendary greatness, then not least because the massing of forces took place at the right time
— namely when the forces still had enough strength to make the retreat an
orderly one. And the same must apply to our fictitious Atlantic (and global)
Marignano. The battle-cry of "Now!" adopted as a constant companion of
every social reform movement from the 1960s to the 1980s, must therefore
become an essential element of the call "Save our global future!"[22]

No less important than the correct timing of the massing is, of course, the
determination of the direction of retreat by the "generals" of this lost battle
— a battle in which all of us participate, directly and indirectly, actively and
passively. But these generals — whose task it is or would be to determine the
direction of the retreat — are the cultural, economic, and ruling elites of the
developed industrial nations, whose economic and political supremacy en-

---

22. *Global Future: Es ist Zeit zu handeln (Global 2000: Die Fortschreibung des
Berichts an den Präsidenten)* is the title of the book by Armin Bechmann and
Gerd Michelsen, Freiburg (1981).

ables them to provide the strongest impetus — and indeed, they must do so, if reorientation is to succeed permanently.

No one whose mental processes are not inextricably enmeshed in the status quo can be unaware of the aim of this reorientation. Its aim can only be the gradual reassumption of ideal conditions of national (with additional moves toward regional and local) autonomy of production, distribution, and consumption — in other words, nothing less than the reversal of the economic dynamics of the world today.

In establishing this aim, the Platonic principle of division of labor (as developed in the *Politeia* dialog between Socrates and Adeimantos[23]) appears to conflict with the Aristotelian idea of self-sufficiency (as expounded in the Ethica *Nichomachea* and in the *Politics*[24]). On closer examination, however, this proves not to be the case.

Division of labor is undeniably a principle based on the diversity of human nature and its entelechy whose final aim is integrity. It is equally undeniable, however, that when precisely this good of the whole is regarded, this principle — despite its tangential concern with integrity — cannot claim any absolute validity for itself. Its extent corresponds to its aim. Up to a certain point, overstepping the bounds of self-sufficiency can serve the good of the individual as well as that of the whole. However, if this critical point is exceeded the good deed turns sour. It has already been made clear that this is increasingly the case in the world's economic system under today's economic, ecological, and political auspices. It cannot be mere coincidence that Plato took the postulate of division of labor already mentioned, with its aim of self-sufficiency and justice, to apply to the individual polis, not to the whole of the Greek or Mediterranean theater of states. The social cost of a global division of labor distorted through many layers of supremacy and structures of exploitation is, at any rate, so high today that it represents a significant danger not only to peace between man and man, but also to peace between man and nature. Neither the dealings of the highly developed industrial nations nor the dealings of nations with less highly developed or undeveloped industries would satisfy the categorical imperative of a global system of ethics supporting the general good of global society as well as the natural environment which gave that society shelter and nourishment. Such a system of ethics, given today's global conditions, would have to take its orientation from a world culture with more emphasis on spiritual joy and more material asceti-

---

23. Cf. Plato, *Republic*, Book 1, Chapter 10 ff., margin numbers 368 ff.

24. Cf. Aristotle, *Nichomachean Ethics*, Book 1, Chapter 5 (margin number 1097b); and Aristotle, *Politics*, Book 1 (margin numbers 1252a ff.).

cism.[25] A victory of the "International of the Carriers-On" (Sloterdijk[26]) would, however, lead in the foreseeable future to the large-scale destruction of life on the planet and could thus hardly be taken as the basis of a general law for which human beings would accept responsibility, as Immanuel Kant rightly demands "categorically" in his version of the Christian commandment of charity and brotherly love.[27]

It is obvious that an immediate retreat — quite apart from the illusionistic nature of such a vision — would be impossible. The short-term effects would be catastrophic for the economies of almost every country in the world. Only an orderly retreat would come into question — that is, a retreat in which a shelter and refuge for the retreating army of civilization would be set up, as the second phase of the "massing" after the decision to retreat and the choice of direction.

Such a "shelter and refuge" can only be attained in the form of a mixed economy oriented toward the ideal of extensive autonomy, in which every country produces as much as possible the ingredients it needs for survival and a good life. Both foodstuffs and other items of daily life as well as those means of fulfilling needs "beyond those of every day" (Aristotle[28]), would have to be produced in an increasingly socially and environmentally acceptable way. This would mean that large-scale technological structures would have to be replaced by so-called intermediate technology oriented intelligently toward integrity. Such restructuring of economic and industrial systems would necessarily mean a drop in export production, and redundant labor from this sector would — also of necessity — be transferred to agriculture, trades and crafts, and small businesses. A not insignificant consequence of this transfer would be a considerable increase in the quality of products.

Only worldwide adoption of a mixed economy of this kind could hinder the progress of the economic, ecological, and political power dynamics of destruction I have outlined. Only then would the more or less costly, environmentally destructive, and peace-endangering dipping of all too many (State)

---

25. The terminology, if not the idea, of the demand for an "ascetic world culture" comes from Carl Friedrich von Weizsäcker, *Die Zeit drängt. Eine Weltversammlung der Christen für Gerechtigkeit, Frieden und die Bewahrung der Schöpfung,* Munich (1986), p. 94.

26. Cf. Peter Sloterdijk, *Kritik der zynischen Vernunft,* Frankfurt (1989).

27. Cf. Immanuel Kant, *Metaphysik der Sitten, Rechtslehre, Einleitung in die Metaphysik der Sitten, IV, Vorbegriffe zur Metaphysik der Sitten* (K. Vorländer (ed.), Hamburg (1959), p. 28): *"Handle nach einer Maxime, welche zugleich als ein allgemeines Gesetz gelten kann"* ("So act that the maxim of your action can be willed without contradiction as a universal law").

28. Cf. Aristotle, *Politics,* Book 1, Chapter 2 (margin number 1252b).

hands into all too many (national) pockets disappear. Only then would the motive disappear for the all-too-ardent wooing of the poor by the rich, and the all-too-eager submission of the poor to the rich.

The ordered structure of global society's retreat from the lost battle of civilization should thus aim for a kind of global middle-class policy to stabilize the world's economy, ecology, and power politics. The recommendations for the creation and maintenance of internal national order put forward by such political thinkers as Aristotle, Thomas Aquinas, and Rousseau, as precursors of the 19th and 20th-century concept of the social state,[29] can also be recommended for the creation of order within a community of states. But one important condition would arise. Pursuing the concept of a social state encouraged social peace but endangered peace with nature, since then as now capital and employment tended to make their arrangements at the expense of the environment. This is not at all the case with the global middle-class policy envisaged here. Its aim is not least to protect nature from the ecological exploitation stemming both from greed and from need.

Such reorientation will be easy for neither rich nor poor countries: the rich are in the position of the New Testament's "rich man" (Matthew 19,22), and such a reorientation means abandoning cherished patterns of growth, prosperity and progress, plus radically restructuring their own economies; the poor largely do not have, or have lost, the know-how and the skills of craftsmanship and technology to restore the autonomy of their economy — leaving aside historically based blockades of development and illusionary horizons of hope. The times when one wanted to echo Paracelsus's demand "that the islands of those happy naked people"[30] should be left in peace are long past. Because we have not left them in peace, it is now our responsibility to ensure that they can return to a balanced peace.

In other words, the global community will not be able to manage without "development" policies, not even under the auspices of an orderly retreat. This new kind of "development" policy, however, will only be permitted as the complete form of what it is only partial today — genuine help in a brand of self-help which will save the developing countries from the stranglehold (partly from outsiders, partly self-inflicted) of both exploitation and existential need, without turning them into mere carbon copies of their industrialized "development helpers," complete with unsuccessful structural policies.

---

29. Cf. Peter C. Mayer-Tasch in cooperation with Armin Adam, F. Kohout, B.M. Malunat, and Hans-Martin Schönherr, *Politische Theorie des Verfassungsstaates*, Munich (1991), pp. 105–138.

30. Cf. Theophrastus Bombastus von Hohenheim (Paracelsus), *Vom Licht der Natur und des Geistes*, edited with an introduction by Kurt Goldammer in cooperation with Karl-Heinz Weimann, Stuttgart (1976), pp. 170 f.

A global cleanup of structural policies of the kind outlined would lead —
also of necessity — to a gradual drawing apart in international economic relations, while at the same time intensifying national and above all regional
attenuation of the world market. To be able to accept certain compensatory
functions, the world market would have to continue to exist, albeit at a comparatively modest level and along socially and ecologically acceptable lines.

In encouraging this process of global restructuring and directing compensatory functions on the remaining world market, the United Nations could
retain a significant role in its task as global peacekeeper. This traditional
peace-keeping role would be simplified, as the global process of (re)estab-
lishing socio-economic self-sufficiency, and the socio-ecological rehabilitation
that goes with it, progresses. Population migrations with aggressive political
consequences and other acts of forcible expansion have generally arisen out
of either ecological catastrophes or disturbances to the internal or external
equilibrium of a region or nation that has slipped into the shadows. These
imbalances naturally include an oversupply of armament and faulty orientations in arms policy. By the Gulf War the industrial nations must have realized what is lying in wait for them — and other smaller countries — if they
continue to tolerate arms dealings. Just as the détente in the East-West conflict was the signal for extensive disarmament for both the members of the
Atlantic Treaty Organization and the former Soviet Union, the Gulf War
could and should be the prelude to worldwide disarmament. However, such a
perspective is only realistic if the industrialized countries which produce arms
not only strictly forbid arms trading and take equally strict measures to prevent its occurring, but also give further material aid for structural development in the Third World dependent on progressive disarmament in developing countries. Precisely this Atlantic alliance could prove itself to be an alliance of reason by leading the field as an example, to provide a guarantee of
its credibility, and thus to draw the Soviet Union as well as the whole of the
global community into the spell of reason. As well as encouraging and supervising global procedures for restoring economic autonomy, the United Nations could and should play a significant role in encouraging and supervising
global disarmament.

If this path were consistently followed, the success of an "orderly retreat"
would be assured. Even those ideological and religious differences which
constantly cause political upheaval in the global community would be able to
encounter a definite détente, in the shape of an army of civilization with-
drawing along a wide front from a dead end of civilization; further moves involving military force would be abandoned and (thus direct and indirect)
ecological weakening and destruction of life would be stopped. A social environment reformed in this way would provide conditions under which the ge-

netically determined potential for self-preservation and self-realization would be very much easier to deal with than has been the case up to now.

4. Marignano Utopos: What Are Our Chances?

Naming one's aims is one thing, achieving them quite another. Even when we consider the new world (economic) order, we must still ask what are our chances of attaining a global Marignano. In other words, we will have to ask ourselves whether we are dealing with a concrete aim or whether this is just another Erewhon,[31] a long line of political Utopias.

As essential as it may seem to hurl an intellectual spear into the straits of possibilities — to recall Emperor Otto the Great (936–973) and his "possession" of the North Sea — it is indispensable to provide this spear with the force it needs to reach its target. The achievement of this goal needs far more than a mere awareness of the problem, arising from the availability of increasing quantities of information and from an increase in possibilities of processing it. Awareness of the problem must be backed up by awareness of the aim. Not merely an intellectual confirmation of the existence and extent of a crisis, but also confirmation of the aim and the paths leading to a resolution of the crisis; these are conditions *sine qua non* of every potentially successful strategy of renewal. When the young Hegel spoke of reality not being able to resist the "revolutionizing of the realm of imagination,"[32] he was probably thinking of both aspects — awareness of the problem and of the aim. Awareness of the problem and aim can only attain a politically relevant level if a milieu of social energy is formed out of reciprocal confirmation at all levels of society, thus making consistency, purposeful behavior possible. Consequently, the question is whether such a milieu can be expected to form among the leading Atlantic powers — and at a global level.

It is obvious that the socio-psychological conditions necessary for the formation of such a milieu are not exactly at their most favorable at the start of the 1990s. In Germany, the debate on reunification, at first colored by euphoria and then, on realization of the financial burdens looming ahead,

---

31. Cf. Samuel Butler, *Erewhon*, (1st ed. 1872), New York (1935), pp. 1970 ff. (Introduction by Peter Mudford).

32. Cf. Georg F.W. Hegel, in his letter of October 28, 1808 to Niethammer, reprinted in Johannes Hoffmeister (ed.), *Briefe von und an Hegel*, 1785–1812, vol. 1, Hamburg (1955), p. 253.

swinging over to worry, is leaving very little scope for the creation of such a milieu. And what applies to Germany applies just as much to the whole of Europe; the triumph of the (social) free market economy over the (socialist) planned economy creates but slight inclination to clip one's own economic and political wings when their span is constantly broadened by the rapidly growing dynamics of integration. The United States sees its prime aim as the struggle to find answers to the economic challenge posed by its Pacific partner Japan and its Atlantic partner Europe. This struggle, with other themes, takes priority over reorientation at the moment. The competitive struggle over world markets creates structural tension, which will probably scarcely be altered by "trans-Atlantic declarations" or the temporary comradeship-in-arms at the Gulf.[33] The expression of this tension is still, despite all the rhetoric of goodwill, a certain distrust comparable to the developing countries' distrust of the industrial nations, which leads them to meet suggestions of reform, even those arising out of primarily socio-economic motives, with an unmistakable suspicion of neo-colonialism. "You say Christ, and mean cotton," was once the cry, referring to the intertwining of mission work and colonial politics; "you say ecology and mean economy," would be the up-to-date equivalent. Since the Stockholm Environmental Conference in 1972, this suspicion has permeated all debates on structural reform in the North-South dialog. When one examines the attitude of many of the industrialized nations — including, unfortunately, the United States — at the global climate conferences in Montreal, Geneva and Washington, such a suspicion is hard to allay.[34]

Neither did any real change result from the Environmental Conference in Rio de Janeiro (1992). This mega-eco-show, attended by over 100 heads of state and government leaders and around 30,000 national and press representatives, developed at best into a festival of goodwill, impotent helplessness and superficiality, at worst into one of cynicism with a veneer of hypocrisy. This had naturally been clear from the outset. Even if the drafts produced by the Convention on Climate and Biological Diversity, watered down to insignificance in the run-up to the conference, had actually borne the stamp of any serious desire for change, they could hardly have been expected to supply

---

33. In the "Trans-Atlantic Declaration" published in Washington and Rome in November 1990, the USA and the EC committed themselves to fundamental and long-term cooperation. Cf. on this also *Neue Züricher Zeitung*, November 25/26, 1990, p. 2. In this context also Klaus-Michael Meyer-Abich, "Entwicklung statt Fortschritt," *Scheidewege*, 1989/1990, pp. 245 ff.

34. Cf. Ernst-Ulrich von Weizsäcker, "Klimapolitik als Erdpolitik," *Scheidewege*, 1990/1991, pp. 14 ff. (16) and the report in the *Neue Zürcher Zeitung*, November 19, 1990, on the World Climate Conference in Geneva in 1990, p. 2.

a remedy for even the most urgent ecological problems of the world. This was not least the case because the UNCED, as its full name runs, was shaped by what sociologists call a "built-in-conflict." For while the ruling and economic elites of the industrialized nations assume today that "the world has developed enough" (Meadows) and thus attempt to stabilize their own position by means of a sort of eco-imperialism, the countries of the Third and Fourth World, plagued by population explosions and poverty, are frantically striving for all the joys of civilization which neither the selfishness of the industrialized nations, focused on the politics of power and development, nor the voice of environmental reason want to grant them.

The so-called Rio Declaration passed in 1992 clearly reflects this situation. It can be seen from most of the twenty-seven principles of the declaration, which is aimed at establishing a rhetorical consensus, that it follows the principle of making an omelette without breaking eggs. There is talk of the sovereign right of states to use their resources at their own discretion; it is stated that both conservation and development are the issues, that the goals are "sustainable development" *and* economic growth, that no country's progressive conservativism may lead to restrictions on trade, and so on and so on — such a document, as fugacious as a leaping Cossack, must surely bring tears to the eyes of professional cynics, but also delineates the present limits of what is politically attainable.

What is there, then, which could confirm the hope of a neo-Galilean *epur' si muove?*

Three developments paradoxically may give grounds for hope that something will move in the right direction after all. Their consequences are difficult to predict; the developments themselves are in any case catastrophic. The possibility that catastrophes can (also) be reasons for hope is indicated in the very ambivalence of the word itself. Its meaning of *reversal* can have a positive as well as a negative meaning. If a catastrophe means, on the one hand, the destructive collapse or breaking off of a development, it can equally well be a signal of a new beginning in the right direction.

The first of the three catastrophic developments I mentioned is the catastrophic famine in many Third World countries, breaking out again and again and calling attention to serious structural faults in agricultural and economic policies. The second is the environmental catastrophe whose effects are visible the world over and whose global extent can be observed not least in the climatic alterations already taking place or on the horizon. And the third catastrophe is the virulent dialectics of civilization manifested in the Gulf War. All these catastrophes — together with their countless ominous implications — show that we are truly adrift in that "spaceship Earth," which

Kenneth Boulding spoke about twenty-five years ago,[35] in great danger from turbulence within and without. And all these catastrophes also show the dark side mentioned earlier of what one could see as civilization's karma. It is the distorted image of that unceasing "wanting more" (pleonexia[36]) already execrated by Greek classical philosophers, with which the whole world is now reproached, and above all those industrialized nations threatened directly and indirectly by not only the vengeance of nature, but also the vengeance of mistreated and misled Third World countries.

The hope spoken of here is founded on the expectation that the writing on the wall is clear and striking enough to bring a global Marignano into sight. This perspective is to be hoped above all from those Atlantic partner states — especially affected by the Gulf War — who must maintain their role of leadership precisely during the massing, ordering and acceleration of the retreat. If they cannot fulfill this role, they will in all probability be visited by "plagues" (to keep up the Biblical imagery) of the kind mentioned here until they both tolerate and take the lead in the exodus of today's world out of the Egyptian-Babylonian captivity of an obviously necrophiliac civilization. With every "plague" the elite leaders' motivation to retreat, and the social acceptability of such a move, will increase; awareness of the problems and the aims will accelerate, the milieu of social energy forming refuge from the orderly retreat will expand. And this all the more because such a retreat does not merely involve relinquishment, but can also mean an increase in the quality of life, albeit measured on a scale different from the present one.

It is possible to imagine happier scenarios — scenarios in which the salvation of the *reversal* arises not under the pressure of catastrophes, but rather under the auspices of the "third" kingdom of the Holy Spirit, proclaimed at the closing of the Middle Ages and the threshold of the Renaissance by Joachim von Fiore (1130–1202).[37] At the moment, admittedly, this kingdom is not yet within reach. The rationalists' still-unconcluded "demystification of the world" (Max Weber[38]), which constantly referred to Joachim, has, in the face of its own insights and effects, made the hope of an inspiration of hu-

---

35. Kenneth Boulding, "The Economics of the Coming Spaceship Earth," in Henry Jarrett (ed.), *Environmental Quality in a Growing Society,* Baltimore (1966).

36. Cf. Aristotle, *Nichomachean Ethics,* Book 5, Chapter 2 (margin number 1129b).

37. Cf. Joachim von Fiore, *Das Zeitalter des heiligen Geistes,* edited and introduced by Alfons von Rosenberg, 1937. Cf. also Wolfgang Schickler, *Ewiges Evangelium: Aus dem Leben Joachims von Floris und Franziskus von Assisi.* Including extracts from the Gospels, by Ewiges Evangelium, Stuttgart (1937).

38. Cf. Max Weber, "Wissenschaft als Beruf," in Max Weber, *Gesammelte Aufsätze zur Wissenschaftslehre,* 4th edition, Tubingen (1973), p. 594.

manity as all-embracing as it would be unexpected recede further into the distance than it has ever been since the cyclical philosophy of ancient times was abandoned.

Should anyone decide, in the face of such experiences, to hope not so much for sudden inspiration as for respectable progress based on trial and error, he may reckon on having better chances of worthwhile life and survival in time and space. The only questions are whether we do not take our attempts too far, whether we can recognize our mistakes early enough, and whether we can begin the orderly retreat while there is still time. Despite all skepticism we will probably be able to live — as, indeed, we must — with the hypotheses of hope that an Atlantic — and in its wake a global — Marignano may still be possible today. It is more than likely that this Marignano may soon degenerate to a mere utopian Fata Morgana in the maelstrom of the "plagues" increasing in both number and ferocity. Each forceful step we take now in the right direction increases our chance of contradicting that cry of capitulation "No Future," heard most frequently throughout the industrialized nations and, alas, not entirely unfounded.

5. Epilogue

It is anything but coincidence that the successors both of those who on that 14 September 1515 called mass ranks and sounded to retreat and of those who followed this signal live today in a country whose name is a worldwide symbol of peace, prosperity, and security. Even today, as Switzerland prepares to celebrate its 700-year anniversary, there is certainly no reason to go in for euphorically uncritical apotheosizing of this country, whose riches hardly fell from the sky as manna of gold. And yet it is undeniable that its policies of moderation (of which the retreat into neutrality which began at Marignano is merely a particularly striking example) have proved their worth in many respects. With this in mind, the "orderly retreat" of the confederates at Marignano may be chosen with full justification as a global symbol of hope.

2

The State of the Global Environment:
Is There a Need
for an "Orderly Retreat"?

Bo R. Döös

1. Introduction

The basic message of Peter Mayer-Tasch's essay is a very important one, namely, that there are already alarming indications that the present overexploitation of the Earth's resources and degradation of the environment will eventually lead to a catastrophe. Consequently, he argues that there is an urgent need for the nations of the world to reconsider their direction of development, or, to use his words, "all the signs appear to point to nothing less than a retreat in order to avert, or at least moderate a coming disaster."

2. Major Stresses on the Global Ecological System

Perhaps the most basic questions to be asked at this point would be: How severe is the situation with regard to the global ecological system? Is it as critical as Mayer-Tasch fears? Unfortunately, this must be judged to be the case. Since the realization about three decades ago that the global ecosystem is not an inexhaustible resource, the situation has worsened at an accelerated rate. At first the environmental problems were only of limited extent and concentrated in industrialized areas where the pollution of the air and water were becoming disturbing. Since then, seemingly unexpected, new environmental problems have appeared (see Figure 2.1) one after the other, and their integrated effect is of such a magnitude that it is beginning to affect the global life-support system. Some international efforts have been made to reduce these threats to the global ecological system.

FIGURE 2.1

Timetable of Major International Acceptance of Currently Known Environmental Issues

Time	Environmental Issues	First Identification as a Potential Problem
1960	Pollution of Air and Water	1962 Carson
	Tropical Deforestation	1874 Marsh
	Acidification of Lakes	1872 Smith
1970		
	Stratospheric Ozone Depletion	1974 Molina-Rowland
	Carbon Dioxide induced Climatic Change	1896 Arrhenius
1980	Additional Greenhouse Gases	1976 Wang
	Acidification and Decline of Forests	
1990	?	

Source: Döös 1990.

FIGURE 2.2

Schematic Map Showing Regions that Currently Have Acidification Problems and Regions Which Might Become Severely Affected in the Near Future

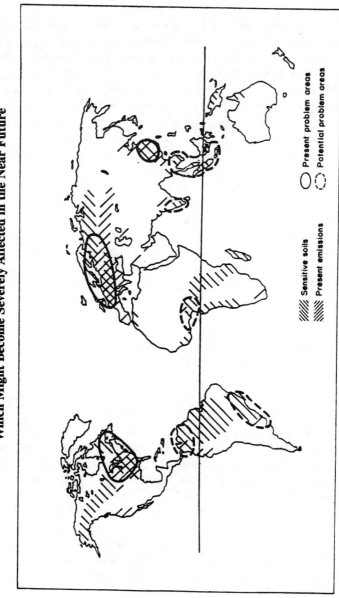

Source: Rhode et al. 1988.

2.1 Acidification of Terrestrial Ecosystems

The first observation that increasing emission of sulfur dioxide caused damage to lakes was made in 1968. However, several years passed before it was recognized that acidification is a long-range transboundary problem, that it is a severe threat to forests, and that in addition to sulfur dioxide, nitrogen oxides and ammonia nitrogen contribute significantly to acidification.

Certain progress has been made in Europe with regard to both accepting that the scientific knowledge, although not perfect, is sufficient for taking corrective action and agreeing to lower the amount of emissions of sulfur dioxide and nitrogen oxides according to the protocols of the United Nations Economic Commission for Europe (UN/ECE). It should be recognized, however, that the present substantial commitments by the Western European nations (amounting to many billions of US$) to reducing emissions are far from providing sufficient protection.

According to a study by Rodhe et al. (1988) it can be expected that the problem of acidification will spread to many parts of the world, including the tropics (see Figure 2.2) as a consequence of a combination of several factors, e.g., sensitive soils, increasing population, industrialization, and biomass burning.

2.2 Anthropogenic Modification of the Earth's
Radiation Budget: The Greenhouse Effect

It was only in the late 1970s that this problem began to receive international attention and concern. At that time it was referred to as a problem caused by increasing atmospheric concentration of carbon dioxide.

Some years later it became clear that anthropogenic activities were also responsible for the emission of several other gases (methane, chlorofluorocarbons, and nitrous oxide). Taken together, these gases contribute an almost equally high share to the modification of the Earth's radiation budget (the greenhouse effect), thereby causing a climatic change and climate variability.

Through the efforts of the World Meteorological Organization (WMO)/ UNEP Intergovernmental Panel on Climatic Change (IPCC) it was possible to achieve a comparatively unified scientific consensus with regard to both the magnitude of the expected climatic change and its various harmful impacts on human activities and the response strategies required to delay significantly a climatic change. Nevertheless, the response from governments has been very limited. Only a few countries (representing less than 10 percent of the current emissions of carbon dioxide) have agreed to reduce emissions by 20 percent. Some other minor contributors have stated their intentions not to increase their emissions. These planned reductions should be compared with the reduction of net emissions by more than 60 percent that would be required to stabilize the concentrations at today's levels.

Thus recent estimates of the anticipated emission of greenhouse gases can not be expected to be optimistic. Figure 2.3 shows the projection of carbon dioxide according to the International Energy Workshop (1990). This projection, which includes only the emission caused by energy production (excluding the emission from the tropical deforestation), is compared with the corresponding emission scenarios developed by the IPCC.

2.3 The Destruction of the Stratospheric Ozone Layer

In 1974 the first hypothesis was presented about another kind of degradation of the global ecosystem caused by the increasing use of chemicals produced by the "developed" world, namely, the destruction of the stratospheric ozone layer by chlorofluorocarbons (CFCs). This family of non-toxic chemicals have many qualities which make them extremely useful, for example as coolant in refrigerators, as propellant in spray cans, and for the manufacturing of plastic-foam materials. Although the theory presented at that time about the reactions in the stratosphere provided a good base for an intense debate on the aerosol industry, it was not sufficient in explaining the extensive destruction of the ozone in the stratosphere (the "ozone hole") over Antarctica a decade later. The latest measurements indicate that this destruction is not confined to the Antarctic region.

This destruction of the stratospheric ozone is leading to increased ultraviolet radiation on the Earth's surface which can be expected to have a severe impact on human health (e.g., skin cancer and effects on the body's autoimmune system).

CFC's also contribute significantly to the greenhouse gas effect. However, it is probably their indirect impact on human health that has made it possible to reach a comparatively effective international agreement on a phaseout of the production of these chemicals, by 2000 in industrialized countries and by 2010 in developing countries.

FIGURE 2.3

The International Energy Workshop's Projection of Emission of Carbon Dioxide from Commercial Energy Production[1]

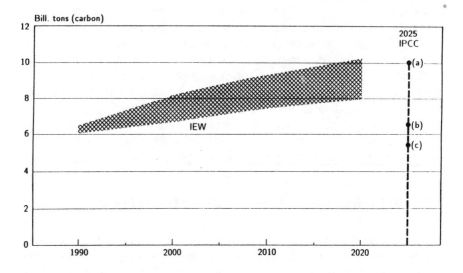

1   excluding the emission from deforestation compared with the scenarios developed by the WMO/UNEP IPCC

(a) Business as usual
(b) Low emissions
(c) Control policies.

Source: International Institute for Applied Systems Analysis (IIASA) 1990.

2.4   The Pollution and Toxification of Ecosystems

The concern about the environment began with the increasing use of chemicals which caused visible pollution of air and water. However, the seriousness of this problem, which has so far been mainly concentrated in the industrialized world, particularly within the (formerly) centrally planned economies, seems to have not yet been fully recognized. One of the reasons for this is that most ecosystems (e.g., soils, sediments, and wetlands) have a capability to store and immobilize large amounts of harmful chemicals. The accumulation may occur over long periods of time, but sooner or later, and with very little warning, the maximum storage capacity of the ecosystem will be reached and it will begin to leak; this can have devastating impacts. Considering the length of time during which emission of harmful chemicals has occurred, and the characteristic time for the saturation of ecosystems (years and decades), it can be expected that this kind of seemingly unexpected environmental problems (the so-called chemical time bombs) will increase in the near future.

Another aspect of this problem is that present efforts to reduce pollution are often limited to reducing the emissions of chemicals at the point of entry to the environment. What is needed is to take a more systematic and comprehensive view of the stocks and flows of manufactured chemicals through the industrial economy prior to their entry to the environment.

3. Is There a Need for "An Orderly Retreat"?

In view of its fundamental importance for global security, the question about the future capacity of the global life-support system requires particular attention. Actually, considering recent developments, the stresses are already beginning to be so apparent that the question is not so much whether the global life-support system will be able to meet future demands, but rather when it will become insufficient unless decisive response measures will be taken. Several problems must be addressed.

3.1 The Growing World Population

Before the middle of the next century the world population is expected to have grown from the present 5.3 billion to about 10 billion (United Nations Medium Variant assuming increased fertility and mortality decline; UN 1989). This increase is almost entirely concentrated in the less developed countries (see Figure 2.4). If the present fertility and mortality rates remain unchanged, the 10 billion value will be reached before 2030.

3.2 Limitation and Degradation of Agricultural Land

Most developing countries have little or no potential arable land to develop to support their rapidly increasing population. Consequently, in spite

FIGURE 2.4

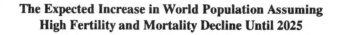

The Expected Increase in World Population Assuming
High Fertility and Mortality Decline Until 2025

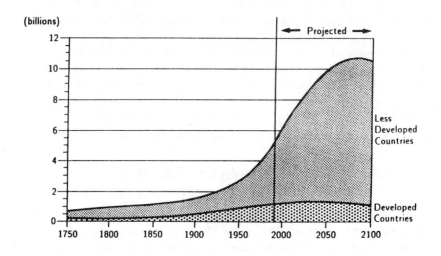

Source: The UN Medium Variant, UN 1989.

of the fact that the total cultivable area is increasing, the land available per capita will decrease (see Table 2.1). Also the global value for the grainland per capita is decreasing (Brown 1990; and see Figure 2.5).

TABLE 2.1

**Decline in Potentially Cultivable Land Per Capita in the Developing
Countries (ha/capita)**

Region	1990	2020
Sub-Saharan Africa	1.6	0.63
West Asia and North Africa	0.22	0.11
Rest of Asia, excluding China	0.20	0.12
Central and South America	2.0	1.17

Source: Oldeman 1990.

FIGURE 2.5

World Grainland[a] and Per Capita[b] With Projection to 2000

World grainland

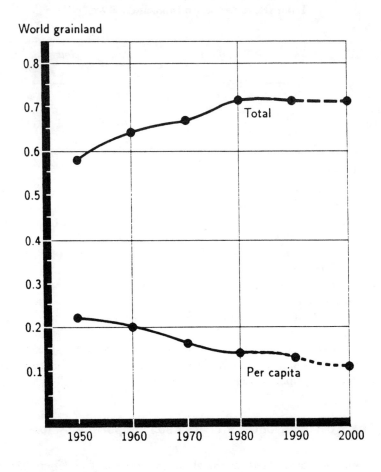

a   in billions of hectares
b   in hectares

Source: Brown 1990.

In addition, there is increasing degradation of available land due to various anthropogenic activities, e.g., soil erosion caused by mismanagement and
overgrazing and increased runoff of precipitation and flooding caused by
deforestation. Other causes of land degradation are, for example, water log-

TABLE 2.2

**Areas of Different Regions Affected by Various Types of Human-Induced
Land Degradation (in thousands of km^2)**

Type	Africa	Asia	South and Central America
Water erosion	1700	3150	770
Wind erosion	980	900	160
Nutrient loss	250	100	430
Salinization	100	260	

Source: Oldeman 1990.

ging and salinization, acidification, and loss of organic soil matter. An
estimate of the extent of the different types of land degradation has been
made by Oldeman (1990), and is given in Table 2.2.

The shortage of agricultural land has also led to a competition for land.
This is particularly evident in the tropics where about half of the deforestation has been caused by the need for the expansion of the agricultural land.
Thus, a successful retardation of the tropical deforestation would reduce significantly the potential for expansion of agriculture in areas where it is criti-
cally needed.

There is also a competition between agriculture and urban-industrial development. By the year 2025 it is expected that about 3 million km^2 will be
lost, and it can be expected that much of this loss will be of high-quality land.

3.3 The Weakening of the World's Food Supporting System

Although substantial gains in the global grain output (see Figure 2.6), can
be accomplished by, e.g., improved technology and management, these gains
have been reduced to less than 1 percent because of the various kinds of environmental degradation identified above. This net value of about 1 percent
increase in grain production per year is thus much more than counterbalanced by the almost 2 percent annual population growth (Brown 1990).

It should be recognized that in these calculations of the present trends of
the world's food-supporting system no account has been taken of the need
for accommodating justice and equity for the less developing countries. Nor

do they take into account the problems which may occur as a result of the expected greenhouse effect.

FIGURE 2.6

World Total Grain Production[a] and Per Capita[b] Projected to 2000

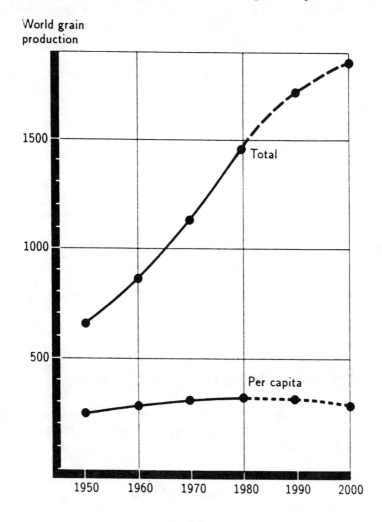

a   in million tons
b   in kilograms

Source: Brown 1990.

3.4 Disintegration of the World's Forests

The world's forests resources are threatened in different ways. In Europe and in some parts of the world the damage is mainly caused by acidifying chemicals. Recent evaluation of the situation points to the fact that only quick action to make drastic reductions in the emission of these chemicals will make a difference, and even then it is probably too late for some forests in Eastern Europe, which will simply disintegrate over the next decades (Nilsson 1991).

The boreal forests in the high latitudes of North America, Europe, and Asia are expected to be severely affected by the greenhouse gas-induced climate warming which will be particularly pronounced in these latitudes. Because this type of forest is very sensitive to warm temperatures, the southern parts of this type of forest will be significantly reduced. Although it may be based in the north and even extend into the tundra zone, the net loss of the boreal forest area is expected to be from about 30 percent to 40 percent.

In the tropics deforestation continues at an accelerated rate in spite of the worldwide attention given to this problem. In 1980 it was estimated that the loss of total (open and closed) tropical forest (FAO/UNEP 1981) was about 110,000 km^2/year. As is illustrated in Figure 2.7, this rate has increased in one decade to about 170,000 km^2/year (FAO 1991). For the closed tropical forests the corresponding figures are equally dramatic.

Comparing these trends of the loss of tropical forests with the estimates of the remaining tropical forest areas, 8 million km^2 closed forest and 17 million total forest, it can be estimated that the main parts of the tropical forests will disappear by the middle of the next century.

3.5 Limitation of the World's Fresh Water Resources

Similar to the problem of the limitation of potentially arable land, we are also confronted with the fact that the world's fresh water resources are fixed, but the population is not.

It is becoming more and more apparent that in many parts of the world the lack of sufficiently good-quality water will be the main obstacle to socio-economic development. As the demand for water increases due to the growing population and an increasing need for irrigation to augment agricultural production, the currently available water resources are being exposed to several stresses. For example, there is a general consensus among hydrologists that the vulnerability of water systems to a greenhouse gas induced climatic

FIGURE 2.7

Present Trends in the Decline of Total and Closed Tropical Forests[a]

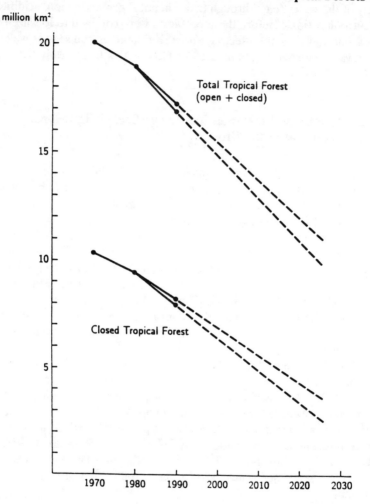

a The two versions represent the trends based on estimates from FAO/UNEP (the slower rate of deforestation), from World Resources Institute (WRI) and Food and Agriculture Organization (FAO) a decade later (the faster rate of deforestation)

Source: FAO/UNEP 1981; WRI 1990; FAO 1991.

change may be particularly high in regions where the current level of water stress is already high.

Furthermore, there is a shift in the magnitude of pollution reducing the quality of the water (e.g., through toxic chemical contamination, acidification, and eutrophication). Before these problems were confined to localized water bodies, but now they are affecting whole river systems and seas as well as the groundwater. In some areas in Eastern Europe this has already led to acute health problems.

3.6 Environmental Degradation, Large-Scale Migrations, and Political Instability

The increase of the world population will, to a large extent, be concentrated in areas of poverty, where the life-support system has obvious limitations, including low-level coastal zones being threatened by a climatic change induced sea level rise. It does not require too much imagination to recognize that this is bound to result in large-scale migrations. People will flee to places with better possibilities of better livelihoods and a better life. Actually such migrations are now taking place; for example, in North Africa famines have resulted from the occurrence of extended droughts and desertification and have forced people to migrate. In Figure 2.8 an attempt is made to identify such regions which are particularly vulnerable because of population growth and insufficient local food production, regions which may become sources of large-scale migrations.

It should not be excluded that in some regions the environmental degradation may be so severe that it may lead to national and international political instabilities. A possible cause-effect chain is shown in Figure 2.9. It links the environmental degradation caused by population pressure with such consequences as a dramatic reduction in food production, which in turn causes starvation and famines. Migration may follow, which will break the social and political stability both nationally and internationally. The figure also shows the feedback processes which result in an amplification of this negative development.

4. What Can Be Done?

In the second section of his essay, Mayer-Tasch attempts to identify what is needed to "save our global future." Clearly he realizes that the ecological problems are intimately connected with other global issues which bear on global security and risk management, e.g., the issues of economy and technology and those of a political and social nature. He is concentrating his discussion on how to achieve an orderly retreat based on the economic aspects of the problem. He very bravely states that what is required is "nothing less than a reversal of the economic dynamics of the world today," which would require a "gradual reassumption of national autonomy of production, distribution and consumption." It would also require the replacement of large-scale technological structures by "intermediate technology oriented intelligently toward integrity." Very rightly he emphasizes that an orderly retreat must include a "retreat from the race of progress which has degenerated into an inglorious material battle."

FIGURE 2.8

Scenarios of Large-Scale Migration[a]

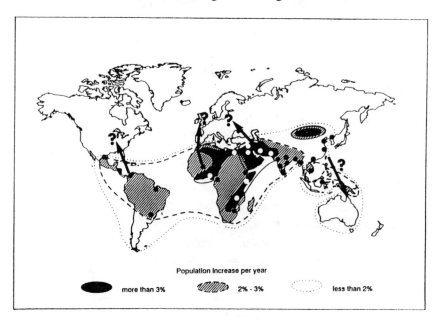

Population increase per year

more than 3%   2% - 3%   less than 2%

a   caused mainly by rapid population increase and insufficient local food production. The dots indicate regions where the population will have increased by 100 million prior to 2025

Source: Öberg 1991.

FIGURE 2.9

**The Cause-Effect Chain Linking Population Increase, Environmental
Degradation, and Political Instability with Positive Feedbacks
Which May Reinforce and Accelerate this Process**

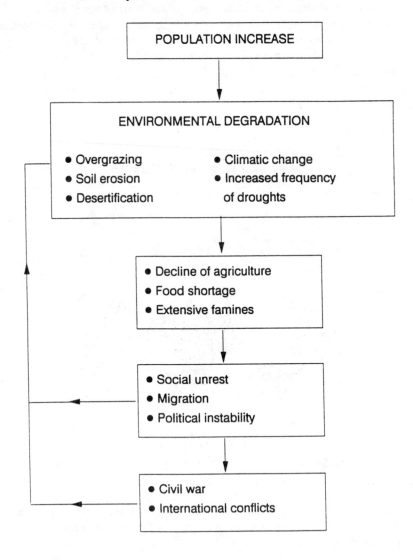

Source: Döös 1992.

Now the question arises whether such a radical statement as "the world economy as it stands today has no future," followed by the recommendation to reverse its dynamics, would help to focus attention on the need to attain global socio-economic, socio-ecological, and socio-political equilibrium? Most likely it would, but even the most optimistic politician or economist supporting such a change of the present economic system would admit that it could not be easily achieved. No doubt, many would argue that the present development of the world economic system, given the gradual adoption of the free market economy in the Eastern bloc, is very promising in the attempt to achieve global economic-ecological-sociological-political equilibrium. Actually, Mayer-Tasch himself refers to "the free market economy's triumph over planned economy and of the disintegration of the Eastern bloc" (with its catastrophically rundown environment).

In trying to design a realistic and efficient plan of action to reduce the threats to global security it appears to be more strategic to apply a direct approach that identifies specifically the factors having an influence on the present undesirable direction of developments rather than attacks the existing world economic system, but still maintains the philosophy of an orderly retreat. Certainly there are many such factors, but a few should be singled out as being particularly important:

— the lack of understanding and recognition in many industrial countries of the environmental consequences of the present technological and socio-economic developments;

— the difficulties in building up a political base for the acceptance of a sound environmental policy which is often due to the erratic way the public is being informed. For example, the media are often emphasizing the sensational aspects rather than providing factual and objective information;

— the reluctance of politicians to suggest decisive actions to reduce the degradations of the environment (often due to their limited terms of appointment). Instead they argue that the knowledge is insufficient for taking action, while the real reason is short-term economic concerns;

— the lack of financial resources and suitable technologies in less developed countries. This results in the fact that they have little choice but to repeat the mistakes now being made in the so-called developed world.

References

Arrhenius, S., "On the Influence of Carbonic Acid in the Air upon the Temperature of the Ground," *Philosophical Magazine* 41 (1896), p. 237.

Brown, L.R., "Feeding the World in the Nineties," *Sustainable Development, Science and Technology,* The Norwegian Research Council for Science and the Humanities (1990).

Carson, R.L., *Silent Spring,* Boston (1962).

FAO, "Global Overview of Status of Worlds Forest," Paper presented at the Technical Workshop to Explore the Feasibility of Forest Options, Bangkok, April 1991.

FAO–UNEP, "Tropical Forest Resources Assessment Project," Food and Agriculture Organization and United Nations Environment Program, Rome (1981).

Houghton, J.T., G.J. Jenkins, and J.J. Ephraums (eds.), Intergovernmental Panel on Climate Change, Scientific Assessment (IPCC), Report prepared for IPCC by Working Group 1, Cambridge, U.K. (1990).

Manne, A.S. and L. Schrattenholzer, International Energy Workshop-Overview of Poll Responses (IEW), International Institute of Applied Systems Analysis, Laxenburg (1990).

Marsh, G.P., *The Earth as Modified by Human Actions,* London and New York (1874).

Molina, M.J. and F.S. Rowland, "Stratospheric Sink for Chlorofluoromethanes: Chlorine Atom Catalyzed Destruction of Ozone," *Nature* 249 (1974), pp. 810–814.

Nilsson, S. (ed.), *European Forest Decline: The Effects of Air Pollutants and Suggested Remedial Policies,* International Institute for Applied Systems Analysis, Laxenburg (1991).

Öberg, S., Personal communication, 1991.

Oldeman, L.R., R.T.A. Hakkeling, and W.G. Sombroek, "Global Assessment of Soil Degradation," *ISRIC/UNEP Study,* 1990.

Rodhe, H., E. Cowling, I.E. Galbally, J.N. Galloway, and N. Herrera, "Acidification and Regional Air Pollution in the Tropics," in H. Rodhe and R. Herrera (eds.), *Acidification in Tropical Countries,* Chichester (1988), pp. 3–39.

Smith, R.A., *Air and Rain: The Beginnings of a Chemical Climatology,* London (1972).

United Nations, "World Population Prospects 1988," United Nations Department of International Economic and Social Affairs, New York (1989).

Wang, W.C., Y.L. Yung, A.A. Lacis, T. Mo, and J.E. Hansen, "Greenhouse Effects Due to Manmade Perturbations of Other Gases," *Science* 194 (1976), pp. 685–690.

WRI (World Resources Institute), *World Resources 1990–1991,* New York (1990).

3

Global Cooperation for Sustainable Development: Challenges to the North on the Road from Rio

Irene Freudenschuss

1. Introduction

Many of the more than 100 speakers who took the floor in the plenary of the UN General Assembly in November 1992 to address agenda item 79, entitled "Report of the UNCED," agreed that the success or failure of the Rio conference would be determined by the speed and effectiveness with which the recommendations of the conference are implemented. Maurice Strong, the Secretary General of UNCED, had the foresight to coin the phrase "the Road from Rio" early on, and he left no doubts that the "Road from Rio" would be longer and more arduous than the "Road to Rio."

There are indeed many road blocks, potholes, and even deep chasms that need to be overcome by the international community on the Road from Rio. Many of the difficulties are more acute for the developing countries, some challenges are equally felt in countries across the North-South divide, but there are also challenges targeted more specifically to the industrialized countries. In the limited scope of this chapter I will focus on the last two categories.

Irene Freudenschuss was a member of the Austrian delegation to the United Nations in New York. The article reflects her personal views.

2. From "The Rio Spirit" to a New North-South Relationship

To implement the UNCED recommendations smoothly and effectively, delegations emphasized in the plenary debate and during the subsequent negotiations, under the Chairmanship of Ambassador Razali Ismail (Malaysia), that it was imperative to keep the "spirit of Rio" alive. For example: Canada saw this spirit of Rio characterized by transparency, accountability, and inclusiveness;[1] Finland underlined partnership and shared responsibility;[2] Bulgaria held that UNCED broke new ground in multilateral decision making, public participation, and active involvement of NGOs.[3]

This Rio spirit of shared responsibility and partnership represents more than just a good negotiating climate. In Rio the industrialized countries formally recognized, as it was spelled out explicitly in the context of the negotiations on a Framework Convention on Climate Change,[4] the concept of a shared but differentiated responsibility for the well-being of the planet and its inhabitants. They also agreed to take the lead in this endeavor. Art. 3, para. 1 of the Framework Convention on Climate Change unequivocally states:

> The Parties should protect the climate system for the benefit of present and future generations of mankind, on the basis of equity and in accordance with their common but differentiated responsibilities and respective capabilities. Accordingly, the developed country Parties should take the lead in combating climate change and the adverse effects thereof.

Throughout the text of the Convention on Climate Change the differentiation between the commitments of the industrialized countries and the commitments of the developing countries is maintained. Principle 7 of the Rio Declaration on Environment and Development restates the responsibility of the North in very similar terms:

---

1. Statement by Jean Charest, Minister of the Environment of Canada, November 2, 1992.
2. Statement by Sirpa Pietikaeinen, Minister of the Environment of Finland, November 2, 1992.
3. Statement by Slavi Pashovsky, Permanent Representative of Bulgaria to the UN in New York, November 4, 1992.
4. UN-Framework Convention on Climate Change, Doc. DPI/1300.

States shall cooperate in a spirit of global partnership to conserve, protect and restore the health and integrity of the Earth's ecosystem. In view of the different contributions to global environmental degradation, states have common but differentiated responsibilities. The developed countries acknowledge the responsibility that they bear in the international pursuit of sustainable development in view of the pressures their societies place on the global environment and of the technologies and financial resources they command.[5]

In the plenary debate of the 47th General Assembly a number of representatives from developing countries went to great lengths to remind the North of its responsibility and its commitment to take the first step toward remedial action. In his capacity of spokesman of the Group of 77 (G-77, founded in 1964), Akram Zaki, Secretary General for Foreign Affairs of Pakistan stated on November 2:

Much of the world's finite resources are being depleted or degraded due to unsustainable patterns of consumption and production in the developed countries. It is well recognized that the present environmental crisis is mainly due to unrestrained and unsustainable consumption patterns and life styles in the developed countries.

He goes on to deplore the lack of specific commitments by developed countries in Agenda 21. Furthermore, he points out that the "solidarity demanded by the new paradigm of environmentally sound development is limited if not absent in [the policies of the developed countries] relating to development assistance, trade liberalization and technological cooperation."

Malaysia was also highly critical and addressed the inequalities of the international economic structures. Ambassador Razali Ismail said on November 3, 1992:

Follow-up after UNCED must make up for this lapse examining issues such as the reverse South-North outflow of resources, improved South's terms of trade and reduction of the debt burden. Such reform is essential if the South is to gain the necessary economic space to implement a transition to ecologically sound and socially equitable development.

Ambassador Razali also called for a total ban on the export of hazardous waste and dirty industries from the North to the South and deplored the absence of leadership from the countries of the North in the Rio process which expressed itself, he said, in a tendency to hide behind one another. This was evidenced in particular with regard to the financial resources issue, which for the South lies at the very heart of the UNCED outcome. "Present status is not encouraging," Razali underlined, "as by the end of UNCED, we are still not in the position to estimate the amount of new moneys that had been

5. Rio Declaration on Environment and Development, Doc.A/Conf. 151/26.

committed by the North. Indications are that they fall far short of the estimated amount."

A compilation of the UNCED statements made during the plenary debate in New York, which included indications of current funding commitments for sustainable development-related activities, lists statements by
Austria, the EC, France, Germany, Japan, the Netherlands, Norway,
Switzerland, and the United States.[6]

These quotes show with great clarity that what is really at stake in the
UNCED follow-up is the transformation of the North-South relationship
with a view to achieving sustainable development for all people, in all countries.

The intervention of the Minister of External Relations of Brazil, Fer-
nando Henrique Cardoso, on November 2, put it bluntly:

---

6. *Austria:* has pledged 400 millions AS (US$ 38.10 million) to the initial three-year
   pilot phase of GEF; earmarked 200 million AS (US$ 19.05 million) to
   sustainable forest management activities; will participate in International
   Development Association (IDA) replenishment; will increase its contribution to
   United Nations Development Program (UNDP) and allocate US$ 1 million to
   Capacity 21.
   European Community: has committed 3 billion European Currency Unit (ECU)
   (priority to various sustainable development sectors, poverty reduction,
   technology transfer, and capacity building).
   France: has reiterated its commitment to reach the Official Development
   Assistance (ODA) target of 0.7% by 2000. In 1992, ODA will be 40 billion FF or
   US$ 8 billion. In 1993, it will be 43 billion FF. Specifically for Agenda 21: its
   assistance will amount to 4 billion FF in three years (urban, water, energy, soil,
   forests) of which 1.2 billion FF will be contributed in 1993.
   Germany: IDA 10 maintained in real terms; debt relief in context of Paris Club if
   resources generated are for environmental protection.
   Japan: ODA target: US$ 50 billion in five years (1988-1992) (+100%); Rio:
   Environment ODA to 900 billion yen-1 trillion yen/(US$ 7 to 7.7 billion) in
   1992-1996 (five years).
   Netherlands: supports IDA replenishment with an Earth increment; ODA is
   greater than 0.7%. 0.1% for environment will be added to current level.
   Norway: IDA 10 should be at least equal to IDA 9 in real terms.
   Switzerland: infrastructure for Less Developed Countries (LDC) missions in
   Geneva; transport costs for LDC delegates.
   United States: in 1993, US ODA US$ 11 billion (+4%); contribution to UNDP
   US$ 125 million (+9%); contribution to UNEP US$ 22 million (+21%).
   Montreal Protocol: US$ 28 million (1993) up from 18 million in 1992;
   multilateral banks: US$ 1.6 billion including US$ 90 million for Inter-American
   Development Bank (new fund).

The main virtue of this consensus [achieved at UNCED] lies in a vigorous contribution given to the promotion of a major shift in international relations, particularly in the way which the North and the South interrelate. All countries are now partners in a common enterprise. The simple categories of donor and recipient countries no longer apply. This new partnership expresses a logic of cooperation that rules out both confrontation and patronizing attitudes. A trend in which global negotiations are "relegitimized" as a process for the fostering of worldwide understanding. Multilateralism has been strengthened by the realization that solutions to universal problems require universal and equitable participation.

Under the heading "Partnership for Solutions," the World Bank Development Report of 1992 states in a very analogous way that "finding, implementing, and financing solutions will require a partnership of effort among nations." The World Bank Report goes on to say:

Improved know-how, new technologies, and increased investment are essential. Open trade and capital markets, the restoration of creditworthiness through policy reform and selective debt relief, and robust, environmentally responsible growth in the world economy will all be needed.

The close link between poverty and environmental problems makes a compelling case for increasing assistance to reduce poverty and slow population growth and for addressing environmental damage that hurts the poor.

High-income countries must play a major role in financing the protection of natural habitats in developing countries from which the whole world benefits. They must also assume the primary responsibility for addressing worldwide problems of which they are the primary cause (greenhouse warming and depletion of stratospheric ozone).[7]

There is a compelling logic in this line of argumentation. The problems UNCED sought to address cannot be solved by any one country nor by any one group of countries. All countries, indeed all people, need to cooperate to solve these problems. The industrialized countries need the cooperation of the South, just as the developing countries need the cooperation of the North in order to achieve global sustainability. These conditions give greater negotiating clout to the South and contain the potential for generating greater equality in the North-South dialogue. At the Conference in Rio this potentiality had not been realized; UNCED barely touched such core parameters of the North-South relations as commodities, trade, ODA, and transfer of technology.

Whether the industrialized countries are going to accept the logic of the need for a *redefinition* of the scope and the quality of North-South-relations

---

7. World Bank, World Development Report 1992, *Development and Environment.* Oxford (1992), p. 3.

in the service of sustainable development is the most profound challenge to the North on the road from Rio. Such a redefinition would of course require give and take on both sides; this burden cannot be laid only on the North. But if the North reverts to business-as-usual, perhaps with a little added sensitivity to environmental protection and worldwide poverty, and some sectoral activities of more or less limited scope, UNCED will have failed.

The willingness and capability of industrialized countries to give concrete financial and technological expression to the "Rio Spirit" of shared but differentiated responsibility will be tested shortly. The Commission on Sustainable Development (CSD) will have a role in overseeing the transfer of technology and money, a role that is deemed to be of primary importance by the developing countries.[8] In addition a number of follow-up conferences and negotiating processes that were spawned during UNCED will test the North's commitment even more since they are likely to generate less public interest and hence will be less high up on most political agendas.

A case in point is the "Intergovernmental Negotiating Committee for the Elaboration of an International Convention to Combat Desertification in those Countries Experiencing Serious Drought and/or Desertification, Particularly in Africa," created by General Assembly Resolution 47/188 on December 22, 1992 in response to the recommendations in Agenda 21. Doubtlessly, desertification is a serious problem given the fact that almost 40 percent of the Earth's land area (6.1 billion hectares) is dryland, some 0.9 billion hectares of which are hyper-arid lifeless deserts. Of the 5.2 billion hectares of potentially productive drylands, 84 percent are prone to drought and desertification. It is estimated that about 3.6 billion hectares are currently threatened by various forms of land degradation known as desertification and that some 900 million people are affected by it.

Doubtlessly prevention of any further land degradation which is often the consequence of overexploitation by a population that has no other means of subsistence, should be encouraged.

Of course the gravity of the desertification problem was recognized years ago, long before UNCED. In 1977 the General Assembly adopted Resolution 32/172 which endorses a rather detailed program of action to combat desertification. Many of the measures detailed in chapter 12 of Agenda 21 were already touched on in the 1977 resolution.[9] Yet there was never enough money forthcoming to really implement the program of action. The cost of the programs detailed in Agenda 21 in chapter 12 is estimated at US$ 12.2

8. General Assembly Resolution 47/191 in particular, paragraphs 3c) 5.

9. Agenda 21, A/Conf, 151/26 (Volume I–III). Chapter 12, "Managing Fragile Ecosystems: Combating Desertification and Drought," is contained in vol. II, pp. 42–61.

billion, about half of which would have to be provided through external sources. Can we be confident that moneys will be flowing more readily and more copiously now?

The secretariat of the Intergovernmental Negotiating Committee seems to be duly aware of this uncertainty and has tried to overcome it by foreseeing a two-track approach: in addition to the convention proper, it aims to develop specific programs for particular countries, which supposedly will not only spell out the measures to be taken but correlate them with concrete commitments from donor countries. Since the substantive negotiations haven't started, it is too early to say whether all partners will agree to this approach.

Other test cases for the North's willingness to "deliver" could arise from the results of the Conference on Sustainable Development of Small Developing Island States that was decided upon by General Assembly Resolution 47/189. The conference took place in April 1994 in Barbados. This resolution was a major concern of the small developing island states that had grouped together in the UNCED process to form the Alliance of Small Island States (AOSIS). AOSIS was able to make itself heard on the road to Rio. However, it has been pointed out, that its strength came from having a clearly defined agenda which it pursued from within the G-77. Will it be able to continue to generate enough political interest now that it has stepped outside the G-77 group solidarity and invited the international community to focus on its specific needs and problems (which may even set it up for competition with other groups of developing countries)?

The population problematique presents yet another test case for the North's willingness to act. Because of the many sensitivities surrounding this issue, Agenda 21 is worded extremely carefully when it comes to population questions; so carefully that it may be felt that the issue has not been addressed adequately. At the International Conference on Population and Development, to be held in Cairo in September 1994, the international community will get the chance to take another (more in-depth) look at the issue. A lot will depend on the North's equitable and sensitive leadership. The recent move of US President Bill Clinton to request again more money from Congress to contribute to the funding of UN population activities is a hopeful sign in this regard.

The transformation of the North-South relationship clearly resorts to the level of political decision-making. Concomitant adjustments are necessary at the institutional level and at the level of data management, which are examined briefly in the next section.

3. Integration of Environment and Development

In the process leading up to the Rio Conference the North was very much pursuing an environmental agenda driven by environmental protection agencies and environmental grassroot groups. The South arrived at the Conference with a development agenda. In Rio the inescapable link between both agendas was brought to the center of world-wide public awareness.

"The innovative approach made in Rio . . . lies in integrating environment and development, two sides of the same coin," Klaus Toepfer, Federal Minister for the Environment, Nature Conservation and Nuclear Safety of Germany said on November 2 in New York. A number of speakers echoed this insight. This approach is also enshrined in the Rio Declaration on Environment and Development, in particular in principle 4, which reads: "In order to achieve sustainable development, environmental protection shall constitute an integral part of the development process and cannot be considered in isolation from it." Put in different terms, attacking poverty is not only a moral imperative, but also essential for environmental stewardship.[10]

While there is no disagreement in theory about the necessity to look at environment and development in an integrated way, this integration has yet to happen in the management of relevant data and in the institutional realities at the local, national, and international levels.

The risk is that the concerned actors will only pay lip service to the integration of environment and development and will withdraw to their initial positions. In this regard I think it was not a good sign that the dozen or so ministers from industrialized countries who attended the plenary debate of the UN General Assembly in November 1992 were practically all ministers of the environment. Why were there no ministers of development cooperation or finance or science and technology present?

Decision-making processes and institutions in which decisions are taken on sustainable-development-related issues are still predominantly sectoral; they do not build upon the integrated approach.

Even in the UN proper the integrated approach to environment and development has not yet been achieved. A Non-Paper circulated by the Austrian Mission to the UN dated December 1, 1992, makes the following points:

> The proper elaboration of statistics and data which form the basis for any sound economic and social analysis in the context of environmental

---

10. World Bank, *World Development Report* 1992, supra, p. 25.

sustainability is one of the riches in the UN. This collective asset, however, has not yet been fully realized. Data and analysis in the UN system are fragmented, presented in different formats, and compartmentalized in a multitude of reports which are produced upon request by an overburdened Secretariat and often not properly absorbed by equally overworked delegations.

Information flows at present do not adequately take into account neither vertical interdependences as they exist between the effects of local, national, regional and global decision-making processes nor the multiplying horizontal inter-sectoral relationships which are relevant in view of the need to achieve sustainable development (i.e., integration of economic development, social development and the changes in the available natural resources endowment).

There is no adequate hierarchization of data and analysis. Therefore the wealth of data and analysis 'stored' in the UN system does often not crystallize into the clear articulation of development perspectives and the formulation of policy options. There is no comprehensive 'State of the World Report' published by the UN.

The Austrian Non-Paper, brainchild of the then Head of the Department for UN Affairs at the Austrian Ministry for Foreign Affairs, Walther Lichem, recommends the creation of a system of integrated reports in the economic, social, and natural resources endowment fields. This system of integrated reports would consist of three sectoral reports (which might be called "Report on World Economic Development," "Report on World Social Development," and "Report on the Status of the Natural and Environmental Resource Endowment," respectively) and a fourth report, a comprehensive and integrated "Report on Environment and Development." This last report would highlight the interrelationship existing between economic development, social development, and environmental and natural resources on a global scale, and define problem areas and policy requirements.

The Austrian Non-Paper draws the conclusion that the creation of such a system of integrated reports would have far-reaching institutional implications by streamlining and coordinating through the factual weight of its data and by providing policy analysis and policy formulation:

The three integrated sectoral reports and the comprehensive Report on Environment and Development in conjunction with assessments and policy recommendations articulated by the Commission on Sustainable Development, ECOSOC and the General Assembly, would serve as a common basis and a reference point for policy-making and program design by all other decision-making bodies of the UN system including specialized agencies and regional commissions. It would also be able to influence and guide national and local government authorities in their decisions. It would offer a common data base for individual decisions of other actors in the area of sustainable development. Such integrated reports would help create the communality of purpose required in the leadership and management of the complex UN system.

This Austrian initiative goes to the very heart of the challenge that the international community faces in terms of creating the tools for an effective integration of environment and development. It is a challenge to both the North and the South, a challenge on which the North should take the lead for decisive action.

Integrating the data is, of course, only the first step. The next step is institutional reform. In this area, too, developments occurred during the 47th General Assembly. With Resolution 47/191, adopted on December 22, 1992 and entitled "Institutional Arrangements to Follow-up the UNCED," the General Assembly decided upon the parameters for the Commission on Sustainable Development which was established as a Functional Commission at the Economic and Social Committee's (ECOSOC) organizational session in February 1993. A major sticking point in the difficult negotiations on this resolution was the question of the location of the secretariat to the Commission and the venue of its meetings. Switzerland had conducted a well-orchestrated and generously funded campaign to have the secretariat in Geneva. The Swiss offer was strongly supported by France which was reflected in the EC position. Other countries and groups of countries favored New York. The G-77's position was that the secretariat should be in New York where all countries are fully represented and that the secretariat of the CSD should be distinct from the then Department of Social and Economic Development (DESD) headed by Under-Secretary-General Ji and should be headed also by an Under-Secretary-General.

Things were complicated by the fact that by the middle of November it had become clear that Secretary-General Boutros-Boutros Ghali was about to announce the second phase of his endeavors to restructure the UN secretariat. On December 3, the Secretary-General announced the creation of a new secretariat structure in the economic, social, and environmental field. In his note A/47/753, dated December 3, 1992, the Secretary-General refers back to his annual report on the work of the organization (A/47/1) which he submitted to the General Assembly in September and in which he had stated:

> An integrated approach to . . . development, can only be promoted through a stronger UN. It has to become:
>
> An organization which views its objectives in respect of economic and social cooperation and development with the same sense of responsibility and urgency as its commitments in the political and security area . . .
>
> An organization which takes fully advantage of the central coordinating capacity available to it on economic, social and humanitarian issues, and of the inter-sectoral capabilities at its disposal in the regional commissions and in the various United Nations programmes and organs.

In an attempt to translate these insights into institutional realities the Secretary-General decided that, according to the new organigram, the secretariat of the Commission on Sustainable Development would be part of the new Department for Policy Coordination and Sustainable Development, to be headquartered in New York and to be headed by the Deputy-Secretary-General of UNCED, Nitin Desai.

The Department for Policy Coordination and Sustainable Development would also give substantive support to ECOSOC and to the General Assembly in the economic, social, and environmental areas as well as to their subsidiary organs, a function that DESD had fulfilled until then.

The Secretary-General thus disappointed those who wanted to "shield" the work of the CSD from the "harmful political climate" of New York by headquartering it in Geneva as if it were possible to deal with sustainable development at a purely technical level. He must have also disappointed those who felt that the secretariat of the Commission on Sustainable Development should be outside DESD, so that DESD could continue to devote its resources to the many burning issues of economic development that are of such great concern to the developing countries (as if it were still possible to deal with questions of economic and social development, on the one hand, and questions of sustainable development, on the other).

In his decision of 3 December the Secretary-General followed a course of action that seems detached from the give-and-take of political compromise: he created a department to deal with all three dimensions of sustainable development — the economic, the social and the natural resource endowment dimensions — at the level of policy formulation. That the decision had to be taken while the major partners in the new global partnership were passionately lobbying for solutions that they hoped would give them respective political advantages is indicative of the difficult process that lies ahead.

In creating the new Department for Policy Coordination and Sustainable Development the Secretary-General took a step delegations have yet to take with regard to the intergovernmental structure. The decision taken at Rio to create the Commission on Sustainable Development as a Functional Commission of ECOSOC (rather than to assign the responsibility for UNCED follow-up directly to the competent charter body, namely, ECOSOC) has lead to a further increase of the maze of intergovernmental structures in the economic, social, and environmental fields.

While certainly enjoying greater celebrity than most other subsidiary organs of ECOSOC, the Commission on Sustainable Development will still report to ECOSOC alongside other functional commissions (such as the Commission on Science and Technology for Development, the Human Rights Commission, and the Population Commission), expert bodies (such as the Committee on New and Renewable Sources of Energy and Energy for

Development and the Committee on Natural Resources etc.) and other sub-committees. Unfortunately, adding a new body, namely, the Commission on Sustainable Development, does not automatically guarantee that the UN will become an "organization where the intergovernmental bodies promote policy coherence, and where the ECOSOC plays a central role envisaged for it in the Charter of the UN" as the Secretary-General had put it.[11]

Much work remains to be done to determine the best way these different bodies can support one another, to find a good division of labor, and to avoid sterile duplication and fruitless overlap. Many of these modalities will have to be determined by the Commission on Sustainable Development itself in the course of its first sessions, since the relevant passages of Resolution 47/191 are sketchy at best. It is to be hoped that the industrialized countries will be able to exercise greater leadership in the future. In regard to this the negotiating position of the European Community will be of great importance. The need to focus so much energy and tactics on defending Geneva as the site for the meetings of the CSD seemed to be a rather heavy liability during the 47th General Assembly that sapped time and used up negotiating chips that might have been used to address questions related more directly to the work of the Commission on Sustainable Development.

4. Challenges to the Political Reality in the North

The point is sometimes made that the political process in Western democracies is not conducive to addressing global problems. The argument in support of this view runs like this: Western democracies rely on periodic elections. The outcome of the elections are increasingly influenced by the electronic media which reduce even complex questions to 30-second sound-bites. Politicians must face elections; the powerful incentive to be elected and re-elected induces them to avoid tackling issues which would demand unpopular decisions and long-term strategies. Instant gratification is the name of the game. Furthermore, global problems are by definition confusingly complicated; it is very easy to feel overwhelmed or inadequately equipped to handle them properly. This then opens the door to fatalism and to throwing-up one's hands: "If the problem is so big and so complicated, surely nothing that I could do would really make a difference." Of course this attitude is self-fulfilling in the most direct way possible.

I am convinced that while these shortcomings are clearly evidenced in current practice, the democratic system is still the only one that has the po-

---

11. Report on the Work of the Organization, Doc. A/47/1, paragraph 105.

tential to address global problems effectively. The Rio Declaration on Environment and Development acknowledges the importance of wide participation in the decision-making process relating to sustainable development in Principle 10 (which reflects one of the negotiating achievements of the North): "Environmental issues are best handled with the participation of all concerned citizens, at the relevant level."

An increasing body of evidence exists that connects democratic systems and successful management of scarce resources.[12] Only democratic systems allow for the wide participation of all sectors and groups of society without which solutions will remain elusive.

It would be naive, however, to think that political business as usual in the democratic societies of the North will be sufficient to bring about the dramatic changes in the North-South relations, including changes in the consumption and production patterns in the North, without which Agenda 21 will remain an interesting piece of paper devoid of any real significance.

For behavioral patterns to change a new set of values needs to be developed, propagated, and interiorized by significant groups of citizens in the industrialized countries. A good example of what this new set of values might look like was given by the Swedish Minister of Environment and Natural Resources, Olaf Johannsen, on November 2, 1992, in New York when he spoke with great urgency of the window of opportunity in the next twenty-five to fifty years that the world has to change unsustainable patterns of lifestyle and consumption and to take radical steps to eradicate poverty. He continued to say that in Sweden, the government is currently preparing a bill to define what he termed the "eco-cycle society" which would have at its center the concepts of "reduce, reuse, and recycle." "This is a difficult but necessary transition," he added, "a transition which would necessitate much educational effort and awareness building."

The representative of the Holy See, Archbishop Renato Martino, also warned against the danger of succumbing to the inertial tendency of "wait and see" and against acting as if sustainable development were somebody else's problem. He underlined the grave moral obligations of exercising both responsible stewardship with regard to the environment and genuine solidarity with all other people in the process of development:

> What is urgently needed is a new education in ecological responsibility, that inculcates human values such as respect for one's neighbors, love of nature, a sense of responsibility and solidarity, so that each individual will relinquish

---

12. For example, an article published in the *New York Times* on January 17, 1993, entitled "It's Never Fair Just to Blame the Weather," establishes an interesting connection between dictatorial political regimes and higher rates of starvation during droughts.

egoistic behavior in order that communities assume more responsible lifestyles.

How can such a new set of values, whether based on religious or secular
ethics, come to replace the consumerism that is currently prevailing in the
North? How can concern for short-term advantages, the long-term implications of which are not even registered, grow into a willingness to see the
larger picture and to take into account the interests of future generations?

It sounds trivial, but ignorance is an important cause of environmental
damage and a serious impediment to finding solutions. To overcome this impediment, it is necessary, first, to know the facts; second to determine values
and analyze the benefits and costs of alternative measures; and, third, to ensure that information is available to inform public and private choices.

Whenever there is a sudden expansion of collective consciousness, edu-
cators in the wide sense — teachers, opinion-leaders, and the media — play a
particularly important role. It is their responsibility to promote understanding of the complex correlations between environment and development as
accurately as possible to the widest possible audience. While it is always important for the proper functioning of democracy that citizens be able to take
truly informed political decisions, it is outright crucial in the areas of environment and development. Sustainable development for all humankind cannot be imposed from the top down; rather it requires the responsible cooperation of all political actors, of each and every man and woman.

In democracies, the political practice will improve when groups of voters
that influence the outcome of elections give high priority to the objective of
achieving sustainable development and start thinking and acting in long-term
perspectives.

Overall patterns of consumption can and will change if large groups develop and credibly adhere to alternative lifestyles. Already, the behavior of
consumers and producers is changing:

> In many countries people are willing to recycle, to think about using energy
> and materials more efficiently and to alter their consumption patterns ...
> Companies often respond by using the environment as a selling point. Green
> labeling, increased use of recyclable and biodegradable packaging, and more
> energy efficient technology are most common in industrial countries, but the
> same trends are appearing in some developing countries.[13]

Production processes will incorporate newly won insights if buyers insist
on it. *Changing Course*, a report published by the Business Council for Sustainable Development for UNCED, forcefully advances the idea and pro-

---

13. World Bank, *World Development Report* 1992, supra, p. 84.

vides ample evidence that good environmental management is also good business.[14]

A number of new tools have already been forged by environmentalists, think tanks, and concerned groups. These tools (such as "green taxes," tradeable emission permits, and internalization of environmental costs in pricing) may need fine-tuning. More than anything else, however, they need to be brought out of ivory-tower discussions and into the mainstream of political debate.

In this mission of education, nongovernmental organizations have a special, irreplaceable function to fulfill. NGOs were one of the driving engines of the UNCED process. They will have a special role in the Commission on Sustainable Development, and it is likely that as a result of the UNCED experiences their status within the intergovernmental machinery of the UN in general will be enhanced.

Clearly they will continue to serve as the "watchdogs" of multilateral diplomacy and to provide expert input with regard to the areas of their specialization. Even more important, however, will be the activities of nongovernmental organizations at home; these activities may include lobbying national administrations, mobilizing legislative action, as well as promoting awareness and creating networks of solidarity and concern across all divisions of social sectors, nationalities, economic interests, and ideologies.

Education in the broad sense is necessary at several levels. First of all, it is necessary to highlight the global interdependency, to paint a realistic picture of the problems that already exist and to extrapolate the consequences if current trends persist (e.g., global warming, water contamination, and destruction of biodiversity).

Then alternative behavior patterns that support the achievement of sustainable development need to be demonstrated at the individual, local, national, international, and global level.

Finally, we are faced with the challenge to develop and to spread values which will enable us to forgo short-term advantages out of solidarity for the sake of the greater good of the Earth and all her inhabitants, including future generations.

Without this transformation of the political climate in industrialized countries there will not be enough incentives for administrations to tackle seriously the tremendously thorny task of transforming the North-South relationship into a true partnership based on equity and shared responsibility for the planet Earth. Without serious political will at home, the most clever ways of integrating data, managing information, and setting up international structures will not be more than an intellectual game.

---

14. Stephan Schmidheiny, *Changing Course,* Cambridge, Mass. (1992).

5. Conclusions

The greatest challenge to the North on the Road from Rio clearly lies at home.

The current macroeconomic situation of recession plaguing many countries does not make the challenge any smaller. Under these circumstances, psychological defenses are bound to start operating vigorously: denial will make us try to believe that the environmental problem is really not too bad, and that we can come back to it once the economy has picked up, once the social security system has been reformed, and once unemployment rates have been brought down. Projection will lure us into identifying groups or countries that are so much more guilty of environmental destruction and of exploitation of the poor than we are.

We can fool ourselves for a while with these mind games. But the more time we allow to pass, the greater the adjustment will have to be once we decide to face reality. The reality is that the Earth is one; that the carrying capacity of ecosystems is not unlimited; that every little act has repercussions on the whole for better and for worse; and that we can solve the pressing problems of global environmental threats only if we also address the absolute poverty besetting over one billion men, women, and children. The reality is that we need to truly cooperate. And that we need to do it now. We all stand to gain from it.

PART TWO

Economic and Institutional Capacities for International Environmental Cooperation

4

Affluence and Scarceness: The Effect of Economic and Sociocultural Capacities on Environmental Cooperation

Volker von Prittwitz

1. Disaster Paradox and Capacity for Action

The analysis of environmental policy is traditionally based on a concept of "problem pressure," interpreting environmental policy as a response to the threat of ecological disaster or growing environmental hazards. As this response fulfills a social function, the pressure approach may be regarded as functionalist in character.

Environmental policy is not simply a reaction to environmental problems, however, but should also be seen against a particular social and political background exerting its influence regardless of the actual state of the environment; this becomes obvious if we compare the intensity of environmental efforts with the particular ecological damage to be repaired. Environmental policy is only rarely a delayed reaction to a growing environmental hazard. On the contrary, systematic environmental policies often are omitted at

---

1. Cf. Niklas Luhmann, *Ökologische Kommunikation,* 3rd ed., Opladen (1990); Peter C. Mayer-Tasch, Aus dem Wörterbuch der politischen Ökologie, Munich (1985), and Heinrich Pehle, "Umweltpolitik im internationalen Vergleich," in Volker von Prittwitz (ed.), *Umweltpolitik als Modernisierungsprozeß. Politikwissenschaftliche Umweltforschung und -lehre in der Bundesrepublik Deutschland,* Opladen (1993), pp. 113–136.

times of increased ecological strain while action is taken in periods when stresses are comparatively small or on the decline. This "disaster paradox," for which smog alarm regulations in the big cities in Germany and radiation safety policies before and after the Chernobyl reactor accident are good examples, also becomes manifest in numerous other fields of environmental and health policy. One such instance is the disastrous radioactive contamination of large areas of the former Soviet Union, which was kept secret for decades and has been made public only after the collapse of the socialist regime in the USSR, another one the introduction of meaningful anti-smoking laws in Germany, which do not date back to the fifties or sixties, when smoking was a kind of epidemic playing havoc with the nation's health, but were issued since the beginning of the seventies, when the number of smokers was going down to about half of that of 1950.[2]

If we follow the capacity approach[3] the development of environmental policy mainly reflects a society's existing or possible capacity for environmental action. It is true that as a rule the environment is insulted, polluted, destroyed even in countries with satisfactory capacities; the main factors giving rise to an effective environmental policy are not connected with ecological concerns, however, but with a number of capacity factors which may be quite independent of environmental issues, such as

— economic and technological capacities, i.e., satisfaction of basic material and psychological needs, and technological flexibility;

— socio-cultural capacities, i.e., common value orientations, communicativeness and knowledge;

— institutional capacities, i.e., structures of a vital democracy (established civil rights, representative formulation and implementation of political objectives, i.e., via elections and majority decisions, participation and public information).

If such conditions are met, political awareness increases and existing damage to or stresses on the environment are publicly discussed and made an object of public action. The more advanced these capacities are, the

---

2.   Volker von Prittwitz, "Katastrophenparadox und Handlungskapazität. Theoretische Orientierungen der Politikanalyse," in Adrienne Héritier, *Policy-Analyse. Kritik und Neuorientierung,* special volume of Politische Vierteljahresschrift, vol. 24 (1993), pp. 328–355.

3.   Volker von Prittwitz, *Das Katastrophenparadox. Elemente einer Theorie der Umweltpolitik,* Opladen (1990), and ibidem (footnote 2); Martin Jaenicke, "Erfolgsbedingungen von Umweltpolitik im internationalen Vergleich," *Zeitschrift für Umweltpolitik und Umweltrecht* 13, pp. 213–232, and ibidem "Ökologische und politische Modernisierung in entwickelten Industriegesellschaften," in Volker von Prittwitz (ed.), op. cit. (footnote 1), pp. 15–29.

greater environmental sensitivity and awareness will be; a correlation explaining the occurrence of the disaster paradox referred to above. As the increase in capacity — reflected by environmental action — usually is accompanied by a decrease in environmental stress while it promotes political awareness of environmental problems, ecological hazards and the perception of these hazards will frequently develop in opposite directions, at least at certain stages. At times when the burden on the environment is relatively small or on the decline, problem awareness will grow, whereas it is likely to decrease in ecologically more harmful periods.

While the theory of "problem pressure" uses a functionalist approach when explaining environmental policy, i.e., in terms of functions to be fulfilled, the capacity theory is structural in character. The environmental and analytical conclusions to be drawn from the two approaches are not clearly formulated; there are certain associations in a scientific and political context, however, that are connected with them. The theory of "problem pressure" corresponds to the environmental policy approach common during the seventies, when environmental issues were made a public topic by means of citizens' initiatives, their solution was delegated to the authority of the state, however. It was the state as the authority implementing the decisions made by society as a whole, upon whom pressure had to be exerted; conversely, authoritative action taken by the state in order to solve the accumulated problems was legitimate. Emphasizing the need for action served to legitimize concerted authoritative acts: a theory in line with the concept of central state authority and, in particular, with socialist approaches. According to the capacity theory, on the other hand, practical conclusions are largely determined by the conditions permitting an effective environmental policy. A successful environmental policy depends on the extent to which basic economic and psychological needs have been satisfied (personal security, material demands), and on the existence of socio-cultural communication and value commitment as well as conditions of vital democracy. Classical regulatory environmental policy (rules, injunctions, limits, etc.) can be effective only to the extent to which these structural conditions exist. In the absence of such conditions a regulatory approach along the line of thought that environmental pressure must be met by a corresponding normative pressure (limits, rules, etc.) is unrealistic or even dangerous. In the context of North-South and West-East relations the central strategy of international environmental policy is not to exert pressure via norms and standards, etc., but to assist in developing the necessary capacities for action, i.e., by giving economic and technological support and pleading for the international acceptance of human rights and forms of vital democracy.

2. Ecology of Affluence – Ecology of Scarceness

If the ecology movement and environmental policy are interpreted as manifestations of postmaterialistic value change (basic material needs having been satisfied), the change over time in attitudes towards environmental topics, i.e., whether they are given priority or neglected, may be explained in terms of affluence ecology: Postmaterialistic value change and methodical environmental policy can only emerge when basic material needs have been satisfied. Relative poverty on the other hand requires primary accumulation, the building of an economy even at the expense of the ecology. It is therefore quite understandable that many countries of scarce economic resources, such as Brazil or Malaysia, do not pay much attention to ecological issues. The reasoning that economic recession must be countered by a cut in expenses for environmental protection is in accordance with this interpretation.

In the North-South context particularly, environmental policy is discussed from this perspective and is seen as inseparable from economic affluence. As early as in 1972, at the United Nations Conference on the Human Environment held in Stockholm, the developing countries rejected any responsibility of their own for the environment, pointing to their right of development even at the risk of inflicting ecological harm. Whereas in the then-discussion the capacity argument, in terms of a country's title to economic development even at the expense of the environment, was barely touched upon, a much firmer stand has been taken in the past few years, especially at the meetings before and after the June 1992 Conference on Environment and Development in Rio de Janeiro, where it was clearly pronounced that environmental protection depends on the available means, with a view to setting up an environmental fund for the benefit of the developing countries.[4]

Although such reasoning may be felt to be most appropriate from the capacity point of view, it seems unsatisfactory and even controversial if it leads to the conclusion that Western lifestyle is a prerequisite for ecological thinking and action. As a general introduction of this kind of lifestyle would endanger the ecological system of our planet to an even greater extent, this would imply that we would tolerate and even promote further damage to the

---

4. A survey of the bargaining positions is found in Sebastian Oberthür, "Die internationale Zusammenarbeit zum Schutz des Weltklimas," *Aus Politik und Zeitgeschichte* (Beilage zur Wochenzeitung "Das Parlament"), no. B 16/1992, pp. 9–20; Udo-Ernst Simonis, "Kooperation oder Konfrontation: Chancen einer globalen Klimapolitik," *Aus Politik und Zeitgeschichte* (Beilage zur Wochenzeitung "Das Parlament"), no. B 16/1992, pp. 21–32.

global environment as a prerequisite for the development of suitable remedies. For this reason the uncritical acceptance of the capacity theory would lead into an economic-ecological development trap.

By linking ecology to economic prosperity we fail to realize that a behaviour reflecting environmental awareness and responsibility is in itself a fundamental resource of societal development and thus of a society's capacity for economic development. If a society ranks its economy above its ecology, for example, in a period of economic recession, it will damage or even destroy vital development potentials of this economy:

1. The conservation of nature and environment not only contributes to the immediate protection of human health against environmental hazards, but preserves future biological potentials relevant for agricultural development, for instance. The increasing susceptibility of crops to diseases, for example, should be seen against the background of the massive decline in species diversity and the fact that in view of bacteria and viruses adapting to monocultures, survival will eventually depend on this very diversity;

2. Environmental technology and environmentally sound behaviour represent development potentials, i.e., present and future potentials of the economy and society of a country, that are increasingly important in international competition. The development or reduction of environmental research and development capacities may be vital for the future prospects of an economy, in particular in the services sector. As the President of the German Federal Office for the Environment, Heinrich v. Lersner, has pointed out, it would be to the disadvantage of the German industry if environmental policy came to a standstill. In that case ecologically beneficial technologies would increasingly have to be purchased abroad, and Germany's present top position on the world market (with an export volume of DM 35 billion for environmental technologies) would be jeopardized;[5]

3. The conservation of nature and environment itself has become a decisive factor for preserving jobs. If conservation efforts are diminished mass unemployment will rise. In Germany in 1992 a total of 600,000 were employed directly, and 200,000 indirectly in technologically-additive environmental protection — whose impact on the environment is somewhat ambiguous, though;[6]

---

5. Press information of the Federal Environmental Agency of the FRG, October 19, 1993.

6. Directly employed in environmental technology are persons concerned with the production of systems and technologies for the purification of air and waste air,

4. Ecological rationalization, i.e., systematic reduction of the consumption of natural resources such as energy, land, water, raw materials, and the corresponding optimization of operations, from purchasing to selling and distributing, will pave the way for a comparatively labour-intensive, low-cost production manner. It is thus a job-preserving, even job-creating form of structural rationalization tending to reduce employment.[7]

An analytical escape from the ecological development trap discussed before and the blind spot obscuring ecological-economic development potentials in periods of recession is offered by emphasizing the multidimensionality of societal and individual affluence: A society's wealth and its capacity for ecological action do not only depend on technological and economic factors, but also on its socio-cultural and institutional capacities, i.e., the development of values and behaviours oriented towards responsible action, and of mutual communication and exchange relations, shared responsibilities and active commitment. Recent studies in economics investigating innovation prospects in the new German provinces and Eastern Europe, have illustrated the relevance of socio-cultural and institutional networks as a basis for economic, social and ecological innovation.[8] Last but not least the knowledge of the relatively independent character of value and lifestyle orientations corresponds to the experience of alternative and ecological movements.

If the satisfaction of basic material needs, the development of ecological awareness and of institutional facilities encouraging environmentally friendly action are not rigidly coupled to each other, different combinations will become possible, such as affluence ecology, environmental destruction by superabundance, excessive exploitation or depletion of scarce resources and ecology of scarceness.

2.1 Ecology of Affluence

If postmaterialistic value change, ecological movements and a well-conceived environmental policy have evolved on the basis of satisfied primary needs and vital democracy, an ecology of affluence has developed. An afflu-

---

water and effluent treatment systems, waste processing and recycling techniques, control and analysis techniques (see Möller in G. Altner, B. Mettler-Meibom, U.E. Simonis, E.U. v. Weizsäcker (eds.), *Jahrbuch Ökologie*, Munich (1994), p. 154. Indirectly employed are system suppliers and operating personnel.

7. See Möller, op. cit. (footnote 6), pp. 144–145, 152 ff.

8. Cf. Jaenicke, op. cit. (footnote 3).

ent society's ecological behaviour is determined by its tendency to interpret environmental issues in the established terms of pollution and ecological stress,[9] and to utilize its specific technological and socio-cultural as well as institutional facilities and procedures for solving ecological problems. Activities involve a combination of expert-supported forms of technologically advanced risk management and efforts of developing ecologically oriented structures across society. Such efforts rely on developed procedures of democratic decision-making, as they have become established in the comparatively wealthy industrial societies.

2.2 Environmental Destruction Due to Superabundance

Economic affluence may also assume an uncivilized character, often by being founded on the continual destruction of a civilization's very background. As the threats it imposes on the climate and ozone layer of our planet illustrate, this characterization still is true for numerous industrialized countries and the oil-producing countries — despite all attempts of change in values and lifestyle initiated by the ecological movement.

2.3 Depletion of Scarce Resources

If the basic material and psychological needs have not been satisfied an over-exploitation of scarce resources may follow, a (self-)annihilating race for the remaining scarce resources and thus a rapid advance of ecological degradation. Current signs of such depletion in the name of poverty are found in many regions (the Sahel, for example), with dramatic consequences for the directly afflicted population, and often with potential consequences for the world population as a whole (destruction of tropical rain forests).

2.4 Ecology of Scarceness

Scarce resources may also lead to processes of adaptation based on socio-cultural adapting capacities. Examples are intensified efforts at collecting and recycling scarce resources, increased waste processing, meaningful strategies for economizing on resources, and social-institutional forms of a recycling

---

9. Resource scarcities usually are discussed in terms of ecological stress, such as pollution and waste problems.

economy in general aimed at preserving scarce resources. Usually such behaviours and the appropriate implementation mechanisms are regarded not so much as ecological than economic in character, although their impact is one of environmental compatibility and conservation. They can therefore be considered as scarceness-ecological forms of behaviour.

Ecology of affluence and ecology of scarceness are different ideal-typical patterns of environmental behaviour, environmental policy and their prerequisites: affluence ecology is based on the relative satisfaction of primary material needs and on post-materialistic value change, and is centered on the safety risks immanent in a prosperous society. Its main concerns are ecological problems related to superabundance and safety, such as pollution (of atmosphere, water and soil) and waste problems. A more careful management of resources is only obtained if efforts are made to solve the problems arising from an overstrained environment. The individual forms of affluence-ecological policy are highly differentiated (defence against dangers, risk management, development of ecologically oriented structures), and involve forms of management on a high technological and organizational level. The basic tenet of affluence ecology is in line with the pattern of reflexive modernization, according to which civilization problems caused by simple modernization are perceived via economic, socio-cultural and institutional capacities and are absorbed in new forms of socio-political commitment, a pattern of socio-political learning based on action capacity and experience.

Ecology of scarceness on the other hand is typical of societies and/or socio-political situations whose main emphasis is less on postmaterialistic value change or forms of environment-related surplus management, but on the compensation of an acute lack of resources. Scarceness management too may take different forms, such as the combination of recovery, recycling and demand minimization of scarce goods. Simpler forms of selective problem management and individual behaviour patterns predominate, however. There is no comprehensive awareness of environmental issues including the perception of potential problems and costs of economic surplus resources. Rather, scarceness ecology is a synonym of scarceness economy whose representatives are conscious of an acute scarceness of resources and the possibility of effective scarceness management.

Both socio-political ideal types, i.e., the ecology of affluence founded on post-materialistic value change, and the ecology of scarceness based on the awareness of economic scarceness, represent functioning forms of ecological adaptation. Essential to both are ecologically meaningful socio-cultural value and behaviour orientations. In the long run these socio-cultural patterns give rise to the corresponding political and institutional instruments, or rather a change in institutions depending on the particular type of ecology: Ecologically incompatible regulation structures are routinely penalized and replaced by ecologically compatible forms. Socio-cultural patterns of affluence or scarceness ecology are internalized and/or determined authoritatively.

Affluence- and scarceness-ecological structures are mutually exclusive only to the extent to which primary material needs are satisfied or unsatisfied. A society whose material needs have been largely satisfied is more likely to develop and perceive post-materialistic structures of awareness and ecological problems of superabundance than a society which is haunted by material want. Connections and mutual relations between an ecology of affluence and an ecology of scarceness will develop under several aspects:

1. Awareness structures, value orientations and routine behaviour orientations are not necessarily a function of given material and economic conditions. Like all factors of the socio-political process, socio-cultural factors to a certain extent are independent of technological and economic factors. An educated person, for instance, may be a fervent advocate of post-materialistic value orientations (at least at times), even if his own material circumstances are miserable;

2. Wealthy societies can reproduce their favourable situation for the very reason that their members are constantly aware of the possible loss of their abundant resources, i.e., of their potential poverty. The (idealtypical) market economy is founded on the balancing of scarce factors (supply and demand) and a corresponding formation of prices;

3. In a society certain resources may be provided in abundance whereas others may be scarce. As a consequence, mixed structures are typical.

All forms of methodically collecting and recycling scarce (i.e., non-abundant) resources are scarceness-ecological in character. In Germany public collecting campaigns of this kind date back to the time before World War I (for example, the Berlin system of "tripartition"). During the Hitler regime raw materials required for war purposes were collected systematically, though not always successfully, while the former German Democratic Republic had a system of collecting secondary raw materials, which was abolished after the fall of communism but has since been successfully revived and even exported into the Western provinces. Other examples of scarceness-ecology include early forms of energy-saving by ingenious heating techniques and decentralized heating units, such as tiled stoves, which were built in many parts of Europe and still are of practical importance.

As a superabundance of materials finally becomes manifest only via resulting scarcities, i.e., of drinking and bathing water, good air, health, radition-free soil, etc., and scarcity of economic factors is the underlying principle of the market system, general considerations of theoretical economics also lead to the concept of scarceness ecology. Besides, scarceness ecology is part of what — in spite of all criticism and weaknesses — is the most sensitive and innovation-encouraging type of present-day systems, the market economy. In practice, however, this system can only work if there is a genuinely open market (without any monopolistic or oligopolistic structures) and if the scarceness of environmental factors is taken into account (and not externalized from the market).

3. Conclusions

1. The common position still held even in the scientific world, according to which economy and ecology are uncritically differentiated, compared, added and contrasted, is out of place and politically misleading. Instead, ecological thinking and acting should be understood as economic thinking and acting with a wider horizon of responsibility and calculation whose material, temporal and possibly spatial radius has been extended. This is repeatedly ignored or denied, especially in periods of economic recession, a fact which is related to the fundamental dilemma of collective goods, i.e., the apparent opportunity of taking a free ecological ride. In the long run, however, such free rides are detrimental to a country's national economy and public health, worsening conditions for everyone. The prospects of "location Germany," for example, do not improve in this manner. For the reasons stated above, i.e., the safeguarding of health and natural and aesthetic living conditions, the productivity increase induced by carefully managing nature, and the innovative function of ecology in a cyclical and structural context, everybody thinking along economic lines will acknowledge the importance of ecological requirements and make himself their advocate.

2. While the development of environmental action depends on whether there is sufficient capacity for action, i.e., wealth in a wider sense, environmental action itself is not only the attempt of exerting a direct influence on the quality of the environment under given preconditions, but also the attempt to improve these preconditions. Ecological thinking along this line includes the perception of the ecologically disastrous effects of unemployment and poverty; this refers to the situation in Germany, and to the removal of trade barriers and unfair terms of trade causing or increasing poverty in many countries. Environmental policy must also be understood as a policy encouraging the development and use of flexible technologies and an open exchange of information on technological and civilizatory procedures. Finally, environmental policy is aimed at facilitating specific socio-cultural value

orientations and institutional patterns of decision-making for the benefit of those affected by a damaged environment or profiting from ecological conservation measures. Special concerns are the protection and encouragement of a vital, i.e., representative and participatory democracy.

3. Even in periods of economic recession or structural economic scarceness environmentally friendly behaviour is possible and useful. Statements such as, "Environmental protection is expensive, so we cannot afford it at the moment," do not take into account what has been discussed above, i.e., the productivity- and innovation-increasing properties of ecology. These statements can be countered effectively, however, by stabilizing socio-cultural (value) orientations and meeting organizational requirements for ecological objectives. As regards the relationship between rich and poor countries, it may be justified from the perspective of scarce economic resources to point out the special responsibility of the wealthy industrialized nations: this statement will become an ecological and economic boomerang for the poorer nations, however, if it induces them to neglect or suppress their own efforts to protect their natural environment. Departing from scarceness-ecological considerations — ecological action is possible even if economic resources are scarce, given the appropriate value orientations and organizational patterns — ecological and thus economic innovation and performance potentials will be obtained.

Further Literature

Amery, Carl, *Natur als Politik. Die Ökologische Chance des Menschen,* Reinbek (1978).

Beck, Ulrich, *Risikogesellschaft. Auf dem Weg in eine andere Moderne,* Frankfurt (1986).

Beck, Ulrich, *Gegengifte. Die organisierte Verantwortungslosigkeit,* Frankfurt (1988).

Beyme, Klaus von, "Policy Analysis und traditionelle Politikwissenschaft," in Hans-Herrmann Hartwich (ed.), *Policy-Forschung in der Bundesrepublik Deutschland. Ihr Selbstverständnis und ihr Verhältnis zu den Grundfragen der Politikwissenschaft,* Opladen (1985), pp. 7–29.

Caldwell, Lynton Keith, *In Defense of Earth. International Protection of the Biosphere,* London (1972).

Hauff, Volker (ed.), *Unsere gemeinsame Zukunft. Der Brundtland-Bericht der Weltkommission für Umwelt und Entwicklung*, Greven (1987).

Höpfner, Ulrich et al., PKW, Bus oder Bahn? Schadstoffemissionen und Energieverbrauch im Stadtverkehr 1984 und 1995, IFEU-Institut Heidelberg, IFEU-report no. 48, Heidelberg (1988).

Huber, Joseph, "Ökologische Modernisierung. Zwischen bürokratischem und zivilgesellschaftlichem Handeln," in Volker von Prittwitz (ed.), *Umweltpolitik als Modernisierungsprozeß. Politikwissenschaftliche Umweltforschung und -lehre in der Bundesrepublik Deutschland*, Opladen (1993), pp. 51–69.

Jaenicke, Martin (ed.), *Umweltpolitik. Beiträge zur Politologie des Umweltschutzes*, Opladen (1978).

Jaenicke, Martin, *Wie das Industriesystem von seinen Mißständen profitiert*, Opladen (1979).

Jaenicke, Martin, "Arbeitsplätze durch umweltgerechtes Wirtschaften," Kongreß Zukunft der Arbeit, Bielefeld (1982), pp. 294–301.

Jaenicke, Martin, *Umweltpolitische Prävention als ökologische Modernisierung und Strukturpolitik, Wissenschaftszentrum Berlin* (IIUG discussion paper 84–1), Berlin (1984).

Jaenicke, Martin, *Staatsversagen. Die Ohnmacht der Politik in der Industriegesellschaft*, Munich (1986).

Jaenicke, Martin, "Ökologische Modernisierung. Optionen und Restriktionen präventiver Umweltpolitik," in Udo-Ernst Simonis (ed.), *Präventive Umweltpolitik*, Frankfurt-New York (1988), pp. 12–26.

Knoepfel, Peter and Weidner Helmut, *Luftreinhaltepolitik (stationäre Quellen) im internationalen Vergleich*, 6 vol.: 1. Methodik und Ergebnisse, 2. Bundesrepublik Deutschland, 3. England, 4. Frankreich, 5. Italien, 6. Niederlande, Berlin (1985).

Leipert, Christian, *Die heimlichen Kosten des Fortschritts*, Munich (1989).

Luhmann, Niklas, *Beobachtungen der Moderne*, Opladen (1992).

Mármora, Leopoldo, "Sustainable Development im Nord-Süd-Konflikt: Vom Konzept der Umverteilung des Reichtums zu den Erfordernissen einer globalen Gerechtigkeit," Prokla 22, no. 86 (1992), pp. 34–36.

Maslow, Abraham H., *Towards a Psychology of Being*, New York (1954).

Mayntz, Renate et al., *Vollzugsprobleme der Umweltpolitik*, Stuttgart et al. (1978).

Meadows, Dennis et al., *Die Grenzen des Wachstums,* Stuttgart (1972).

Monheim, Heiner and Rita Monheim-Dandorfer, *Straßen für alle, Analysen und Konzepte zum Stadtverkehr der Zukunft,* Hamburg (1990).

Oberthür, Sebastian, *Politik im Treibhaus. Die Entstehung des internationalen Klimaschutzregimes,* Berlin (1993).

Prittwitz, Volker von and Klaus Dieter Wolf, "Die Politik der globalen Güter," in Volker von Prittwitz (ed.), *Umweltpolitik als Modernisierungsprozeß. Politikwissenschaftliche Umweltforschung und -lehre in der Bundesrepublik Deutschland,* Opladen (1993), pp. 193–218.

Prittwitz, Volker von, "Katastrophenparadox und Handlungskapazität. Theoretische Orientierungen der Politikanalyse," in Adrienne Windhoff-Heritier (ed.), *Policy Analysis. Kritik und Neuorientierung,* PVS-Sonderheft 24 (1993), pp. 328–355.

Seifried, Dieter, *Gute Argumente Verkehr,* Munich (1990).

Simonis, Udo-Ernst (ed.), *Präventive Umweltpolitik,* Frankfurt-New York (1988).

Simonis, Udo-Ernst, *Beyond Growth: Elements of Sustainable Development,* Berlin (1990).

Zilleßen, Horst, Die Modernisierung der Demokratie im Zeichen der Umweltproblematik," in Volker von Prittwitz (ed.), op. cit., Opladen (1993), pp. 81–91.

5

Economic and Institutional Capacities for Environmental Cooperation
(Some Remarks on Volker von Prittwitz)

Peter H. Sand

It is not difficult to concur with the basic approach advocated by Volker von Prittwitz; viz., to relate progress in European environmental cooperation to the different levels of environmental awareness in the countries concerned, which in turn are conditioned by economic and institutional capacities. Not surprisingly, "capacity building" has also become the focus of global cooperative efforts to address the environmental problems of developing countries and economies in transition, especially in the context of *Agenda 21,* the action plan of the United Nations Conference on Environment and Development.[1]

With regard to *economic capacities,* the simple correlation of high gross national product (GNP) and high environmental ranking of state behavior in international relations — as implied by Jänicke and Mönch[2] — may not suffice, and may actually be misleading. For example, while it is correct that

---

Legal Adviser, Environmental Affairs, The World Bank, Washington, D.C.; formerly Principal Programme Officer, UNCED. Views and opinions are those of the author and should not be attributed to any institution with which he is or was associated.

1. *Report of the United Nations Conference on Environment and Development,* A/CONF. 151/26; see especially chapter 37, "National Mechanisms and International Cooperation for Capacity-building in Developing Countries."

2. Martin Jänicke and Harald Mönch, "Ökologischer und wirtschaftlicher Wandel im Industrieländervergleich" in Manfred Schmidt (ed.), *Staatstätigkeit: International und historisch vergleichende Analyse,* Opladen (1988), pp. 389–405; as quoted by Volker von Prittwitz.

domestic pesticide consumption in industrialized countries has *declined* as a result of environmental awareness, their overall pesticide production has continued to *increase*, as more than 95 percent of the pesticides produced by German or Swiss chemical industry are exported.[3] The Jänicke-Mönch correlation also fails to take into account the special situation of small countries, whose international environmental activism is not a matter of choice but the only way in which they can influence developments that otherwise would be beyond their national economic power and control; this explains at least in part the disproportionate prominence of countries like Austria, the Netherlands, Norway, and Switzerland in European environmental diplomacy — not unlike the role of the small island countries threatened by sea-level rise in the negotiations for a global climate convention.[4]

At the same time, there are solid economic reasons for the newly found "environmental foreign policy"[5] of industrialized countries. Rather than resisting international environmental controls, it may be preferable for a country to ensure that its domestic level of constraints is at least extended evenhandedly to all countries (for a "level playing field"). As the negotiations on ozone-depleting substances demonstrated (the Montreal Protocol and its amendments[6]), any environmental benefits of a treaty regime, however quantified, invariably mean pollution control costs — costs to government and costs to industry. In an international setting, countries will first seek to avoid penalizing their own industries and taxpayers; rather than imposing such costs unilaterally, they will instead endeavor to ensure that costs are evenly spread and, in particular, are imposed on foreign competitors. Hence, one way of looking at intergovernmental environmental agreements is as legal mechanisms to ensure a degree of international equalization of costs among competing polluters.[7] Another economic motive which has been

3. According to the 1988 UN/ECE *Annual Review of the Chemical Industry* ECE/CHEM/75, United Nations, New York (1990), pp. 132 f. West German production of disinfectants, insecticides, fungicides, weed-killers, anti-sprouting products, rat poisons, and similar products in 1986 amounted to 144.947 million metric tons, of which 144.590 million metric tons were exported.

4. The AOSIS played an active part in the negotiations both for the UN Framework Convention on Climate Change and for Agenda 21 of the UN Conference on Environment and Development.

5. Volker von Prittwitz, *Umweltaußenpolitik*, Frankfurt (1984).

6. The 1987 Montreal Protocol on Substances That Deplete the Ozone Layer, as amended/adjusted in London 1990; see Richard E. Benedick, *Ozone Diplomacy: New Directions in Safeguarding the Planet*, Harvard University Press, Cambridge, Mass. (1990).

7. See Peter H. Sand, "Regional Approaches to Transboundary Air Pollution," in

identified in the "environmental" position of industrialized countries, especially in the European acid rain negotiations, is a desire to promote the export of a country's advanced pollution control technology.[8]

With regard to *institutional capacities*, Prittwitz rightly emphasizes the significance of mechanisms for democratic public participation in decision-making, and public access to environmental information. While the creation of such mechanisms and procedures in Central and Eastern Europe may be considered as a prerequisite, Janos Vargha has pointed out the mutual interdependence of political reforms and environmental awareness in this region,[9] which had its parallel at the diplomatic level: Not only did the 1975 Helsinki Final Act lead to specific environmental agreements, e.g., on transboundary air pollution,[10] but the technical cooperation so established in turn facilitated and forced further political détente. Among other things, it contributed to the formation of what has been described as "epistemic communities"[11] of technical experts and scientists whose growing involvement in treaty negotiation and implementation added further momentum to the transnational cooperation process.

The participation of non-governmental groups in international environmental regimes in Europe has been more intense than is generally known. For example, at a time when there was still virtually no NGO's participation in the global ozone layer regime,[12] groups like Greenpeace and Friends of the Earth already had observer status at the sessions of the executive body for the Geneva Convention on Long-Range Transboundary Air Pollution (LRTAP);[13] and the position of a number of delegations in the negotiation

---

J.L. Helm (ed.), *Energy Production, Consumption and Consequences*, National Academy Press, Washington, D.C. (1990), pp. 246–264, at 258.

8. With reference to the German position, see the analysis by P. Roqueplo, *Pluies acides: menaces pour l'Europe*, Paris (1988).

9. Quoting H.F. French, "Green Revolution: Environmental Reconstruction in Eastern Europe and the Soviet Union," *Worldwatch Paper* no. 99, Worldwatch Institute, Washington, D.C., November 1990.

10. See E.M. Chossudovsky, '*East-West' Diplomacy for Environment in the United Nations*, United Nations Institute for Training and Research, Geneva (1989).

11. See J.G. Ruggie, "International Responses to Technology: Concepts and Trends," *International Organization*, vol. 29 (1975), pp. 557–583, at 570 (borrowing a term by Michel Foucault, *The Order of Things*); and P.M. Haas, "Do Regimes Matter? Epistemic Communities and Mediterranean Pollution Control," *International Organization*, vol. 43 (1989), pp. 377–403.

12. See Peter H. Sand, "Protecting the Ozone Layer: The Vienna Convention is Adopted," *Environment*, vol. 27, no. 5 (June 1985), p. 42.

13. See list of participants at the Helsinki session in July 1985, which adopted the

and eventual signature and ratification of subsequent protocols under the Convention may be said to have been influenced by active NGO lobbying and public information campaigns.[14]

As regards treaty implementation, however, only the European Community has so far established a formal mechanism for citizen participation in environmental matters. As part of the "custodial" role of the European Community (EC) Commission for the implementation of Community law pursuant to Article 155 of the Rome Treaty, a "complaints registry" has been set up in Brussels, where individuals or citizen groups may report infringements of EC environmental directives by any member government. Under the infringement procedure of Article 169, the Commission may take up the case — based on the complaint or on its own initiative — by way of a "letter of formal notice" of infringement, addressed to the government concerned. After giving the member state an opportunity for responding, the Commission can next render a "reasoned opinion" confirming the infringement in light of all the facts gathered. If the member state still does not comply, the Commission may then refer the matter to the European Court of Justice.[15] The overall number of environmental citizen complaints registered in 1990 was 480. During that year, the Commission initiated a total of 167 letters of notice to governments for infringements of EC environmental directives, 39 reasoned opinions and 14 referrals to the Court.[16] While only a small proportion of complaints thus end up in judicial proceedings, the three-step infringement procedure has resulted in a substantial volume of out-of-court compliance action, in which public participation has played a major role.

---

protocol concerning the reduction of sulfur emissions and their transboundary fluxes by at least 30 percent (ECE/EB.AIR 12). On the negotiations see L. Björkbom, "Resolution of Environmental Problems: The Use of Diplomacy," in J.E. Carroll (ed.), *International Environmental Diplomacy*, Cambridge University Press 1988, pp. 123–137.

14. For example, on the US position regarding the 1988 Sofia Protocol on Nitrogen Oxides see R.N. Mott, "Nitrogen Oxides," *Environmental Policy and Law*, vol. 18 (1988) pp. 52 f.; and R.N. Mott, "An Acid Rain Summons From Europe," *Environmental Forum*, vol. 5, no. 1 (1988), pp. 32 f. See also the newsletter of the Swedish and Norwegian NGO Secretariats on Acid Rain, *Acid News*, and the *ECO* newsletters jointly published by NGOs during the annual sessions of the LRTAP executive body.

15. Peter H. Sand, *Lessons Learned in Global Environmental Governance*, World Resources Institute, Washington, D.C. 1990, pp. 31–33.

16. Commission of the European Communities, "Monitoring Application of Community Law," 8th Report to the European Parliament, *Official Journal of the European Communities* no. C 328/1, 1991; see L. Krämer, *Focus on European Environmental Law*, London (1992), chapter 14.

PART THREE

International Negotiating Processes in the Environmental Field and Their Results

6

Specific Characteristics of Environmental Diplomacy

Winfried Lang

Diplomacy has been defined as "the application of human reason to re-solving conflicts between nations."[1] At the outset this definition seems to cover environmental diplomacy only in an imperfect way, as this type of diplomacy appears to deal mainly with issues beyond traditional inter-state conflicts, namely issues such as the protection of the global commons (high seas, climate, space, etc.) which are of interest to mankind as a whole. Broad objectives such as the well-being of future generations or the protection of nature transcend narrow conflicts between nations. As, however, costs to be borne to attain these objectives are unevenly distributed — some countries may be required to make more sacrifices than others — conflicts over burden sharing, which are among the most traditional conflicts of interest, are likely to arise. A case in point was the gradual elimination of chlorofluorocarbons because of their ozone-depleting capacity; countries that had no industry ac-tively engaged in producing and exporting these substances were much less reluctant to approve their elimination than the producing and exporting countries.[2] Landlocked states are much less affected by the rules on marine pollution contained in the Law of the Sea Convention than coastal or port

---

1. George McGhee, "The State of Diplomacy," in George McGhee (ed.), *Diplomacy for the Future,* Washington, D.C. (1987), p. 3.

2. For an overview of these negotiations see inter alia Richard E. Benedick, *Ozone Diplomacy,* Cambridge, Mass. (1991).

91

states, to whom special responsibilities were assigned in this respect.[3] Thus, as environmental measures affect political actors in different ways — mainly as a consequence of different levels of economic development, differences related to the industrial base or geographic position (downstream versus upstream) — environmental diplomacy is in charge of preventing or settling conflicts between nations.

Environmental diplomacy is also a relatively new branch of international relations.[4] Although disputes about water rights, the elaboration of boundary water treaties and so on have occurred in the past, it was not until the late 1960s and early 1970s that "the environment" became a matter of interest for national and international politics. In 1968 the UN General Assembly decided to convene the 1972 Stockholm Conference on Human Environment. In 1968 the Council of Europe adopted its first declaration on air pollution. During these years too, as a consequence of major oil pollution disasters, the International Maritime Organization drafted numerous international treaties related to activities such as the transport of oil by sea and the dumping of waste at the high seas.[5]

Today, twenty years later, environmental diplomacy comprises a broad field of activities, which are conducted at various levels: neighborhood, regional, and global. These levels depend mainly on the scope of the problem to be addressed. The pollution of a river crossing several countries should be dealt with regionally by the riparian states (Rhine, Danube, and so on). Problems such as climate change, biodiversity, and ozone depletion have to be resolved by the community of states as a whole. Air pollution in Europe has also been considered in a regional context.

Environmental diplomacy is not restricted to meetings of experts. As public opinion pays much attention to environmental matters political lead-

3. On these negotiations see inter alia T.T.B Koh, "Negotiating a New World Order for the Sea," in Alan Henrikson (ed.), *Negotiating World Order*, Wilmington (1983), pp. 33–45.

4. For a broad overview see Winfried Lang, "Negotiations on the Environment," in Victor Kremenyuk (ed.), *International Negotiation*, San Francisco-Oxford (1991), pp. 343–356; a selected reading is provided by Lawrence Susskind and Esther Siskind (eds.), *International Negotiation*, MIT-Harvard Public Disputes Program, April 1990 (Salzburg Seminar 284); John Caroll (ed.), *International Environmental Diplomacy*, Cambridge, Mass. (1988); Peter Chasek, *The System of International Environmental Negotiations*, American Academy of Diplomacy, Background Paper Series BP-1; and most recently Gunnar Sjöstedt (ed.), *International Environmental Negotiation*, Newbury Park, Cal. (1993).

5. This evolution is summarized by Winfried Lang, *Internationaler Umweltschutz, Völkerrecht und Aussenpolitik zwischen Ökonomie und Ökologie*, Vienna (1989), pp. 64–70.

ers have shown a keen interest to be associated with certain environmental "success stories," as for instance those related to ozone depletion or air pollution (the Montreal Protocol and the Helsinki and Sofia Protocols). Thus "high-level" attendance has become customary in many environmental conferences — either at the opening or during the final phase (signing of instruments).[6]

Environmental diplomacy is well rooted in the national context of each state. At first it is to some extent the follow-up of the internal environmental policy of the countries involved, which in itself is the result of many economic and social forces at work.[7] Secondly this branch of diplomacy depends on an especially intense process of internal coordination, because many departments (ministries) have a say in formulating a common national position. In some cases competition may develop between foreign ministries and environment ministries as regards the leadership in certain environmental negotiations. This requirement of coordination especially arises in the phase of pre-negotiation ("getting to the table").[8] It seems to be of particular importance in the field of environment, where some departments may show special allegiance to certain interest groups outside the government.

Environmental diplomacy has become fully embedded in the main stream of international politics. Thus summit meetings of the Group of Seven (G-7) as well as ministerial meetings of the Conference on Security and Cooperation in Europe (CSCE) usually deal with environmental issues or at least treat some related topics in their concluding statements.[9] For some governments introducing environmental language in summit declarations has become a yardstick of success. It remains to be seen whether those high-level pronouncements can be translated into concrete policies thus affecting the real-life environment.

Environmental diplomacy, furthermore, is highly complex by the very nature of its issue area. Whereas the specific nature of environmental problems would require a holistic approach (systems analysis approach), which

---

6. UNCED '92 was attended by numerous heads of state and government and was thus labeled the "Earth Summit."

7. See Lang, op. cit. (footnote 5), p. 175; Volker v. Prittwitz, "Several Approaches to the Analysis of International Environmental Policy," in *Wissenschaftszentrum Berlin 1988*, Papers (Forschungsschwerpunkt Technik-Arbeit-Umwelt), p. 7; and Volker v. Prittwitz, *Umweltaussenpolitik,* Frankfurt-New York (1984), p. 26.

8. This term is explained in Janice Gross-Stein (ed.), *Getting to the Table,* Baltimore (1989).

9. See, for example, numerous references to the environment in Stefan Lehne, *The Vienna Meeting of the Conference on Security and Cooperation in Europe,* 1986–1989, Boulder-San Francisco-Oxford (1991).

takes into account whatever linkages, interdependencies, and other factors that affect issues to be solved, most governments follow a piecemeal and incremental approach.[10] They commit themselves only to targets that seem easily attainable, the costs of which can be evenly and easily distributed in society. This inclination for a step-by-step approach gives support to a well-known pattern: drafting, at first, framework conventions with relatively few and "soft" obligations; these treaties are to be followed at a later stage by "protocols" containing more stringent obligations (reduction schemes with target dates, see the treaties in the field of long-range transboundary air pollution and ozone depletion). It should not be neglected that this complexity of environmental diplomacy is also due to pressures coming from numerous social forces outside government.

Environmental diplomacy is strongly influenced by interest groups (non governmental organizations) which act at several levels.[11] In the national context they try to have their views at least partially reflected in the common national position approved by the respective government. At the international level (conferences) they try to have an at least indirect impact on negotiations by presenting their views to national delegations and by pleading their cause vis-à-vis the media. An impressive number of NGOs participated also in the preparatory process for UNCED. It is, however, difficult to evaluate precisely the real influence of these organizations on the outcome of an intergovernmental negotiation.

Environmental diplomacy is certainly not the secret and private exercise of a few diplomats. It rather comes close to the Wilsonian ideal of "open covenants, openly arrived at," although many negotiations on substance — the real give and take — occur in quiet back rooms among a limited number of chief players. However, these chief players have to take into account not only other governmental actors but also the media; they must sell the outcome of the negotiation to the public at home.[12] This relatively strong influence of the media on environmental negotiations may be explained by the

---

10. This need for a special and comprehensive approach explains to some extent the high degree of attention paid by the IIASA to environmental negotiations, see Sjöstedt, op. cit. (footnote 4).

11. Fritjof Capra and Charlene Spretnak, *Green Politics,* New York (1984); John McCormick, *The Global Environmental Movement,* London (1989); Norita Yap, "NGOs and sustainable development," *International Journal,* vol. XLV, pp. 75–105; and Nancy Lindborg, "Nongovernmental Organizations: Their Past, Present, and Future Role in International Environmental Negotiations," in Lawrence Susskind, Eric J. Dolin, and William J. Breslin, *International Environmental Treatymaking,* Cambridge, Mass. (1992), pp. 1–25.

12. Lang, op. cit. (footnote 4), pp. 348 and 351.

fact that environmental issues are regarded by many individuals as affecting them directly. Strong media involvement does not always have a beneficial impact on negotiations: during negotiations on the transport of hazardous waste (Basel Convention), the general impression prevailed, due to intensive media reporting, that one was confronted with a major North-South dispute, although the huge majority of such transports does take place between industrialized countries.[13]

Environmental diplomacy is also highly dependent on science.[14] The impact of science goes well beyond the narrow scope of negotiations: scientists usually discover new threats to the environment; scientists are expected to propose remedies, to develop alternative substances, and to provide substitutes; finally scientists often play an important role in monitoring the compliance of a government with its commitments. However, during all phases of the involvement of science in political decision making the same questions are likely to arise: Are scientists objective and impartial? Are these scientists on the payroll of organizations which have a vested interest in a specific outcome of their research?

Environmental diplomacy, furthermore, has to take into account the economic feasibility of control measures and of measures combating various types of pollution.[15] Sometimes costs to be expected for certain industries may constitute a stumbling block to environmental progress. As a consequence, legal instruments such as the Convention on Long-Range Transboundary Air Pollution contain numerous "soft provisions," which allow for exceptions on economic grounds. Another consequence of these economic considerations is the special treatment accorded to developing countries in the Montreal Protocol on Substances that Deplete the Ozone Layer; in this

---

13. See Willy Kempel, "Transboundary Movements of Hazardous Wastes," in Sjöstedt, op. cit. (footnote 4).

14. This was especially highlighted during the ASCEND 21 Conference held in November 1991 in Vienna under the auspices of ICSU, see J.C.I. Dooge et al. (eds.), *An Agenda of Science for Environment and Development into the 21st Century*, Cambridge, Mass. (1992).

15. Reading on the overall aspects is provided inter alia by Horst Siebert, *Economics of the Environment*, (1st ed. 1981), Berlin-Heidelberg (1987); Charles Perrings, *Economy and Environment*, Cambridge, Mass. (1987); J.B. Opschoor and H.B. Vos, *Economic Instruments for Environmental Protection*, OECD, Paris 1989; and R.J. Johnston, *Environmental Problems: Nature, Economy and State*, London (1989); see also Wolfgang Weigel (ed.), *Economic Analysis of Law*, Vienna (1991), pp. 41–103 (contributions of Ercmann, Nentjes, Swanson, Ashworth-Papps, and Pearson); and most recently, Stefan Schmidheiny (with the Business Council for Sustainable Development), *Changing Course. A Global Business Perspective on Environment and Development*, Cambridge, Mass. (1992).

agreement developing countries benefit from so-called "differential obligations" which impose upon them less stringent standards than those applicable to developed countries. Furthermore, governments entering into new commitments in the field of environment will have to consider the impact such commitments might have on the competitive position of their respective industries on the world market. Thus they will try to pursue ecology and economy as a twin goal without giving too much priority to one or to the other.

Environmental diplomacy has become a new area for North-South disputes. Traditional claims of developing countries such as transfer of technology at advantageous terms were at center stage not only when the above-mentioned Montreal Protocol was revised (London 1990), but also during the negotiations for a global climate convention. The South feels that it now has much more bargaining leverage than in previous New International Economic Order (NIEO) negotiations.[16] A Southern threat of not participating in certain global conventions — thus eroding the very impact of these instruments — may lure the North into more generosity as regards financing the transfer of alternative or clean technologies. Such threatening behavior could, however, also damage the interests of developing countries themselves, because in the long run they should also care for the state of their environment.[17]

Environmental diplomacy has also moved into the field of development assistance.[18] International financial institutions have made several of their lending activities subject to the environment impact assessment of programs and projects.[19] The Global Environment Facility (GEF) is about to become a focal point for development projects closely associated with environmental

---

16. This assumption is reflected especially in a strategy paper issued by the South Center, *Environment and Development,* Geneva 1991; see also Winfried Lang, "Der Nord-Süd-Konflikt/Ökonomie und Ökologie," in Jürgen Bellers and Reinhard Meyers (eds.), *Europa in der entwicklungspolitischen Verantwortung,* Münster-Hamburg (1992), pp. 58–71; as regards negotiations on global climate change see inter alia Winfried Lang, *Auf der Suche nach einem wirksamen Klima-Regime,* Archiv des Völkerrechts (1993), pp. 13–29.

17. David Adamson, *Defending the World,* London-New York (1990), p. 216.

18. On the environmental problems of the South see inter alia Yves Laulan, *Le Tiers Monde et la Crie de l'Environnement,* Paris (1974); and Jürg Hauser, *Bevölkerungs- und Umweltprobleme der Dritten Welt,* Berne-Stuttgart (1990); for a perspective from the South see Latin American and Caribbean Commission on Development and Environment (IADB – UNDP), *Our Own Agenda,* 1990.

19. The World Bank, *The World Bank and Environment, First Annual Report,* Washington, D.C. (1990).

concerns. "Debt-for-nature-swaps" being mainly organized by private interests have to rely, at least in some cases, on the support of governmental authorities (in the donor or in the recipient country); thus in many cases negotiations at the governmental level are required to put these projects on the appropriate track.[20]

Environmental diplomacy is an activity that, except for bilateral negotiations (neighborhood) heavily relies on international organizations.[21] These institutions do play a wide variety of roles:

— raising awareness of new threats;
— providing a forum for negotiations;
— providing support for negotiators (scientific, legal advice, etc.);
— acting as facilitators (devising compromise formulae etc.);
— acting as "guardians" of legal or political instruments, which reflect the outcome of negotiations; most treaties need institutions to render rights and duties operational.

In many instances UNEP, International Maritime Organization (IMO), the International Atomic Energy Agency (IAEA), and the ECE have played one or more of these roles.

Environmental diplomacy does no present itself as a static endeavor; it is rather an international activity in constant flux[22] as:

— more and more threats to the environment are discovered;
— international treaties once concluded must constantly be adapted to changing circumstances, such as new scientific evidence, technological breakthroughs, etc.; such adaptation and revision must be preceded by new negotiations because not all actors may share the view that changes and amendments are necessary;

---

20. Kristin Dawkins, "Debt for Nature Swaps," in Susskind and Siskind, op. cit. (footnote 4).

21. For a comprehensive review see Michael Kilian, *Umweltschutz durch Internationale Organisationen,* Berlin (1987); and Lynton Keith Caldwell, *International Environmental Policy,* Durham-London (1990), pp. 94–111, and pp. 129–167; Alexandre Kiss, *Droit International de l'Environnement,* Paris (1989), pp. 307–336; Andrew Hurrell and Benedict Kingsbury (eds.), *The International Politics of the Environment,* Oxford (1992), pp. 183–249; for a UN focus see Donald J. Puchala, "The United Nations and Ecosystem Issues," in Lawrence S. Finkelstein (ed.), *Politics in the United Nations System,* Durham-London (1988), pp. 214–245.

22. This flux is most amply demonstrated by the evolution of the Montreal Protocol, see the section "Ozone Layer," in the *Yearbook of International Environmental Law,* vol. 1, pp. 95–99 (Lang and Kempel) and following volumes.

— compliance of states with their obligations has to be monitored — a technical task — and evaluated — a political task; the latter (peer review) may require that states have recourse to efficient mechanisms of dispute settlement.

Environmental diplomacy is conducted by established actors as well as new ones.[23] In addition to national governments, which remain the main actors — building coalitions or assembling within regional or interest groups — the European Economic Community, due to its sheer economic weight and its competence in environmental matters (Single European Act), has become a chief player in this arena (see the negotiations leading to the Montreal Protocol or the preparatory process for UNCED). To some extent science, nongovernmental organizations, and the media may also be considered as actors, although their impact on negotiations is only an indirect one.

As a new branch of intercourse between nations, environmental diplomacy does not substantially differ from diplomacy in other fields as far as working methods are concerned.[24] It strives for the adoption of legal or political instruments ("soft law") which reflect to the largest possible extent the consensus of participants. Unless the text agreed upon covers the interests of all parties, it is threatened by noncompliance or imperfect compliance because the international society — at present — does not have means of coercion such as strong sanctions that would oblige "holdouts" to reconsider their negative attitude. As mentioned above environmental diplomacy relies much on scientific evidence and is strongly influenced by NGOs and the media.

Environmental diplomacy would in traditional terms be considered part of "low politics" such as trade negotiations and other "welfare"-related interactions between states. This division between "high politics" and "low politics" becomes more and more blurred because some governments associate environmental threats with threats to their national security or to global security; risk management and crisis management have become not only focal points of military security but also of environmental security.[25] Further-

23. Lang, op. cit. (footnote 4), p. 345; and Gareth Porter and Janet Welsh Brown, *Global Environmental Politics,* Boulder-San Francisco-London (1991), pp. 35–68.

24. Ibidem, p. 351; see also Richard E. Benedick, "Behind the Diplomatic Curtain, Inner Workings of the New Global Negotiations," *Columbia Journal of World Business,* Fall/Winter 1992, pp. 53–61.

25. Jessica Tuchmann-Mathews, "Redefining Security," *Foreign Affairs,* vol. 68, no. 2 (Spring 1989), pp. 162–177; Anne Ehrlich and Paul Ehrlich, "Die Umwelt als Dimension nationaler Sicherheit," in Mostafa Kamal Tolba et al., *Die Umwelt bewahren,* Bonn-Bad Godesberg (1989), pp. 35–57.

more "power politics" are not totally alien to environmental diplomacy: the Law of the Sea Convention is likely to remain a dead letter as long as the United States refuses to ratify it; a global climate convention setting CO_2 emission targets will be a futile exercise unless ways and means have been found to persuade those countries to sign, which have huge fossil fuel reserves that would have to be left unused in case of their adherence to the treaty; the conventions on nuclear accidents would lose much of their value if countries with important nuclear industries were not ready to become parties. Environmental negotiations are likely to fail, if they do not recognize the respective political and economic interests of countries involved, and in particular those carrying major political weight.

Environmental diplomacy may be considered an international activity that is most strongly confronted with the issue of national sovereignty.[26] Countries which contribute to transboundary pollution or to the pollution of the global commons are expected to accept certain constraints, which may restrict their economic activities to some extent or make these activities more expensive as a consequence of prevention or abatement costs. Countries that are affected by transboundary pollution feel that their sovereignty has been violated by emissions from abroad; such emissions may even be assimilated to military aggression. Either side will have to refrain from postulating unrestricted or absolute sovereignty or unlimited territorial integrity. Only serious harm, beyond a certain threshold, is considered a wrong committed under international law.[27] As there is no general consensus on where that threshold should be located, solutions have to be sought by mutual accommodation on a case-by-case basis. Sovereignty is certainly an obstacle to rapid progress; efforts aimed at redefining its content and making it compatible with the various needs for action — by national or international bodies — should be pursued.

Through its multiple activities environmental diplomacy has contributed to the emergence of a new branch of international law: international environmental law.[28] As there exists only a modest amount of customary law and

---

26. On this issue see also Winfried Lang, "Die Abwehr weiträumiger Umweltgefahren, insbesondere durch internationale Organisationen," in *Umweltschutz im Völkerrecht und Kollisionsrecht,* (Berichte der Deutschen Gesellschaft für Völkerrecht, Bd. 32, Heidelberg (1992), p. 51; Ernst Ulrich von Weizsäcker, *Erdpolitik,* Darmstadt (1989), pp. 203 and 215; and Marvin Soroos, *Beyond Sovereignty,* Columbia, South Carolina (1987), p. 359.

27. As for the respective dictum in the Trail-Smelter case see Kevin Madders, "Trail Smelter Arbitration," *Encyclopedia of Public International Law,* vol. 2 (1981), p. 276.

28. Patricia Birnie and Alan E. Boyle, *International Law and the Environment,*

the number of rulings by international judicial bodies is rather scarce, rule-making (treaties and soft-law texts) has become a major task of environmental diplomacy. Advantages and drawbacks of this approach should be kept in mind: treaties contain relatively clear language, thus determining to a large extent the future behavior of contracting parties; however, states that have not ratified these treaties continue to be free as regards their actual conduct.

Environmental diplomacy could not ignore the issue of international trade.[29] As several legal instruments in the environmental field entitle parties to impose trade restrictions (export and import of ozone-depleting substances, trade with endangered species), international trade law, which is reluctant to accept measures causing trade distortions, would have to be made compatible with these new rules. There again looms a major confrontation between North and South because developing countries are afraid that such adjustments of trade law may legitimize environmental barriers protecting the markets of industrialized states.

Against the background of past and current environmental negotiations a final question has to be asked: Is environmental diplomacy sufficiently transparent and efficient? As regards the issue of transparency one has to draw attention to the growing public interest in problems of foreign policy.[30] This

Oxford (1992); Alexandre Kiss, *Droit international d'environnement*, Paris (1989); Alexandre Kiss and Diane Shelton, *International Environmental Law*, Irvington on Hudson (1991); Winfried Lang, *Internationaler Umweltschutz*, Vienna (1989); Winfried Lang, Hanspeter Neuhold, and Karl Zemanek (eds.), *Environmental Protection and International Law*, London (1991); Allen Springer, *The International Law of Pollution*, Westport (1983).

29. Among recent articles on this issue see Ernst-Ulrich Petersmann, "Trade-Policy, Environmental Policy and the GATT," *Aussenwirtschaft*, 46. Jg. (1991), no. II, pp. 197–221; Gerhard Loibl and Lilly Sucharipa-Behrmann, "Umwelt und Freihandel," *Economy-Fachmagazin* 12/91, pp. 300–304; Hames Cameron and Jonathan Robinson, "The Use of Trade Provisions in International Environmental Agreements and their Compatibility with the GATT," *Yearbook of International Environmental Law* 1991, pp. 3–30; Thomas Schönbaum, "The International Trade and the Protection of the Environment: Irreconcilable Conflict," *American Journal of International Law*, October 1992, pp. 700–727 (followed by a commentary of Edith Brown Weiss); and Kym Anderson and Richard Blackhurst, *The Greening of World Trade Issues*, New York-London (1992); as well as studies undertaken by organizations: General Agreement on Tariffs and Trade (GATT) (Doc. L/6896, *Trade and Environment*), OECD (Doc. COM/ENV/EC/TD 91/66 *The Applicability of the GATT to Trade and Environment Concerns*).

30. Winfried Lang, "Diplomatie im Wandel," in Hans W. Kalyza, Heribert F. Köck, and Herbert Schambeck (eds.), *Glaube und Politik* (in honour of Robert Prantner), Berlin (1991), p. 294.

growing interest being linked to the ever-mounting concern for environmental matters should be strong enough to assure a relatively high degree of transparency. The sometimes important role played by NGOs in this context is another guarantee that environmental diplomacy will take place in a much more open setting than most other types of diplomacy. One should not however believe that transparency and openness necessarily contribute to the efficiency and progress of a specific negotiation.

If one considers efficiency an issue of its own, one should identify its meaning by asking the following questions: Is the outcome (conclusion of a treaty) the primary yardstick of success? What role does the "time" factor play in measuring efficiency? Is real-life compliance with treaty obligations the ultimate test of efficiency? Is efficiency assured if all or at least major interests of parties concerned are taken into account? As none of these questions can receive a clear-cut and simple answer, further research into environmental negotiations is required. Once the sample of negotiations is sufficiently broad, a comprehensive and reliable answer may be given.

Environmental diplomacy should also be understood as a learning process; by drawing on past experience, one may avoid some pitfalls, but one may equally run into new hitherto unknown difficulties. Past negotiations may serve as models, but changes in the negotiating environment should never be neglected.[31]

---

31. Winfried Lang, "Is the Ozone Depletion Regime a Model for an Emerging Regime on Global Warming?," *UCLA Journal of Environmental Law and Policy*, vol. 9, no. 2 (1991), pp. 161–174.

7

Critical Attributes of International Environmental Negotiations

Gunnar Sjöstedt

1. Introduction

Environmental policy-making is increasingly coming under the responsibility of the EC. The competence of the EC is steadily growing in this area. At the same time environmental negotiation between the European Community and various third parties — single countries or groups of nations external to the Community — is becoming more frequent and more complex. As a consequence, internal bargaining within the EC has become more and more intertwined with global negotiations processes. Negotiations over climate change is a good illustration. On the one hand, a constructive and effective agreement between the members of the EC to reduce emissions contributing to global warming would probably facilitate negotiations in this area.[1] On the other hand, progress in global negotiations would probably put pressure on the EC nations to come to an agreement among themselves.

The complex interdependence between regional and global negotiations was, for example, highlighted at the UNCED '92, and is likely to grow in the future. The interdependence between regional and global environmental regimes may be of different kinds. There are physical linkages, in that action in a given policy area, say at the regional level (e.g., transboundary air pollu-

---

1. The "effectiveness" of an international environmental agreement refers to its capacity to contribute to the solution of the ecological problems to which it pertains.

tion in Europe), will also have an effect on global environmental problems (e.g., climate change).

However, a quite different type of influence from global to regional negotiations is also discernible. It ultimately derives from the inherent attributes of environmental issues and their treatment in international negotiations. It is possible to draw useful lessons from negotiations in one environmental issue area which are applicable in another. Thus, international environmental negotiations retain a number of special, or very characteristic, properties which may facilitate, or obstruct, the search for a feasible agreement.[2] The purpose of this chapter is to discuss some of these critical qualities of environmental negotiations and to assess their effect on the outcome. The motive for this exercise is that the knowledge and understanding of the recurrent features of environmental negotiations permit lessons from different issue areas, as well as over time, for the same continuous bargaining process.

2. The Anatomy of Negotiation

An international negotiation can be described as a process, involving at least two parties, in which conflicting values and objectives are combined to form a joint decision over a given issue.[3] An agreement requires the consent of negotiating parties. Participants finding a proposed agreement totally unacceptable will disassociate themselves from the negotiation process. In a two-party situation such a defection will cause the collapse of the negotiation. However in a multilateral negotiation one or even several smaller countries may drop out without having any impact on either the process or the outcome.

Negotiation is a form of peaceful conflict resolution, which, in principle, is applicable to disputes over all sorts of issues.[4] There are always alternative methods of conflict resolution that the parties concerned may choose from, for instance, unilateral action producing a *fait accompli*. However, negotiations not only are contentious but also contain important cooperative elements. In fact, analyses have often tended to exaggerate the distinction be-

---

2. These are the conclusions from a recent book; G. Sjöstedt, *International Environmental Negotiations,* Beverly Hills, Cal. (1993).

3. I.W. Zartman and M. Berman, *The Practical Negotiator,* New Haven, Conn. (1982).

4. O.J. Bartos, *Process and Outcome of Negotiation,* New York (1974).

tween conflict and cooperation in negotiation. Often these two elements of negotiation are fused to such an extent that they may not be disentangled from one another. To use a common metaphor, nations may be interacting to increase their size of the pie — e.g., the values embodied in an international regime — while they are struggling among themselves over the distribution of this common good.[5] A typical example is a negotiated agreement between two countries on a joint venture of high-technology development, such as the coproduction of a new sophisticated aircraft. Neither country is able to construct the aircraft alone. Therefore, they pool their resources in a cooperative enterprise. Both parties will profit from the outcome of this cooperation in various ways, for instance, in the sense that they will have an aircraft which they would otherwise not have possessed. At the same time there are likely to be considerable differences of interest between the two parties, for example, concerning the design and operational capabilities of the airplane or the distribution of work in the construction process or what components each partner is going to manufacture. Thus, this case clearly demonstrates that conflict resolution is an integral part of the process of cooperation.

A negotiation may confront either only two single parties or several countries (for instance, at a conference of the United Nations). Bilateral and multilateral negotiations represent quite different patterns of interaction. Multilateral negotiations often unfold within the context of an international organization and are commonly referred to as conference diplomacy.[6] The more negotiating parties, the higher the degree of complexity of the negotiation from the point of view of each participant.

The composition of the agenda represents another dimension of complexity of international negotiations.[7] Sometimes nations negotiate over a single value (e.g., fishing rights) and other times over many and quite different issues (such as in a GATT round). In some cases a negotiation is but a brief episode requiring only a few days to be completed. In other cases a round of negotiations may continue for years, especially when it concerns a multitude of issues and involves many parties. The GATT rounds in the 1970s and 1980s are good examples.[8]

---

5. J.K. Sebenius, *International Negotiation Analysis,* Prentice-Hall, Englewood Cliffs N.J. (1991).

6. J. Kaufmann, *Conference Diplomacy,* The Hague (1988).

7. G.R. Winham, "Complexity in International Negotiation," in D. Druckman (ed.), *Negotiations: Social-Psychological Perspectives,* Beverly Hills, Cal. (1977).

8. G.R. Winham, *International Trade and the Tokyo Round Negotiations,* Princeton N.J. (1986).

The character of a negotiation process varies considerably depending on the parties, the substance of the agenda, and the special characteristics of the external context in which it evolves (for instance, in an international organization). At the same time all negotiations share a number of basic common features. For example, as seen in an analytical perspective all negotiations can be said to contain five elements. *Actors* refers to who the negotiating parties are; their number and their identity. *Strategy* pertains to how actors choose to pursue their interests and objectives in the negotiation, be it as a "lone ranger" or in co-operation with other parties. *Process* essentially reflects the pattern of interaction at the heart of the negotiation. *Structure* is a representation of circumstances external to the process, which systematically influence negotiations and their outcome. Finally, the *outcome* is the result of the negotiations; all its components need not necessarily be explicitly defined.[9]

Negotiation may also be described in general terms as a sort of production process resulting in a yield or the outcome.[10] As seen in this perspective a negotiation typically originates in a conflict of interest between the parties concerned. In the initial stage of the negotiations parties decide whether they prefer negotiation to alternative methods of conflict resolution. Then follows the stage of agenda setting, which often largely corresponds to partly informal pre-negotiations. Sometimes agenda setting may be described as merely the selection of issues, the definition of which is well known to the negotiators. However, in other cases the establishment of an agenda is an extremely complex and demanding process, presupposing a considerable amount of collective learning.

With the agenda set, parties often begin negotiating on a "formula": guidelines or even operational instructions for the actual distributive bargaining between them. Thereafter comes the actual exchange of concessions, the stage of "horse-trading." Finally, negotiations are terminated with a formal specification of the agreement attained. The agreement may, but need not necessarily, be given a legal dressing such as a convention text.

---

9.   V.A. Kremenyuk, *International Negotiation: Analysis, Approaches, Issues,* San Francisco (1991).

10. I.W. Zartman, *The Negotiation Process: Theories and Applications,* Beverly Hills Cal. (1978).

3. Characteristics of International Environmental Negotiations

Thus, at the highest level of understanding, negotiation may be regarded as a particular type of conflict resolution and collective decision making which has many significant process properties. General descriptions, as well as formal models, of the negotiation process have been developed. This literature tells us that a number of recurrent factors, exogenous to the negotiations, contribute to give each particular negotiation its special process character. Thus, the structure of the negotiations may, in a fairly predictable way, influence how the process unfolds and may have an impact on other negotiation dimensions as well. For instance, the organizational context of a negotiation may considerably condition process and outcome. Hence, trade matters are treated quite differently in UN Conference on Trade and Development (UNCTAD) as compared to GATT, partly due to quite dissimilar organizational cultures.

Issues may also considerably condition an actor's behavior in negotiations in a predictable way. This type of influence is pluri-dimensional. For example, the value elements of issues relate to the interests and motives of actors. It is ultimately the actor's preferences that attribute values to issues. This clear-cut relationship between issue values and actor's interests influences *who participates* with the use of *what strategy* for *what purpose.*

The relative degree of issue complexity is another factor which may have a significant impact on the process of the negotiation and its outcome. Complexity has to do with the amount of knowledge and information parties have available to them on an issue. The greater the need for knowledge building, collective learning, and exchange of information to make issues negotiable, the higher the degree of complexity. For negotiators "at the table" an increasing complexity represents more demands and ultimately a heavier work load. The more complex the issue is, the more pre-negotiation — or agenda setting — activities are probably needed to handle it. Basic issue properties not only affect the process; they also represent conditions that may strongly influence the character of the outcome. For instance, if issues are easily distributive and represent tangible values, it is easier to exchange concessions than if they are nondistributive and intangible. Thus, negotiating parties are likely to find it considerably less problematic from a technical point of view to work out a detailed and binding agreement concerning the distribution of export quotas for cocoa than to exchange losses of sovereignty. Accordingly, the inherent nature of issues represents an important determinant of negotiations and their outcome, the strength of which has often been underestimated in the literature.

Environmental issues are no exception; they retain a number of characteristic, or special, properties which are likely to systematically influence the character of negotiations over them. Each issue property of an environmental problem may be shared by other issues such as trade, human rights, or the distribution of radio frequencies. However, a configuration of several properties typical for environmental negotiations is discernible.[11] Some of the most important general attributes of this configuration are reviewed below.

3.1 The Transboundary Character of Environmental Issues

Their obvious, recurrent transboundary character helps explain why environmental problems are increasingly the subject of international negotiations. Emissions of pollutants in one country easily spread into other countries. In a historical perspective environmental issues are, however, relatively new items on the agenda for international cooperation and negotiation. The 1972 UN Conference on the Human Environment in Stockholm is a landmark in this respect. Since this conference literally hundreds of treaties concerning environmental issues have been signed by two or more countries. As of 1989 the UNEP listed some 140 multilateral agreements. A growing awareness of the transboundary character of most environmental issues is, no doubt, a major explanation for this formidable development.

Environmental issues are transboundary in several different respects. In principle, each type of internationalization represents a different kind of effect on the negotiation process and outcome.

First of all, many forms of degradation of the environment are caused by transboundary processes in a direct physical sense. For example, upstream emissions of pollutants into big European rivers like the Rhine or the Danube affect water consumers in downstream riparian states. Ultimately, the degree of pollution in the Sea will also be affected with consequences for still more nations. Sea pollution through inland waterways causes particular concern in semi-closed seas like the Baltic or the Mediterranean.[12] Acid rain represents another example of the physical transboundary dimension of envi-

---

11. Sjöstedt (ed.), op. cit. (footnote 2).

12. P. Haas, *Saving the Mediterranean: The Politics of International Environmental Cooperation,* New York (1990).

ronmental problems; the winds blow industrial and other emissions from "exporting" countries causing acidification in "importing" countries. In Europe complex computer models (like the Regional Acidification Information and Simulation [RAINS] model developed at the IIASA) have made it possible to attribute the relative responsibility of individual countries to the flows of transboundary air pollution; for instance, to qualify them in very precise, indeed quantitative, terms as net exporters or net importers.[13]

The impact on global commons is another important international dimension of environmental issues. An important case of this type is the global problem of climate change.[14] Human activities in production, transportation, and consumption, as well as their interaction with each other, contribute to cause a process of global warming. Although cause-effect relationships are not fully mapped and clarified, it is clear that nations on all continents and in all stages of political and economic development share the responsibility for this complex development.

It is equally well known that national governments have strong and diverging opinions on exactly how this responsibility should be shared by nations. For instance, as a group, developing countries demand financial and technological assistance from industrialized nations as a condition to undertake measures to curb the process of climate change and to cope with other environmental problems. The argument is that industrialized countries are the main culprits when it comes to global environmental degradation and that Third World countries must give priority to their development needs. Most industrialized nations seem willing to comply with the demands of developing countries, but only to a point. Some "hard-liners," and notably the United States, have argued that no "additional resources" should be created for the sake of the financial and technological assistance to developing countries. Means for such support should be created through, firstly, the reallocation of traditional development assistance from the Organization for Economic Cooperation and Development (OECD) nations and, secondly, rationalization measures within the United Nations. Other, mostly Western European, countries have been more accommodating toward developing countries, in principle, accepting the notion of "additional resources" to help them undertake costly measures to protect the environment.

These international differences of interest may be quite strong but do not seem to undermine the universal concern for the changing climate of the Earth. The outcome of the UNCED with respect to the problem of climate

13. L. Alcamo, R. Shaw, and L. Hordijk, *The RAINS Model of Acidification: Science and Strategies in Europe,* Dordrecht (1990).

14. M. Grubb, "The Greenhouse Effect: Negotiating Targets," *International Affairs,* vol. 45, 1(1990).

warming is probably a disappointment to many observers, particularly natural scientists working in this area. Concrete measures are so far quite modest. However, the UNCED negotiations should also be regarded as a strong acknowledgment that climate changes have to be dealt with in negotiations at the global level. Negotiations on climate changes will certainly continue, probably in the relatively near future.

Still a different type of internationalization derives from the remedial action some governments have taken to cope with certain environmental problems. Waste management is a typical case.[15] Large quantities of nuclear and industrial hazardous waste have been dumped into the oceans over the years. There is also considerable international trade in hazardous waste. This traffic has become a great North-South problem as the importers of waste usually have been poor, developing countries in need of hard currencies. The same countries, however, do not have the technology and equipment to handle hazardous, often strongly toxic, waste. It is very likely that some of the representatives of developing countries who have accepted deals concerning trade in hazardous waste have not fully understood the long-term consequences of their undertakings. However, trade in waste has conditioned international negotiations and agreements (notably, the Basle Convention) to set the terms for this type of commercial activity. It may be added that within the European Community trade in hazardous waste has recently become a bone of contention which will be probably lead to intra-Community bargaining.

3.2 Multiple Issues

As presented in opinion-building campaigns, environmental issues are often related to single, uni-dimensional objectives or simple slogans like "Save the seals in the North Sea," "Prevent the construction of a new dam in the X-river," or "Restrict the emissions of mercury." In international negotiations on the environment, the issues on the agenda often prove to be quite different: multiple and interrelated in complex ways. The basic reason for this kind of complexity is that environmental degradation, to be diminished or controlled by means agreed upon in international negotiation, is usually caused by the interplay of several different human activities, be they economic or social.

An often-used remedy to environmental problem is the reduction of emission of certain kinds of pollutants. In these cases negotiations concern

---

15. W. Kempel, "Transboundary Movement of Hazardous Wastes," in Sjöstedt (ed.), op. cit. (footnote 2).

the reduction, or sometimes the qualitative transformation, of activities producing these emissions: for example, road transports of goods and people, agriculture, or industry. Accordingly, businesses, interest organizations, and regional or national public agencies directly, or indirectly concerned with the activities producing emissions of pollutants are *stakeholders* in the negotiations. For instance, in a negotiation concerning emissions from cars, automotive producers and their subcontractors are likely to become interested parties as well as motorist organizations or regional and national agencies for whom local car factories are important economic actors. Furthermore, organizations and interest groups related to other transport systems competing with cars such as railway companies, may also become concerned, although they may have somewhat different interests. Thus the multiple-issue character is typical for many environmental problems negotiated at the international level.[16]

The frequent occurrence of multiple issues in environmental negotiations often renders it more difficult for the government, or the individual responsible ministry, to take — and defend — a coherent, national position. Different actors involved at the national level may have contradictory interests and therefore pull in different directions.

Multiple issues are, hence, related to another typical, and sometimes complicated, attribute of environmental negotiations, that of *multiple actors*. Multiple issues and interests in the negotiation are often likely to influence the composition of the delegation of individual negotiating parties as well as the pattern of participation in the preparatory work for the negotiations undertaken in the capital. The more issues are perceived to be involved, the more ministries, state agencies, and sectorial interest groups are likely to try to influence the preparations of the conduct to technical or political coordination problems at the level of the individual nation. Some large delegations, e.g., that of the United States, have sometimes been so composed that leading sectorial interests have been able to follow the negotiations "at the table." This is, however, not a common situation.

Sectorial interests are more likely to try to influence national policy making related to the negotiation concerned with the help of external lobbying and opinion-building, mostly in the capital.[17] The historical record seems to demonstrate that opinion building has been particularly important in the area of environmental politics as compared with other issue areas. Furthermore, the role of public opinion seems to increase in environmental issues. One indication of this is the approximately 1,400 NGOs which were accred-

---

16. Sjöstedt (ed.), op. cit. (footnote 2).

17. Kempel, op. cit. (footnote 15).

ited to the United Nations Conference on the Environment and Development.[18]

Environmental negotiations are characterized by multiple actors also for other reasons than the assertiveness of sectorial interests. The relatively high degree of technical complexity, which is typical for many international negotiations on the environment, also requires the participation of a comparatively large number of different types of actors: state agencies, organized interest groups, and other types of organizations. The foreign ministry is often not ably to cope with environmental issues with the exclusive help of in-house administrative and analytical resources. Technical advice must come from other ministries and agencies dealing with, for instance, environmental problems, agriculture, science and research, or industrial affairs. Even this is not always enough. Scientific experts may have to be called in from universities and the research community. This is, in fact, a prominent feature of many international environmental negotiations.

All actors in an environmental negotiation from a particular nation are probably not actively involved simultaneously. There are at least two basic reasons why the configuration of actors "at the table" changes as the negotiation unfolds. Firstly, different stages of the process are likely to attract, or require, different combinations of active participants. Professional diplomats may sometimes need the help of scientific experts to assess the "final" offers of other nations when the negotiation process begins to come to an end. However, at this stage the participation of scientists and the role of the scientific community is likely to be quite modest. Scientific knowledge is particularly relevant and valuable in the pre-negotiation and agenda-setting stages early in the negotiations, when environmental issues are technically difficult to assess and hence need a profound analysis. At this point professional diplomats may simply be dependent on scientists to understand the issues. One good example is represented by the difficulties diplomats and policy makers have had — and still have — in fully comprehending the causes and effects of the process of global warming.[19] In contrast, natural scientists may be less useful advisers to the diplomats when the agreements on substance reached in the negotiation will have to be formalized; then legal expertise is likely to be more in demand than scientific knowledge.

18. This figure has been given by the UNCED secretariat. Many of these NGOs never took part in UNCED. The number of organizations that made a tangible contribution to UNCED was probably not greater than one hundred. Still, the list of accredited organizations is probably a noteworthy indication of the mounting public interest in international environmental cooperation.

19. E. Skolnikoff, "The Policy Gridlock on Global Warming," *Foreign Policy*, Summer (1979), pp. 77–93.

The process of job rotation routines and career cycles is another reason for changing actors in international environmental negotiations. Due to their relative complexity, politically as well as technically, negotiations over environmental issues are likely to unfold as lengthy, often quite protracted processes.[20] This fact may sometimes be hidden by the way the environmental negotiations are organized: as a sequence of formally separate rounds. This has frequently been the case with negotiations dealing with industrial emissions causing air pollution. The implicit strategy has been to achieve stepwise reductions of emissions. As a consequence, it has been meaningful to have relatively low expectations in the initial round of negotiation which, in turn, probably has been a condition for success. However, in reality, different rounds should be regarded as continuous stages in the same process rather than as separate events. There may be a high degree of continuity between the rounds even if they are separated by a time span of several years.[21]

It is fairly common that key individuals in the national delegation during the early stages of environmental negotiations that may go on for several years will change positions before the process has been concluded. For instance, some of the more skillful negotiators and experts will probably be promoted out of the negotiation process. They will be replaced by other diplomats and civil servants who may have little or no insight in the particular negotiation process beforehand. Recall the generalist doctrine of the diplomatic profession; the individual diplomat should, in principle, be able to hold any position in the foreign service. Obviously, the likelihood of "changing actors" increases when a negotiation is organized in two or more separate rounds or when a regime in reality is built up stepwise on the basis of two or more agreements.

It is conceivable that "changing actors" in a negotiation process may have positive effects. Personal relationship between the representatives of negotiating parties may sometimes have a considerable impact on the process. For instance, if the main delegates of two of the leading countries feel animosity toward each other, this relationship may impede compromises or the constructive search for innovative solutions. There are, no doubt, situations in which the replacement of negotiators may help unblock a stalemate "at the table."

However, in complex negotiations, like in the area of environmental problems, "changing actors" are for the most part likely to be dysfunctional. When issues on the agenda are technical and complex, the process of learning may be quite long. It is not enough to study summaries of the problems

---

20. Sjöstedt (ed.), op. cit. (footnote 2).

21. The GATT rounds are good examples, G.R. Winham, op. cit. (footnote 7).

at hand or to go through abridged records of negotiation sessions. The knowledge required not only pertains to the substance of the issues. It is also necessary to acquire a nuanced understanding of how the interests of one's own country, as well as those of other nations active in the process, relate to the substance of the issues. It is a handicap not to be able to fully appreciate the frame of reference and technical jargon that has been developed and employed in earlier stages of the negotiation.

Finally, a protracted multilateral negotiation gradually develops into a social community with various types of ties between the individuals constituting it.[22] It may sometimes be difficult for a new delegate to perform with the same ease in this community as his predecessor who may have participated in it from the very start.

3.3 The Values at Stake in Environmental Negotiations

An actor accepts to engage himself in a negotiation because alternative conceivable approaches to deal with the conflict or problem concerned (for instance, unilateral action) are considered less instrumental or more costly. Some of the motives for taking part in environmental negotiations relate to the joint gains that only they can produce. Such joint gains are often of a conspicuous magnitude in environmental negotiations such as the preservation of the ozone layer over the Arctic and Antarctic zones or the deceleration of the processes of global warming. Thus, the common perception of possible joint gains represents a major motivation in environmental negotiation.

However, environmental stakes also retain a number of attributes that have a tendency to impede negotiations and complicate the search for viable agreements. Firstly, a typical feature of environmental negotiations is that their purpose is to escape or avoid negative values, as manifested by ecological degradation, rather than to produce new collective goods representing positive values. Furthermore, the gains derived from environmental negotiations are diffuse and often comparatively uncertain and accrue but in the long, or even very long, term. In order to achieve an outcome negotiating parties are usually required to accept very specific, short-term sacrifices such as increased costs for the industrial production of goods essential for the national economy.[23] Typically, these costs are caused by the introduction of

---

22. D. Druckman, "Social Psychology and International Negotiations: Processes and Influences," in R.F. Kidd and M.J. Saks (eds.), *Advances in Applied Social Psychology*, vol. 2, Hillsdale N.J. (1983).

23. Grubb, op. cit. (footnote 14).

new technologies necessary for reducing emissions of pollutants according to the stipulations of the agreement reached in the negotiations.

This relationship between the structures of costs and benefits evidently decreases the willingness of governments to engage themselves in environmental negotiations as well as the likelihood that they will accept binding commitments.[24] This tendency is seemingly strengthened by other circumstances. Thus, the character of collective goods, typical for the outcome of environmental negotiations, is believed to influence actor strategies, for example, to increase the temptations of free riding. Good opportunities for free riding can be expected to render agreement more difficult.[25]

3.4   A High Degree of Uncertainty

Environmental negotiations are often characterized by a comparatively high degree of uncertainty as compared to bargaining in other issue areas. In some cases uncertainty is, in fact, a dominant attribute that significantly contributes to the pattern of the negotiation process and the condition of its outcome. In other words, in environmental negotiations alternatives for action are comparatively difficult to assess correctly and the likely outcome, therefore, is more difficult to predict.

Uncertainty is, obviously, a typical feature of any negotiation. The outcome can never be predicted with certainty: If one of the parties can *a priori* determine the outcome there is no need for negotiation, which is essentially a process of give and take. However, in some cases the outcome of a negotiation is indeed quite predictable. This is typically the case with recurrent negotiations between two, or a few, parties concerning a single and easily distributive issue. One example is yearly, bilateral negotiations on permitted fish catches in a certain sea territory. The stakes of the negotiation are usually clearly defined and easily understood; each party is familiar with the concerns of the other party, and tacit "rules of the game" have been established for determining values.

Negotiations concerning fish catches do not represent a unique case. The uncertainty is likely to be quite restricted in negotiations over many types of transparent issues, the values of which from a technical point of view are relatively unproblematic to distribute between contending parties. Negotiated

24. Sjöstedt (ed.), op. cit. (footnote 2).

25. M. Olson and R. Zeckhauser, "An Economic Theory of Alliances," *Review of Economics and Statistics*, 48(1966).

export quotas for cocoa, coffee, or certain textiles products are good examples.

Environmental negotiations are, however, typically very different with respect to the degree of uncertainty that they represent. Hence, environmental issues are usually inherently more complex than questions concerning fish catches or commodities. This complexity has several dimensions. For instance, environmental issues are, as a rule, exceptionally difficult to understand and to relate to national interests. It is a very cumbersome task to attain a full understanding, with acceptable scientific reliability, of all the processes, and the significant interaction between them, leading to large-scale environmental problems such as the depletion of the ozone layer or climate change. Consider the case of climate change.[26] There seems to be a quasi-consensus in the relevant scientific community that emissions of certain pollutants, such as carbon dioxide, produced by various industrial and human activities do indeed contribute to a process of global warming. However, scientists do not fully agree on exactly *how* the predicted climate change will be produced and what effects it will have. For instance, some scientists predict a $1.5^{o}C$ increase in the average temperature of the atmosphere over the next 40 years. Others claim that this figure will be much higher and around $4.5^{o}C$. Likewise, reliable scientific estimates of the likely related elevation of the sea level range between 33 and 100 centimeters. Various hypotheses have been presented with respect to exactly what will happen with the masses in the Arctic and Antarctic for each increase in temperature degree.

Expressed in somewhat more general terms, there is a considerable uncertainty of what benefits will be attained with respect to reduced climate change if certain emissions coming from industrial plants are reduced to a certain percent. Thus, uncertainty contributes further to the problem of "negative perceptions of immediate outcomes," so typical of environmental negotiations.[27]

The prevalent uncertainty with respect to climate change has clearly affected negotiations in this area in various ways. For example, it has seemingly negatively influenced the willingness of some important actors (e.g., the United States) to undertake costly measures designed to reduce climate change and its negative effects. Some of these countries argue that reduced uncertainty is a *sine qua non* for binding commitments.

Scientific uncertainty has also contributed to the character of the process of negotiations. One such effect concerns the somewhat special role of scien-

26. R.E. Benedick et al., *Greenhouse Warming: Negotiating a Global Regime*, Washington, D.C. (1991).

27. Sjöstedt (ed.), op. cit. (footnote 2).

tists in environmental negotiations. Scientists have become directly involved in some environmental negotiations, to an extent that is comparatively unusual in international bargaining processes. Networks of scientists and other competent experts have been actively involved in many environmental negotiations and have thus significantly contributed to the clarification, definition, and analysis of the issues concerned, and they have assessed possible technical solutions: formulas for an agreement. Such so-called "epistemic communities" have not necessarily been formally involved in the negotiations but have still had access to them. Often the deliberations of epistemic communities have represented the main, or only, intersessional activity in the negotiation process. The negotiations for the Barcelona Convention concerning the pollution of the Mediterranean and those related to climate change are two examples of processes in which scientists and epistemic communities are reported to have played an important role.[28]

4. Attributes of Environmental Negotiations: Critical Developments

This overview has primarily focused on two characteristics of environmental negotiations. The first is their increasing transboundary dimension. The second is the high degree of complexity that typically characterizes a negotiation agenda consisting of environmental issues. In fact, "continued internationalization" and "mounting complexity" currently represent two significant tendencies of change with respect to environmental negotiation generally. These developments will have to be carefully assessed in future studies, because they represent potential problems for negotiators dealing with environmental problems.

To some extent "continued internationalization" may also be regarded as a source of complexity with which negotiators are confronted in their intercourse "at the table." Notably, negotiations on the environment taking place at different levels in world politics are likely to become still more interlinked. Emissions from the same factory in a given European country may contribute to local environmental destruction, to air pollution (acid rain) in neighboring countries, and to the global problems of the ozone depletion and global warming. One effect of these interdependencies is that agreements reached at one particular level of world politics, say within a given country, to

---

28. Haas, op. cit. (footnote 12).

reduce the emissions of hazardous pollutants will have positive effects on the environmental problems negotiated on at other levels, in Europe or globally.

Negotiations at different levels are, however, not necessarily conveniently complementary. For instance, some countries may become reluctant to make concessions in global negotiations because they feel they have already had to pay too high a price, for example, in terms of reduced industrial emissions in negotiations at the regional level. Thus, it will presumably become increasingly difficult to separate the agendas of bilateral, regional, and global negotiations. As a consequence the relative significance of regional solutions to environmental problems is likely to decrease. In the same way an individual country, such as Austria and Sweden, cannot solve its own environmental problems in isolation from neighboring countries, Western Europe cannot satisfactorily deal with its own regional problems unilaterally because of their linkage to global environmental problems like climate change or ozone depletion. In turn, for the same reasons countries located on other continents are more and more concerned about emissions of pollutants from Western European sources as well as exports of hazardous waste from the same area.

Thus, the internationalization, indeed globalization, of environmental issues reinforces the need to coordinate environmental negotiation in Europe with global bargaining processes. However, Western European states also have growing stakes in environmental negotiations in neighboring regions, notably the Middle East and Africa. In some cases such intercontinental negotiations are directly interconnected. A prominent example is the negotiations over water pollution in the Mediterranean which resulted in the Barcelona Convention. All riparian states were engaged in these negotiations.[29]

However, Western European governments also have stakes in extra-European negotiations in which they are not naturally engaged. Consider the environmental and water resource problems in the Sahel area, stretching from the Northwestern African coast into the Sudan.[30] The droughts and famines recurrently hitting the extremely poor Sahel region have caused human disasters, economic crises, migration, and political upheavals and have caused concern in European nations, particularly those bordering the Mediterranean Sea. Land erosion and desertification is also closely related to the process of climate change. Accordingly, Western European governments have strong interests in seeing that the Sahel countries master their environmental and resource problems. However, it seems that feasible solutions can only be achieved by means of international cooperation. Such collective solu-

29. Haas, op. cit. (footnote 12).

30. M. Mortimore, "The Sahel," in Sjöstedt (ed.), op. cit. (footnote 2).

tions presuppose international agreements through negotiation. So far, no serious international negotiation has been launched to deal with the Sahel problems. The main reason seems to be that in the countries concerned no actors have emerged that may act as negotiating parties.

Government structures are, as a rule, controlled by an urban power elite that does not directly suffer from drought and desertification otherwise plaguing the rural populations of the Sahel region. Instead the power elite seems to perceive collaborative agreements with neighboring countries as a threat to their own position as well as to the sovereignty of their nation. The poor people living in peripheral areas, who are most hurt by famine and water scarcity have virtually no access to the central decision making processes of their respective countries.[31] Therefore, they are in no position to incite or force their respective government to propose negotiations with other Sahel countries in order to find collaborative solutions to their common resource and environmental problems. It seems that initiatives to launch regional negotiations over the Sahel problems will have to come from outside the region. Maybe, this task will have to fall on the Western European governments that clearly have a stake in the health of the Sahel environment. Similar interventions may become necessary in other parts of the Third World as well.

In spite of the continuously growing environmental problems in the world, cooperation in this area has no doubt attained considerable results in the last decades. In most problem areas regional or global treaties have been signed by governments committing them to undertake often costly measures designed to at least slacken man-made processes of environmental destruction. Even in the complex issue area of climate warming an initial agreement was signed at the UNCED '92 in Rio de Janeiro. On reason for the relative success in environmental cooperation is seemingly the piecemeal overall strategy which had been employed before the UNCED process got under way in 1990. Particular environmental problems had been singled out for individual treatment in a separate *ad hoc* negotiation context. Another common feature of most environmental negotiations has been the comparatively important role played by lawyer negotiators. Especially in the later stages of the process legal expertise has contributed a crucial input; this is the time when the agreement in substance reached during the negotiations is given the legal dressing of a formal convention text.

The highly structured, compartmentalized, and piecemeal approach has evidently contributed considerably to the progress achieved in the area of environmental negotiations. However, the experiences from the UNCED process indicate that this approach has significant limitations. These difficulties

---

31. Mortimore, op. cit. (footnote 30).

essentially derive from the high complexity of environmental issues, and especially those related to issue linkages.

Agenda 21 represents one of the main issues, and at the same time special features, of the UNCED process. Agenda 21 was designed to function as an overall plan of action in the area of environmental problems from the time of the Rio meeting into the twenty-first century. One aspect of this plan is very practical; it concerns the coordination of the many UN institutions and programs partly or wholly related to environmental issues. Agenda 21 may also be considered a call for a more holistic perspective on global environmental cooperation. This ambition is particularly related to the need to actively consider issue linkages in negotiations and other forms of international decision making. In some respects UNCED certainly lived up to these aspirations. As the preparatory work for the Rio conference proceeded, the so-called cross-sectoral issues increasingly came to the forefront. These items on the agenda of UNCED manifested the concept of sustainable development, essentially interlinking the themes of economic development and environmental degradation. In turn, this connection relates to another political linkage: the North-South conflict. Thus, expressed in very general terms the so-called cross-sectoral issues typically pertain to the amounts of financial and technological assistance needed to make developing countries commit themselves to undertake costly measures to protect the environment. Thus, to some extent this support may be regarded as costs that industrialized countries would have to accept in order to have the necessary global participation in negotiations on global environmental problems like ozone depletion and climate change.

The cross-sectoral issues in UNCED are highly controversial highlighting, as they do, the North-South conflict of interest in world environmental diplomacy. Still, they are comparatively unproblematic for negotiators to deal with from a technical point of view. The reason is that the cross-sectoral couplings between issues can be treated as single and clearly delimited items on the UNCED agenda with equally clearly specified stakes. For example, negotiations over financial assistance have largely concentrated on a few key questions such as the amount of "additional" resources that would have to be channeled to developing countries and the mechanism for their transfer; especially the functions of GEF and the governance of this "green fund." In contrast, physical — real world — linkages between different environmental issues evidently represent a higher degree of complexity which negotiating parties seemingly find considerably harder to address.

Accordingly, physical linkages have largely been avoided in the UNCED process, even if their cross-issue impact is likely to be quite strong. In real life such an interdependence exists across several key environmental issues on the UNCED agenda, for example, in relation to climate change — notably the problems of desertification, deforestation, the ozone hole, acid rain, or biological diversity. Physical linkages often manifest themselves as causal and positive relationship. For example, continued deforestation in countries like Brazil, Malaysia, and Indonesia will accelerate the process of climate change. As a consequence, measures undertaken to stop or slow down deforestation will also have a positive effect on climate change. Such cause-effect relationships between issues represent potential opportunities or complications in future negotiations. On the positive side we find possibilities for package deals — trade-offs — across issue areas. One hypothetical case is that of concessions in deforestation; a country like Brazil gets "a bonus" in the negotiations concerning reductions of carbon dioxide emissions contributing to climate warming. The corresponding scenario representing complications in the process is that Brazil, or other countries in a similar position, takes a hardline stand and refuses to make concessions in the bargaining over climate change because it feels that it *should have* a credit for its commitments in the area of deforestation.

Cross-issue causal relationship need not, however, necessarily imply consistency between the measures taken to reduce environmental problems in different issue areas. In some cases the same type of pollutant may, in fact, have opposite effects on different environmental problems. For example, CFC gases contribute to the depletion of the ozone layer in the atmosphere. At the same time the ozone is one component of the atmosphere that significantly helps to accelerate the process of global warming; thus, from this point of view the elimination of the ozone is a good thing. Emissions of sulfur dioxide represent the most important cause for the problems of acidification at the local and regional levels. At the same time the transformation of sulfur dioxide into particles helps to retard the process of global warming.

5. Concluding Remarks

To conclude, the agenda and process of UNCED indicates a mounting complexity of environmental issues which so far has not seriously disturbed negotiations. One reason is probably that the UNCED has not served as a forum for hard bargaining aimed at the exchange of concessions with respect to a given environmental problem. In some issue areas on the UNCED agenda, notably climate change, biological diversity, and deforestation, such negotiations were attempted with varying degrees of success. The solution sought for was typically an agreement in which negotiating parties undertook to reduce their emissions of certain hazardous pollutants. However, these negotiations on costly environmental policy measures took place formally, as well as in reality, outside the UNCED context in special fora set up on an *ad hoc* basis. This was an effective method of retaining the separateness of the various issues, in fact a strategy corresponding to uncertainty — and complexity — avoidance. As a result, the problems of complexity were seemingly to some extent, "swept under the carpet" in the UNCED process. However, they cannot be ignored indefinitely.

The unresolved problems of complexity due to issue linkages should be regarded as part of the legacy of the UNCED process. They will, in all probability, have to be more actively tackled in future global negotiations. Issue linkages and other kinds of complexity will also increasingly concern regional negotiations in Europe and elsewhere. This will follow from a growing interdependence of regional and global environmental negotiations. If issue linkages are put on the agenda of global negotiations they will have to be prepared at the regional level.

8

The Role of International Environmental Law

Michael Bothe

1. The Role of Law in Environmental Protection

The question "What role does law play in environmental protection?" has been answered in different ways in different parts of the world. At least in Western Europe and North America, law has played an important role as an instrument to achieve better environmental protection. It has served as a means to force relevant actors to discontinue environmentally harmful activities or attitudes. The development of national environmental law during the last two decades, which indeed constitutes a formidable legal innovation worldwide, has been based on the belief that law, being an instrument shaping human behavior, is also a suitable tool for the preservation of the environment.[1]

But it is by no means certain that the same holds true for international law. International law is a decentralized legal order based on consensus, and this decentralized character applies both to the formation and to the implementation of the law. This kind of law, it would appear, is rather apt to stabilize the status quo and not to promote change. In other words, how can a better protection of the environment be achieved when a simple "no" by any one state blocks progress? If one looks at the reality of international practice,

---

1. For a comparative survey of this development of national environmental law, see Michael Bothe and Lothar Gündling, *Neuere Tendenzen des Umweltrechts im internationalen Vergleich,* Berlin (1990), pp. 5 et seq.

however, one finds that law is indeed used as a tool of environmental protection in international relations. Experience shows that the law-making process is indeed used as a means not of freezing an existing situation, but indeed of achieving progress in environmental protection and in many other matters. To put it very simply: law-making is a process of talking states into obligations many of them do not want. This is possible based on the peculiarities of the international consensus-building process. It is characterized by certain built-in pressures. The essential question thus is: How is an international consensus on a better environmental protection policy achieved? To answer this question, the political forces present in environmental negotiations must be analyzed. But, as will be shown, legal techniques also play an important role in achieving a consensus. Certain legal obligations are more acceptable than others. The choice of the most acceptable legal technique for solving a particular problem thus is an important element in making an agreement on certain measures of environmental protection possible.

Before turning to the question of legal techniques, however, a brief look at the political forces which determine the negotiating process is necessary.

2. Political Forces Determining Environmental Negotiations

First, there are "positive" forces that promote the cause of environmental protection. A kind of political "ecologism" can be ascertained not only at the national, but also at the international level. Environmental protection has become a political goal of internal as well as foreign policy. There are three major reasons for this phenomenon. The first one is the physical dependence of states on resource protection which requires international measures. Traditionally, this is a problem of the downstream state which wants to protect its water resources by making the upstream state accept restrictions on the use of a water system. Today, the protection of forests and freshwater resources against the consequences of air pollution, the protection of valuable sea areas against marine pollution, and the protection of valuable species against over-exploitation are relevant issues. The second reason for an ecological foreign policy is internal policy. If a progressive environmental stance is favored by the voters, a government will adopt it also in the international sphere. A strong green movement at home will quite often prompt a green governmental attitude abroad. Some of the reasons for the German government's stance on such matters as the protection of the tropical rainforest come under this heading. This is quite often the way it is seen in the countries concerned. Lastly, foreign policy is also inspired by certain social and moral values. This point is related to the two preceding ones, but it has an importance of its own. It is reflected by such notions as "common heritage."

Generally speaking, in recent years, environmental protection has become an accepted goal of the international political system. The Stockholm Conference on the Environment in 1972,[2] the ensuing creation of the UNEP, the adoption of the World Charter for Nature,[3] and the UNCED 1992 are milestones in this political evolution. The forces and actors that want to promote the cause of the environment in the international field, of course, seek to achieve it by using the most effective means and instruments. It is fair to say, however, that the discussion on instruments of international environmental policy and law has somewhat lagged behind the discussion which took place in the internal sphere, at least in those states which may be considered most developed in terms of environmental policy. Measures which are being used in the internal sphere are also proposed and sometimes adopted in the international sphere. A major issue at the international level remains the strictness of international control.

On the other hand, certain attitudes and forces are opposed to the development of environmental protection and to stricter measures for that purpose. The reasons for this may be a general foreign policy stance, internal policy, and a certain economic philosophy.

As far as general foreign policy stances are concerned, the key issue is sovereignty. International obligations to protect the environment limit the freedom of the state to do what it likes in its own internal sphere. It means that other states are concerned with a situation hitherto essentially considered to be a matter of the internal affairs of a state. A sovereignty interest is affected if other states are concerned with the well-being of elephants or trees living in a given state.

This may not only be a matter of the pride of the actors determining foreign policy; it may be the concern of important groups of the population. The foreign policy stance will also in other respects be determined by internal policy considerations. Groups which are politically important in a state may have an important interest in not enforcing certain environmental protection measures. The fishing industry in certain areas may be against restrictive regulations concerning the preservation of some marine animals.

Related to this aspect, economic considerations may in different respects be advanced against environmental protection. Very important today is a

---

2. Declaration of the UN Conference on the Human Environment, June 5, 1972, Text in Harald Hohmann (ed.), *Basic Documents of International Environmental Law*, vol. 1, London (1992), p. 21.

3. General Assembly Resolution 37/7, October 28, 1982, Hohmann, op. cit. (footnote 2), p. 64.

certain market-economy approach, particularly favored by influential circles in the United States, which subjects environmental considerations to particular cost benefit calculations. This approach tries to limit regulation, including international environmental regulation, to a strict minimum. It accepts such regulations only if there is a clear danger that has to be addressed immediately. It would rather rely on market forces to reduce environmentally harmful activities. Another economic consideration, different from the first one, but quite often allied with it in international negotiations, is development consideration. In this perspective, the cost of environmental protection is seen as an impediment to desired development. A variation of this idea is what could be called the weakness stance; certain states claim to be unable to pay for the costs of environmental protection.

In the light of these opposing forces and philosophies, it is quite clear that any progress of international environmental protection can only be a compromise, a compromise between now and never (which means later), or a compromise between all and nothing (which means a little). This compromise is reflected in particular legal approaches, which have become typical and are to a certain extent repeated where a solution of a new environmental problem is sought in the presence of the political forces just described. In a general way, this typical pattern of compromise can be described as the stepwise approach.

3. The Legal Instruments of a Stepwise Approach

A good and typical formulation of this stepwise approach may be found in Art. 2 of the 1979 Convention on Long-Range Transboundary Air Pollution:[4]

> The Contracting Parties, taking due account of the facts and problems involved, are determined to protect man and his environment against air pollution and shall endeavor to limit and, as far as possible, gradually reduce and prevent air pollution including long range transboundary air pollution.

This provision recognizes that air pollution is a problem, but it does not provide for any specific measure to be taken. Measures are envisaged not today, but later, and the reduction is to be stepwise, "gradually" in the language of the treaty. There is no obligation relating to reduction, but one relating to endeavors for that purpose.

---

4. Convention on Long-Range Transboundary Air Pollution, November 13, 1979, Hohmann, op. cit. (footnote 2), vol. 3, p. 1650.

Why are such compromises adopted? They give something to everybody. Although not satisfactory to those advocating stronger environmental protection, these general formulas may be presented to the political clientele as being an important step forward. On the other hand, those provisions do not really hurt actors having an interest in not promoting or in postponing environmental protection. It must be said that these broad and general obligations involve the danger of international regulation which is merely symbolic. But it is also implied in the stepwise approach that legislation must not stop at this compromise level; it is meant to develop into something which is more meaningful, which really serves the purpose of environmental protection. The essential question then is how fast and how good this further development is.

One can distinguish certain kinds of steps which are involved in this stepwise approach:

— from soft law to hard law;
— from general obligations of principle to specific obligations relating to precise measures;
— from uncontrolled to controlled obligations;
— from procedural to substantive obligations.

4. Hard Law and Soft Law in International Environmental Regulation

The use of nonlegal norms has become the common feature in international relations. The protection of the environment is only an example of this general phenomenon. It appears that nonlegal norms, which may take the form of a political agreement or of resolutions adopted by international organizations, are easier to accept and to live with for states having some problems with their content. The development of nonlegal norms may also be faster than that of legal norms, because they are not subject to the same slowly working rules of formation. In certain cases, they are adopted by majority vote (which, however, reduces their value), and the consent to be bound by such obligations is not subject to the same constitutional restraints to which the conclusion of a treaty is generally subject.

In the field of environmental protection, there is, first, a series of declarations concerning several principles which have played an important role in shaping international environmental policy and law:[5] mainly the Stockholm

---

5. Harald Hohmann, *Präventive Rechtspflichten und -prinzipien des modernen Umweltvölkerrechts,* Berlin (1992), pp. 219 et seq.

Declaration of 1972, the Declaration on Shared Natural Resources (adopted by the UNEP Governing Council, not adopted, but only "noted" by the General Assembly), the World Charter for Nature, and, finally, the Rio Declaration adopted by UNCED in 1992. These declarations have indeed served as a general orientation of environmental policy at both the national and international levels and have constituted important elements of an international awareness-building process. They have not been transformed as a whole into "hard" treaty law, but certain elements in these declarations were taken up and developed through international treaties.

Political agreements were also used to address some more specific problems of international environmental protection. A major example is the North Sea, where only a few specific questions of environmental protection are regulated by treaties, but the whole problem is taken up by a series of declarations adopted during the various conferences of the governments of the North Sea's coastal states.[6] In this case, however, it is time that the step from soft law to hard law be taken as other sea areas are governed by treaty regimes.

Last, but not least, many technical regulations and standards are adopted by both governmental and nongovernmental organizations (such as standardization organizations like International Standards Organization [ISO] and European Committee for Standardization [CEN]) which are not legally binding but which constitute, nevertheless, a standard of behavior which enjoys a great degree of acceptance and implementation. This is so because of the technical expertise which goes into these norms and also because of the identity of the actors creating and applying these norms. To a large extent, these norms are created by the national regulatory bureaucracies working together.

5. General Versus Specific, Vague Versus Precise Obligations

Art. 2 of the Geneva Convention on Long-Range Transboundary Air Pollution, quoted earlier, is a major example of a general and vague obligation not related to any precise step. Nevertheless, this convention created a framework of cooperation which gradually produced more specific measures; first the creation of a European monitoring system and then the two proto-

---

6.   Nearly all of these declarations are reprinted in David Freestone and Tom Ijistra (eds.), *The North Sea: Basic Legal Documents on Regional Environmental Cooperation,* Boston and Dordrecht (1991), pp. 3 et seq.

cols of Helsinki in 1985 and Sofia in 1988 concerning the reduction of SO_2 and NO_x emissions, respectively.[7] This approach has been chosen systematically in other cases and developed into what can be called the framework convention approach. As a matter of fact, the Convention on Long-Range Transboundary Air Pollution has proved to be a framework convention. Examples of this approach are the conventions adopted within the Regional Seas Program of UNEP which are composed of a general or framework convention containing general obligations and additional protocols addressing particular problems like land-based pollution, oil pollution, and accidents.[8] Another example is the Vienna Convention on the Protection of the Ozone Layer of 1985, which only contains very general obligations concerning international cooperation and was then supplemented by the Montreal and London Protocols which contain specific obligations relating to substances that endanger the ozone layer.[9] It must be stressed that this framework convention approach is more than a compromise between now and never. Comprehensive approaches are necessary to solve environmental problems. Framework convention approaches allow nations to address specific problems within a larger setting. They also create cooperative institutions, that is, environmental bureaucracies, which as a rule tend to form an effective environmental lobby.

The Climate Convention adopted by UNCED in 1992 is also a compromise between now and never.[10] The provisions which would be essential, i.e., those which prescribe a precise reduction of (or limit to) specific greenhouse gases within a clear time-frame, remain to be elaborated. There were, and still are, major political controversies concerning the approach to be taken toward the greenhouse effect, and a considerable gap still has to be bridged between those who want action now and others who are not convinced that any action is necessary. It can only be hoped that the Climate Convention will take the same development as the 1979 Convention on Long-Range Transboundary Air Pollution and the Vienna Convention on the Protection of the Ozone Layer before it is too late.

---

7. Protocol on the Reduction of Sulfur Emission, Helsinki, July 8, 1985; Protocol on the Control of Emissions of Nitrogen Oxides, Sofia, October 31, 1988, both in Hohmann, op. cit. (footnote 2), vol. 3, pp. 1662–1666.

8. Hohmann, op. cit. (footnote 5), pp. 280 et seq.

9. Convention on the Protection of the Ozone Layer, Vienna, March 22, 1985; Protocol on Substances that Deplete the Ozone Layer, Montreal, September 16, 1987; Decisions of the 2nd Meeting of the Montreal Protocol Parties, London, June 29, 1990; all in Hohmann, op. cit. (footnote 2), vol. 3, pp. 1691 et seq.

10. United Nations Framework Convention on Climate Change, New York, May 9, 1992, 31 ILM 849.

6. The Global Goal Approach

A number of recent environmental protection conventions have adopted a global goal approach, which is to say they are limited to fixing global goals and do not indicate with any precision how states should achieve these goals. The first and major example for this is the Helsinki Protocol on the reduction of SO_2 emissions, which requires states to reduce the overall emissions of SO_2 without indicating any measures to be taken at source.[11] States may fulfill their obligations by using cleaner technology or by switching to nuclear energy, for example. The Montreal and London Protocols concerning substances which endanger the ozone layer also use gross production and consumption limitations, which, however, end up being strict prohibitions when the reduction is down to zero. This approach is a traditional one in the field of water quality agreements where the yardstick of obligation is a certain water-quality, for instance water quality at a border point. In this case too, it is up to the upstream state to decide which measures are to be taken to make sure that the water has the required quality when it reaches the border.

In a way, this approach constitutes a compromise between all and nothing, but in other respects it is a reasonable division of tasks between international and national regulations. As to the compromise character, it seems easier to agree on global goals than to agree on norms relating to particular sources. The controversy between the United Kingdom and the other members of the European Economic Community (EEC) relating to the regulatory approach of the EEC Water Quality Directive is a proof of that. The United Kingdom pleaded that quality standards were sufficient, while most other members wanted something stronger — namely, effluent limitation standards. The history of the implementation (or otherwise) of the convention on the protection of the Rhine against chemical pollution also shows that it is very difficult for states to agree on specific source-related standards.[12] In the field of the EEC law concerning air pollution, it proved to be very difficult, although finally possible to introduce source-related norms on, for instance, stationary internal-combustion engines. Source-related rules are indeed a more severe restriction on political choices of states, and for this reason states are reluctant to accept them.

---

11. See footnote 7.

12. Cf. Johan G. Lammers in Wil D. Verwey (ed.), Nature Management and Sustainable Development, Amsterdam et al. (1989), p. 446.

On the other hand, it is legitimate to ask whether it is really necessary to have an international harmonization of source-related rules if global quality standards, or global emission/production limits are indeed respected. As modern monitoring systems make it possible to verify compliance with such global obligations, it can be left, at least in many cases, to the states' discretion how to achieve the desired result. In this way, meaningful international obligations are achieved much faster, as source-related negotiations tend to last longer. On the other hand, the global goal approach, as is shown by the example of switching to a nuclear power, entails the danger of environmental problems being transferred from one area to the other, from air pollution to waste problems or water pollution, for example.

7. Procedural Versus Substantive Obligations

The Geneva Convention on Long-Range Transboundary Air Pollution contains a very weak substantive obligation to limit, reduce, or prevent air pollution. But its procedural obligations are rather strong. There is a provision on exchange of information (Art. 8) and on a monitoring and evaluation program (European Monitoring and Evaluation Program [EMEP], Art. 9). Finally, there is an executive body with powers to review the implementation of the convention. The relevant and important substantive obligations were established later with the additional Helsinki and Sofia Protocols. The same holds true for the Vienna Convention on the Protection of the Ozone Layer.

In a way, the choice of procedural obligations thus constitutes a compromise between now and never. If substantive obligations cannot be agreed upon now, procedural obligations are adopted with the hope that they will finally produce the necessary substantive obligations. But this statement has to be nuanced in a certain way. The choice of procedural obligations is also well known in national environmental law because it is not always possible and still less practicable to make rules which determine a specific substantive result for each and every case. Substantive decisions must very often be left to the solution of each case. In this situation, procedural obligations, which ensure that environmental concerns are duly taken into account, are both necessary and sufficient. A major example of this kind of procedural obligation is the environmental impact assessment, which first was developed at the national level, but which has become an important part of international obligations.

8. Uncontrolled Versus Controlled Obligations

In certain cases, international treaties are acceptable only because there are no controls; in others, only if there is one. International controls, be they controls enforced by other states or by an international organization, pose problems from the point of view of sovereignty interests and also due to economic considerations. This can even be shown for a treaty regime which is highly controlled, namely, the Nuclear Nonproliferation Treaty. In this case, the inspection rights of the International Atomic Energy Agency are very well defined in order to minimize interference and to safeguard a state's security and economic interests.[13] On the other hand, if a certain obligation entails serious economic consequences, a lack of implementation poses serious problems of reciprocity and some controls may be needed to make a treaty regime work on the necessary reciprocity basis.

It is fair to say that in the field of international environmental law, states have been slow in accepting regimes with a meaningful control. But there is a clear trend toward closer supervision. This general statement, however, has to be modified according to each case.

There are situations when unilateral controls by state parties pose no problems. Thus, national means of verification concerning treaty compliance play an important role. The respect for obligations concerning the control of commerce in endangered species from the countries where these species live can be ascertained by strict border controls of the importing countries. Water quality can be measured at border points. Another possibility, which is important for air pollution and the protection of natural resources, is control by remote sensing. It must be admitted that in this case, there is a reciprocity problem because the relevant technology is only available in a limited number of countries.

A cooperative method of ascertaining relevant facts, i.e., environmental data, entails the use of common monitoring schemes. In this connection as well, vague or specific obligations may be distinguished. General provisions concerning exchange of information, which are quite common, are less meaningful and have less real impact than monitoring schemes such as the EMEP. Generally speaking, the value of a monitoring system very much depends on the kind of data it has access to, whether the data are supplied by or filtered by a government, or taken directly from a relevant physical source.

---

13. Torsten Lohmann, *Die rechtliche Struktur der Sicherungsmaßnahmen der Internationalen Atomenergie-Organisation,* Berlin (1992).

There is still some reluctance of governments to give up control over data which go into international monitoring systems.

Another means of ascertaining relevant facts are reporting systems. Reporting duties are a very general feature in many areas of international regulations. They were developed by the International Labor Organization, and play a prominent role in the enforcement of human rights' obligations. None of the more recent environmental protection conventions omits this feature of cooperative control. But in this connection again, the information is generated by governments. Demands have been made to increase the role of nongovernmental organizations in this and other processes which are relevant to the practical implementation of international environmental law. So far, these attempts have not been included in treaty law. Governments want to retain control of the monitoring process.

With regard to processes of information gathering, the essential problem is the practical impact which these processes may have. In other words, some kind of evaluation must follow the information-gathering phase. As a rule, it is the function of the assembly of the parties to a particular convention to evaluate that information, in particular the reports submitted by states. In contradistinction to the field of human rights, no independent institution has been created for this purpose in the environmental field. It is interesting to speculate about the reasons for this difference. It may well be because the development of human rights' law has extended over a longer period of time; human rights' law is more mature. But it may also be because the environment is a more sensitive area in many respects, as compliance or noncompliance with environmental obligations is a matter of economic resources.

Provisions on cooperative or common reactions to violations still are very scarce. Under the Convention on International Trade in Endangered Species of Wild Fauna and Flora (CITES), there is the possibility of suspending trade with a noncomplying state.[14] On the other hand, it is quite significant that the question of responsibility and compensation for damages as a possible sanction of noncompliance was left open in both the 1979 Convention on Long-Range Transboundary Air Pollution and the Basel Convention on the Transboundary Movement of Hazardous Waste. However, negotiations on the issue of compensation for damages are also in progress within the framework of ECE.

It is fair to say that there is a trend toward more international supervision of compliance. Thus, the 1991 London Protocol amending the Montreal Protocol, provides for additional reporting duties. Negotiations are under

---

14. Convention on International Trade in Endangered Species of Wild Fauna and Flora, Washington, March 3, 1973, June 22, 1979, April 30, 1983, Hohmann, op. cit. (footnote 2), vol. 3, p. 1346.

way to establish a more thorough enforcement process. The issue is certainly of fundamental importance for additional protocols to the Climate Convention, as a limit to CO_2 emissions would certainly require elaborate monitoring and supervisory schemes.

9. Institutions

Law is an indispensable framework for institutions, and environment cannot be protected without regional and international institutions. They are a necessary framework for both law-creating and implementation procedures. There are a number of organizations possessing certain powers and functions in the field of environmental protection. But if one takes a closer look at them, it becomes evident that they, too, constitute a compromise between the opposing interests and forces described earlier.

But what is the scope of powers of such organizations?[15] There are few "pure" environmental organizations, but many existing organizations have begun to deal with environmental concerns. This explains the existing confusion and the duplication of research. If new organizations are created, their scope is very limited; they are, as a rule, only concerned with one particular convention regime. Combining the functions of some conventions has occurred in several cases, and this is certainly laudable.

The decision-making bodies and organs of these organizations are composed of assemblies where member states are represented. This is different only in some regional economic integration organizations. However, the secretariat of these organizations also plays an important role, at least in some cases such as CITES. But independent expert bodies with some powers of control have so far not been created.

As to the powers of these organizations, it is quite striking that the governing assemblies do not possess the power to take decisions binding the member states. When regulations are elaborated in the framework of such bodies, either they constitute norms which are not legally binding or they must be submitted to the governments in order to be formally adopted. In a number of cases, however, silence may be equated to consent, and it is thus easier to make such regulations legally binding.

---

15. Alexandre Kiss and Dinah Shelton, *International Environmental Law,* Ardsley-on-Hudson-New York-London (1991), pp. 56 et seq.

10. Conclusions

It appears that international law indeed is regarded in practice as a major tool to promote environmental protection. International regulations must reflect the conflicts and power structures of the international system, and accommodate the interests and forces going in different directions. For this very reason in many cases laws are rather symbolic than serious. But today there seems to be a clear tendency from symbolic to serious international environmental protection laws.

9

Comments on the Objective of Regional International Environmental Law

Gerhard Hafner

1. Introduction

The title of this chapter has a double meaning:

1. To describe the existing state of regional international environmental law;
2. To explain the necessary objectives international law must pursue and the possibilities international law possesses of coping with existing and imminent dangers.

This contribution addresses the latter meaning.

It must be stressed that international environmental protection in a strictly regional framework is rarely able to produce an overall effective solution. International environmental law very often resembles the Rubik's cube; any change on one side of the Earth necessarily generates an effect on the other. Consequently, European environmental regulations with specific and controlled obligations, although easier to achieve, will produce only a limited effect unless the sources of the pollution are identified and dealt with in the regulations. This consideration also underscores the necessity to rely on international law, as the natural environment does not necessarily correspond to national borders. Nevertheless, such regional regulation could become the first step to a global instrument.

2. Objectives

2.1 The Ultimate Goal of Environmental Law

Any rule relating to the protection of the environment has to aim at ensuring the survival of mankind. However, divergent views exist on the meaning of the environment; what is needed is:

— non-anthropocentric understanding;
— a holistic approach;
— a long-term perspective.

Understanding must proceed from the view that man himself is both cre-
ator and molder of his environment as stated in the Stockholm declaration.[1]

2.2 Preventive Measures

Different means are available to ensure mankind's survival. One means,
as to preventive measures, consists in prescriptions prohibiting individuals
from performing certain activities which are likely to damage the environment; another entails the obligation to internalize the external effects of activities. The latter is reflected in the polluter pays principle as established in
various acts of the OECD and the EC.[2] In addition, specific procedural regulations are designed to produce communication links through which the individuals concerned are able to reach agreement on necessary protection
measures. A striking example is the ECE Convention on Environmental Impact Assessment in a Transboundary Context in 1991.[3]

Both methods have their pros and cons; therefore, they must be applied
in a complementary manner.

---

1. UN Doc. A/CONF.48/14/Rev.1, p. 3.

2. Cf. Gerhard Hafner, "Das Verursacherprinzip," *Economy-Fachmagazin,* 4/90
    (1990), F 23.

3. Text in XXX *ILM* (1991), pp. 800; cf. also "IMO International Convention on
    Oil Pollution Preparedness, Response and Cooperation of 30 November 1990,"
    text in XXX *ILM* (1991), p. 733.

2.3 Reparative Measures

In addition to the function of problem avoidance, international law must also find solutions to problems resulting from incidents: it must provide effective solutions which are considered just, equitable, and acceptable to the parties involved. Thus, the solutions must provide a clear distribution of responsibilities and liabilities. Those solutions should also include educational measures that teach people to internalize environmental effects. But not many of these types of solutions have been found in Europe so far.

3. Impediments to Such Legal Solutions

A difficult situation arises when rules should be worked out dealing with the environment and the threats it faces today. The rules have to be based on fuzzy assumptions which cannot be verified or falsified. If evidence about the real causes and effects of certain activities can be produced, it is already too late for prevention, as most phenomena are irreversible or reversible only with great costs.

Furthermore, the international community holds different views on the environment according to different time perspectives. Most developing states are inclined to view anthropocentric activities and environmental problems in the short term, whereas other states proceed from a long-term perspective. It is also extremely difficult to induce a state to share a concept of the environment at the international level when this concept does not apply domestically. Even European countries are divided in this respect.

States hesitate to shoulder environmental obligations. According to the prisoner's dilemma, states act in a reasonable way when they avoid incurring obligations concerning environmental protection.[4] Hence, they tend to become free riders or to reduce the obligations according to their economic capacity. Double standards and restrictions of obligations according to economic viability result from, and are further enhanced by, the decentralized nature of international law.

In addition, the actual structure of international law is still based on the traditional system of "reciprocity, prohibition, and sanctions" and marked by a strong relational nature; accordingly, it cannot come to grips with frictions arising between one state and the global environment. The environment is

---

4. See Anatol Rapoport and Albert M. Chammoh, *Prisoner's Dilemma,* Ann Arbor (1970), p. 24.

not a subject of international law and has no agent acting on its behalf unless a state is substantially affected. Thus, even if two states agree on certain measures for protecting the environment in their bilateral relations, this does not necessarily result in the most appropriate solution for the specific environmental problem.

Environmental conflicts are also characterized by a temporal problem; the effects of damaging activities could have a delayed reaction and could surface years later, producing intergeneration conflicts.[5]

Environmental conflicts suffer from the difficulty of determining the actor causing the damage in a manner which is required by legal doctrine. This is due to the complex character of the natural phenomena constituting the environment. These conflicts do not conform to the traditional dichotomy of relations among individuals which are governed by domestic law and relations among states governed by international law. These conflicts can result from activities set by one category of actors affecting the another category.

4. Means and Tools to Overcome These Impediments

How could international law overcome these problems?

In order to produce shared values and conceptions, common understandings of what is sometimes called soft law or prenormative instruments have to be reached, mostly through international resolutions.[6] NGOs could function as transmission belts of common conceptions. However, a way has to be found to escape the Scylla and Charybdis dilemma when formulations are either too soft or will not be accepted because of their rigid obligations. Regulations that are nonbinding, but nevertheless provide a certain autonomous status and value to the environment have recently proved useful in evoking a certain consciousness among states.[7]

---

5. As to the intergeneration conflict, see Edith Brown Weiss, "Our Rights and Obligations to Future Generations for the Environment," 84 *AJIL* 1990, p. 198; Lothar Gündling, "Our Responsibility to Future Generations," ibidem, p. 207.

6. Winfried Lang, "Die Verrechtlichung des internationalen Umweltschutzes: Vom 'soft law' zum 'hard law'," *Archiv des Völkerrechts* 22, 1984, p. 284; Günther Handl, "Environmental Security and Global Change: The Challenge to International Law," 1 *YBIEL* 1990, p. 7.

7. Various recommendations of the OECD and the ECE relate to issues of environmental law such as the equal access of foreigners to domestic procedures in transboundary pollution cases. See, e.g., *The ECE Code of Conduct on Accidental Pollution of Transboundary Inland Waters,* doc. ECE/ENVWA/16.

Since much depends on scientific evidence and assumptions a greater role should be accorded to the international scientific community in the various systems. This enlarged involvement could be modeled on the role which is accorded to the Scientific Committee on Antarctic Research of the International Council of Scientific Unions (SCAR) in the Convention for the Conservation of Antarctic Seals.[8]

To overcome the impasse caused by the prisoner's dilemma, confidence in the willingness of the other states to assume the obligations must be established. Actually, sovereignty still forms an almost insurmountable impediment in this respect which can only be surmounted step by step. The contribution of confidence-building measures, such as the involvement of nonprofitable scientific NGOs needs further discussion.

A further means to expand the effectiveness of international conventions in this field is contained in the Convention on International Trade with Endangered Species of Wild Fauna and Flora which requires a certain amount of third-party participation.[9] Generally, positive sanctions mixed with negative ones could establish a balance which makes a convention more attractive to the states.

To overcome the reluctance of states a step-by-step approach seems most useful. This approach must apply to:

— the matters covered by the regulation;
— the geographic area;
— the concrete nature and devices provided by the regulation.

In regard to these steps, a European regulation could be very fruitful in view of the relatively high sensitivity of European states to environmental concerns.

Procedural problems need certain uncommon legal devices such as a shift of burden of proof and recognition of, and reliance on, stochastic and proba-

---

8. Text in XI *ILM* 1972, p. 251; according to art. 5 of this convention, each contracting party shall provide to SCAR certain information, SCAR shall assess this information and report whether the permissible catch limits are likely to be exceeded.

9. Art. X of this convention relates to the trade with states not parties to the convention and provides that "(w)here export or re-export is to, or import is from, a State not Party to the present Convention, comparable documentation issued by the competent authorities in that State which substantially conforms with the requirements of the present Convention for permits and certificates may be accepted in lieu thereof by any Party" (text: Bernd Rüster and Bruno Simma, *International Protection of the Environment: Treaties and Related Documents,* vol. V, 1976, p. 2228). This provision aims at preventing a shift of the trade with such species to third states.

bilistic assumptions. These devices are required particularly in view of the uncertainties of scientific knowledge likely to be falsified in Popper's sense.[10] Furthermore, institutions are necessary to bridge the gap between individuals and states.[11] Once again, scientific NGOs that are studying environmental problems should function as some sort of agent of the environment. Only a few steps have been taken in this regard.[12]

5. Conclusion

This paper concludes with a warning: One should expect not more from international law than states are prepared to put into it. Thus, due to the basic nature of this environmental law, the lessons from international law are very limited. But as states are more prepared to agree upon a nonbinding text than upon a binding one, the burden of developing further general concepts of international environmental law should be placed on these instruments. Only when the gist of these instruments has penetrated the policies of the states, can binding rules on specific items be elaborated entailing specific controlled obligations.

---

10. In Popper's view any scientific hypothesis has to be subjected to a critical review so that mistakes can be eliminated; any scientific progress can only be an approximation to truth, but we are unable to know whether we have reached truth; Karl Popper, "Über Wissen und Nichtwissen," in Karl Popper, *Auf der Suche nach einer besseren Welt*, Munich/Zurich (1984), p. 51.

11. Attempts pointing in this direction are made in the ECE and in the preparatory stage of the United Nations Conference on Environment and Development.

12. See, e.g., the amended draft directive on civil liability for damage caused by wastes, OJ Nr. C 192 of July 23, 1991, Art. 4 para. 3, which accords nonprofit organizations a restricted *ius standi*.

PART FOUR

Regional Environmental Policies in Europe

10

The Environmental Policy of the European Community

Robert Hull

The European Community has had an environmental policy for almost 20 years. It was not provided for in the original treaties which set up the Community in 1957. The environment first became a matter of concern for the Community as a consequence of the Paris Summit of Community Heads of State and Government in October 1972. The Summit's concern had been precipitated by the warnings issued in 1972 by the Club of Rome and the United Nations Conference on the Human Environment held in Stockholm.

These past two decades have witnessed four Community action programs on the environment.[1] These programs have given rise to about 200 pieces of legislation covering pollution of the atmosphere, water, and soil; waste management; safeguards in relation to chemicals and biotechnology; product standards; environmental impact assessments; and protection of nature. Much has been achieved over this period in terms of both elaboration of an extensive legislative framework in the member states and actual improvements in environmental protection and quality.

The first goals of the Community were to halt the decline in environmental conditions which was beginning to threaten the chances of creating the new Europe. Systematic legislation began to be introduced in the early 1970s to set common standards in the main problem areas: water and air pollution, chemicals, waste, nature conservation, and nuclear safety, which

---

This contribution reflects the personal opinion of the author and should in no way be taken as the opinion of the European Community.

1. C112/1, December 20, 1973; C139/1, June 13, 1977; C46/1,1 February 17, 1983; C 328, December 7, 1987. The Fourth Program ended in 1992.

is now treated as an environmental policy component though it has a history which goes back to the founding of the Community.

From the early 1980s, after ten years of sectoral legislation and with the first signs of an end to the decline of air and water pollution in particular, it became evident that, to improve the situation, it was necessary to broaden the scope of environmental policy and the range of instruments used. In the first place, a proper response to environmental problems caused by action in other policy areas could only come through the integration of environmental considerations into those policy areas, which has meant adapting instruments of a different nature to those controlling emissions, for example. In the second place, the Brundtland Report forced the world to think about better management of our common heritage; this would be the key to continued development.[2] Thus "integration" is now becoming a means of moving toward sustainable development, as well as one of ensuring improvement in environmental conditions per se.

A further turning point was reached very soon after the publication of the Brundtland Report, when it came to be understood that the cumulative consequences of economic decisions created risks for mankind as a whole, and for the well-being of the planet. These required an unparalleled level of cooperation to replace the piece-meal approach which had characterized the initial phase of environmental legislation.

One of the principal characteristics of the Community, as distinct from international organizations such as the UN or OECD, is that it is a legislative body and that when it acts in a legislative capacity its acts are binding upon the member states. One consequence of this is that after 20 years the Community and its member states now have a body of law which, though relatively young and as yet incomplete, provides a very solid basis for further steps which must be undertaken in the decade ahead to ensure environmental protection.

The Community has two basic methods of action: the introduction of common policies and the coordination of national policies. In the first case, there is a transfer of responsibilities to the Community; in the second, responsibility remains with the member states. In all cases the crucial point is that Community action is the expression of the common political will of the peoples of the member states, found in the Community's constitution and operated through the working arrangements of its institutions.

All action is taken on the basis of joint decisions of the twelve equal countries, by majority vote or in certain circumstances unanimously. All legislative action taken applies equally in all member states. Moreover action is always taken at the Community level when the member states agree that

---

2. Brundtland Report, *Our Common Future*, New York (1987).

there is added value in working at this level rather than at the country level. This means that Community action frequently complements national action. Thus, environmental policy is not the policy of each and every member state; it is that part of the member states' environmental policy which they have agreed is better defined and implemented at the Community level.

Legislation in the areas of Community competence is proposed by the Commission and decided upon by the Council with the advice or cooperation of the Parliament. The areas of competence have been expanded as common interests continue to grow. It is important to remember that Community policy is in constant evolution.

The basic principles on which Community environmental legislation is based are the following:

— the best environment policy consists in preventing the creation of pollution and nuisance at the source, rather than subsequently trying to remedy the effects;
— effects on the environment should be taken into account at the earliest possible stage in all technical, planning, and decision-making processes;
— any exploitation of natural resources or of nature which causes significant damage must be avoided, in view of the limited capacity of the natural environment to absorb pollution and to neutralize its harmful effects;
— the cost of preventing and eliminating nuisances must, in principle, be borne by the polluter;
— care should be taken to ensure that activities carried out in one state do not cause any degradation of the environment in another state.

In the middle of the 1980s the Community's environmental activities moved into another gear. The insertion into the treaties in 1986, through the Single European Act (SEA),[3] of a new chapter on the environment and the inclusion of a significant environmental element in the key article relating to the completion of the internal market gave a new thrust to the Community's environment policy at the institutional level. This reflected the extraordinary growth in public awareness, scientific perception, and political importance of environmental issues during the 1980s, and provided a formal mandate, legal basis, objectives, and criteria for Community policy and action in the field of the environment.

The SEA set out the objectives of environmental policy following the principles already established in the earlier action programs. The Treaty now

3.   Single European Act, OJ L 169, November 29, 1987.

requires that the Community pursue environmental objectives as an end in themselves in order to:

— preserve, protect, and improve the quality of the environment;
— contribute toward protecting human health;
— ensure a prudent and rational utilization of natural resources.

Environmental requirements have to be a necessary component of all other Community policies (Art. 130r). Other objectives include a preventive approach, the polluter pays principle, and rectification of environmental damage at the source. An innovation was that measures under Art. 100a which are related to the completion of the internal market, such as establishing product standards, could be agreed upon by majority voting by the Council of Ministers; in these cases the European Parliament has substantial power to influence the outcome of such proposals. Measures which help to establish or operate in the internal market have to be given "a high level of protection." For other environmental measures, unanimous voting remains the norm unless the Council decides otherwise.

The Treaty of Maastricht,[4] which entered into force on November 1, 1993, will strengthen even further the existing Treaty elements on the environment. It incorporates in Art. B and in Art. 2 the idea of sustainable development respecting the environment as a fundamental objective of the Community. There is now to be an environment policy as opposed to the environmental actions specified in the Single Act and in Art. 103r. One of the main objectives of this policy is to be promoting measures at the international level to deal with regional and worldwide problems. The revised Art. 130s specifies that environmental protection requirements must be integrated into the definition and implementation of the Community's other policies. A high level of protection is now specified (Art. 130r) as underpinning environment policy. Importantly too, the provision on subsidiarity, the principle that the Community should act only where action at the Community level is the most efficient approach, has been generalized (Art. 3b) and, as a result, strengthened in relation to environmental actions.

The amendments to the Treaty will also involve modifications to decision making procedures introducing the principle of qualified majority voting for most environmental decisions although with unanimity being retained in a number of exceptional cases. Moreover, action programs will henceforth be adopted by a new co-decision making procedure with the European Parliament (Art. 130s). In addition a new Cohesion Fund has been set up which will be able to make a financial contribution to environmental projects in

---

4. Treaty on European Union (1992), Office for Official Publications of the European Communities.

those member states whose GNP is less than 90 percent of the Community average (currently Spain, Greece, Portugal and Ireland) (Art. 130s).

If the present situation in the Community is examined, environmental legislation currently broadly falls into three major categories. First, there is legislation aimed primarily at harmonizing national approaches to environmental problems, with an additional aim of avoiding distortion of competition within the Community. This category includes, for example, common standards on the quality of drinking and bathing water. This is also the underlying basis for the creation of a common environment within the Community, for example in relation to habitats. The second category covers pollution problems which cross borders within the EC, for example, toxic waste and air pollution. It also includes legislation to underpin the internal market. The third category covers problems which go beyond the Community's borders. Prime examples of these problems are the regulations on CFCs, which enabled the Community to ratify the Montreal Protocol, and trade in endangered species.

The problems of monitoring and enforcing legislation have grown almost as fast as the volume of Community environmental legislation itself. A number of member states have weak traditions of law enforcement and of public participation in environmental decision making. Almost all member states have been guilty of noncompliance in one area or another. The Commission finds it hard to monitor compliance itself, owing to insufficient staff and inadequate reporting requirements for member states, as well as other factors. The Commission relies almost entirely therefore on outside complaints, essentially from individuals or environmental groups. The numbers of these have rapidly risen, from eleven in 1984 to 460 in 1990. Legal proceedings have been instituted against member states in over 360 instances. Even when the European Court of Justice rules against member states the problem is often far from solved, since there are no sanctions (other than political) for the failure to comply with a judgment of the European Court.

By the end of the 1980s, against this background, it became apparent that the European Community was at a turning point in its thinking about the environment. There was a clear awareness of the need to protect the environment acting on principles of sustainable development and preventive and precautionary action. It was generally recognized that environmental policy was inextricably bound to economic strategy and that concerted action was needed at the Community level. This new approach was to some extent codified by Community Heads of State and Government at their Summit Meeting in Dublin in June 1990[5]:

---

5. 1990 Dublin Summit, Declaration by the European Council of the Environment, June 25/26, 1990.

We recognize our special responsibility for the environment both to our own citizens and to the wider world. We undertake to intensify our efforts to protect and enhance the natural environment of the Community itself and the world of which it is part. We intend that action by the Community and its Member States will be developed on a coordinated basis and on the principles of sustainable development and preventive and precautionary action ... The objective of such action must be to guarantee citizens the right to a clean and healthy environment ... The full achievement of this objective must be a shared responsibility.

That meeting set out the approach and objectives to be followed in the 1990s. It considered how the new environmental goals could be met. It addressed the question of whether the Community should continue to follow and strengthen the traditional centralized regulatory approach, setting obligatory environmental norms and standards and emission limits to specific sources of pollution. These have certainly slowed down the process of environmental degradation but have patently failed to halt it. In addition, the meeting considered whether the Community should seek to harness market forces in an attempt to create a sustainable and environmentally sound market economy through the use of economic and fiscal instruments. In the end they decided to follow both approaches. In a wide-ranging declaration on the environment they agreed that these approaches were complementary and provided the basis for the development of policy in the next decade.

The June Dublin declaration recognized the need to build on what had already been achieved through legislation: the legal and regulatory approach. Such a command and control approach would continue to form one of the pillars of EC environmental policy.

It has become apparent, though, in recent years, that legislation and regulation cannot solve all problems. There is a need to look at complementary methods. It is accepted that the new approach will involve the increased use of economic and fiscal instruments, agreed to at the Community level, and designed to encourage better environmental protection. This is vital if environmental considerations are to be fully integrated into other policy areas, if pollution is to be prevented at its source and if the polluter is to pay. Allied with existing measures in the legislative sector, this would have an important economic and psychological impact.

Another element of the Community's approach has been the creation of a financial instrument to underpin its policies and to complement legislation and economic and fiscal instruments. A financial instrument called LIFE[6] was adopted in 1991.

---

6. LIFE Community financial instrument for the environment, OJ L63/1, March 9, 1991.

It allows the Community to consolidate existing financial resources such as the Mediterranean Special Program of Action (MEDSPA)[7] and the North Sea Special Program of Action (NORSPA)[8] and in this way to have some impact on attitude changes through positive incentives, demonstration projects, and preventive operations. It will not, however, replace the funds designed to bring about more cohesion in the Community.

Another area which the Community had to address was the effect of environmental policy in the southern member states. The problem lies in different perceptions of the environment; in the southern states economic growth is given higher priority and environmental concerns are given lower emphasis than in the northern states. Part of this attitude lies in the lack of training and technical skills. Given that for a number of economic, geographic, and other reasons, the largest unspoiled and environmentally rich habitats are in the south, this is a serious problem that must be dealt with in the future.

All of this is given form in the Fifth Action Program on the Environment entitled "Towards Sustainability" which the Commission put forward in March 1992 and the general strategy of which was approved by the Parliament and the Council in Resolutions of November[9] and December[10] 1992 respectively. It will be the first such action program that will have a firm legal base as its foundation. The previous four programs, which were the means of moving Community environment policy forward, contained only lists of actions required and vague principles. The Fifth Program is radically different and defines a long-term strategy to provide a clear sense of purpose and direction for future Community actions, as well as a series of medium-term and short-term objectives.

The point of departure for the Fifth Action Program was the new "Report on the State of the Environment" which was published at the same time as the program. This report indicated that the present approach and existing instruments were insufficient for dealing with the current levels of environmental degradation in the Community; moreover, they were not designed to cope with the anticipated pace of change and development both within the Community and in the wider international arena in this final decade of the millennium.

---

7. MEDSPA, Council regulation on action by the Community for the protection of the environment in the Mediterranean region, L 563/91, March 4, 1991.

8. NORSPA, Council regulation on a specific action to protect the environment in the coastal areas and coastal waters of the Irish Sea, North Sea, Baltic Sea, and Northeast Atlantic, OJ L 370, December 31, 1991, Regulation No. 3908.

9. OJ C 337, December 21, 1992: European Parliament Resolution.

10. OJ C 138, May 17, 1993: Council Resolution.

The approach adopted in drawing up the new program differs fundamentally from that which applied in previous environmental action programs:

— it focuses on the *agents and activities* which deplete natural resources
  and damage the environment, rather than wait for problems to
  emerge;
— it endeavors to initiate *changes in current trends and practices* which
  are detrimental to the environment, so as to ensure socio-economic
  well-being and growth for present and future generations;
— it aims to achieve such changes in behavior in the Community through
  the optimum involvement of all sectors of society in a spirit of *shared
  responsibility,* including public administration, public and private enterprise, the general public, as both individual citizens and consumers;
— responsibility will be shared through a significant *broadening of the
  range of instruments* to be applied to the resolution of particular issues
  or problems;
— rather than be specifically geared toward protection of particular environmental media, the measures to be undertaken will be primarily directed at the *principal economic sectors;* at Community level these
  comprise industry, energy, transport, agriculture and tourism. A striking feature of the approach to the targets sectors is that it is designed
  not only for the protection of the environment as such, but for the
  benefit and sustainability of the sectors themselves.

Previous action programs have relied almost exclusively on legislative
measures. In order to bring about substantial changes in current trends and
practices and to involve all sectors of society in a full sharing of responsibility, a broader mix of instruments is needed. The mix proposed can be catego-
rized under four headings:

1. legislative instruments;
2. market-based instruments, geared toward the internalization of external environmental costs and "getting the prices right";
3. horizontal, supporting instruments including improved base-line data,
   scientific research and technological development, improved planning
   as well as what some have called social instruments, environmental
   information, education and training;
4. financial support mechanisms including the Community's structural
   funds (LIFE, European Investment Bank — EIB) and the new conver-
   gence/environment fund.

The new program also differs from its predecessors insofar as it sets out
indicative objectives, targets, actions and time-frames covering the period up
to the year 2000. These do not constitute legal commitments but, rather,

performance levels or achievements to be aimed at now in the interest of attaining a sustainable development path.

While the Program adopts the end of the decade as its operative horizon, the intention is to have a comprehensive reappraisal of the situation undertaken and an up-dated report on the state of the environment published before the end of 1995. Apart from the expected improvement in relevant information and availability of results from the Community's current research program on the environment (1990–1994), there will be major reviews of Community policies on industry, energy, transport, agriculture and the structural funds over the next few years.

Integration of the environmental dimension into economic and other policies is the heart of the approach to attaining sustainable development. This is clearly included in the Maastricht Treaty and in the Rio Declaration and is reflected in the Commission's 1993 work and legislative programs. Instead of trying to solve problems of pollution and environmental damage as they emerge, integration of environmental considerations into other policies is one of the key means of preventing pollution and of changing the patterns of human consumption and behavior which cause these problems.

The Commission itself has recently adopted measures to ensure the integration of environmental protection requirements into the definition and implementation of Community policies. A number of mechanisms to improve and strengthen existing procedures and practices have been agreed which seek to include environmental aspects at the early stages of definition of Commission policy and action. There has already been progress in this direction in proposals on the CO_2-energy strategy,[11] the Green paper on sustainable mobility,[12] the White paper on transport,[13] the Communications on industrial competitiveness and environment protection[14] and on energy and environment,[15] work on environment and employment and on economic indicators and the recent proposal on the revision of the structural funds.[16]

The Community is aware too of the need to inform and educate if changes in attitude are to be brought about. Insofar as environmental awareness and sensitivity on the part of the general public derives from availability

---

11. OJ C 196, August 3, 1992.

12. Document COM (92) 46 final of February 20, 1992.

13. COM (92) 494, December 2, 1992.

14. OJ C 331, December 16, 1992.

15. COM (89) 369 final February 8, 1990.

16. OJ C 118, April 28, 1993.

of information or knowledge, the Community has already taken a number of major steps:

— Firstly, under the directive on environmental impact assessments which came into effect in 1988, all major projects likely to have a significant effect on the environment must be subjected to a comprehensive assessment of potential environmental impacts which must be made available to the public before any authorizations are granted;[17]
— Secondly, the directive on the freedom of access to information on the environment which came into effect on January 1, 1993, will be seen by many as a milestone in the development of environmental awareness and in the involvement of the public in the guardianship of the environment.[18] The purpose of the directive is to ensure freedom of access to and dissemination of information on the environment held by public authorities and to set out the basic terms and conditions on which such information should be made available;
— Above all, the establishment of the European Environment Agency and the monitoring and information network associated with it will provide both the Community and member states with objective, reliable, and comparable information at the European level on the basis of research and comparative studies.[19] This Agency will enable them to take the necessary measures to protect the environment, as well as to assess the results of such measures, and to ensure that the public is properly informed about the state of the environment.

As a complement to the development of its internal policies the Community has also laid down the foundation for an approach to international environment issues. According to the rulings of the European Court, when the Community adopts legislation it acquires competences in that field to negotiate with other countries and the member states simultaneously lose their powers to act on their own. This clearly may create confusion with other countries and may create some tensions within the Community.

The Maastricht Treaty makes it clear that a basic objective of Community environment policy includes action at global and regional levels. There is, already, increasing acceptance of the Community's responsibility to play a leading role in promoting concerted and effective action at the global level. A

---

17. Council Directive on the assessment of the effects of certain public and private projects on the environment OJ L 175/40, June 27, 1985, Modification COM(91) 270/5.

18. 1990 Directive on the freedom of access to information on the environment OJ L 150/56, June 7, 1990.

19. OJ L 120/1, May 11, 1990.

landmark was the Community's signature of the Vienna Convention on the protection of the ozone layer and the subsequent Montreal Protocol. The Community will also be party to the Basle convention controlling cross-frontier movement of toxic wastes. Having recognized the need to build a wide international consensus, the Community took a leading role in the 1992 UN Conference on Environment and Development (UNCED) in Rio de Janeiro. It emphasized the need for a global political commitment to establish regional and national strategies built on sustainable development. It has recognized it has a responsibility to both present and future generations to put its own house in order and to provide an example to developed and developing countries in relation to the protection of the environment and the sustainable use of the natural resources. Already in October 1990, the Community had agreed in principle to stabilize its own CO_2 emissions by 2000 at the 1990 level and to subsequent reductions. In Rio, it signed the global framework conventions on climate change and biodiversity and will actively promote the rapid conclusion of protocols which translate the framework into concrete measures, timetables and targets. In addition, the Community will contribute to the effective implementation of the package of measures adopted at UNCED including Agenda 21, the Rio declaration on environment and development and the forest principles. It has already announced a financial package of 3 billion ECU to enable a prompt start to the implementation of Agenda 21 and plans to ratify the global climate change and biodiversity conventions in the near future.

Apart from the UNCED process, the Community has particular relations with specific groups of developing countries, notably the Lomé convention countries. These countries, basically composed of all ex-French, ex-Portuguese and ex-British colonial territories in Africa, the Pacific and the Caribbean, are the recipients of the bulk of Community third world aid. The 4th Convention,[20] signed in December 1989, makes environmental protection and conservation basic objectives and contains special provisions for assessing the direct and indirect environment impact of Community aid programs and of the movement of toxic and radioactive waste.

Cooperation with Latin America and Asian developing countries takes place in the context of Community Cooperation programs and 10 percent of Community funding for these programs is directed to environmental purposes. At the European level there are issues of a regional nature which need treatment in common with other European countries. Eastern and Central Europe and the Soviet Union have inevitably become a high priority for Community policy and a percentage of Community aid under the Pologne-Hongrie Actions pour la Reconversion Economique (PHARE) and Trans-

---

20. OJ L 229, August 17, 1991.

European Mobility Scheme for University Studies (TEMPUS) programs and under bilateral cooperation agreements with East European countries is earmarked for environmental purposes. The Commission is designated as coordinator of the broader Western G-24 efforts to promote democracy and economic reform in the area as well as in relation to nuclear safety assistance and it works closely with the new European Bank for Reconstruction and Development. A small Community environment aid program for the Soviet Union has also been established in the context of the Technical Assistance for the CIS (TACIS) program.

Equally important has been the development of close relations with the EFTA countries where there has been close informal cooperation on environmental issues since 1987. Environment will form an essential part of the work in the newly created European Economic Area when it comes into effect in 1994. Environment issues figure largely in the current discussions on accession to the Community of a number of EFTA countries.

The Mediterranean is another region where the Community is heavily involved through the Mediterranean Regional Seas Program and it is a signatory of the Barcelona Convention. The MEDSPA program,[21] coordinated in the context of follow-up to the 1990 Cyprus Mediterranean Conference with a parallel program, Mediterranean Technical Assistance Program (METAP), funded by the World Bank and EIB, provides funding for relevant clean-up and conservation programs in both member states and in non-EC southern and eastern Mediterranean countries. The NORSPA program[22] provides for parallel actions in the North Sea. Both MEDSPA and NORSPA have now been incorporated into the LIFE programs.

Conclusion

Environment policy in the Community, developed in fits and starts over the last two decades, has now moved to the center of policy making in the European Community and is seen as being a key element in its future economic development. Internal and external aspects of policy are changing and developing very rapidly and the Fifth Action Program will be the means by which this change is channelled and given direction. This will be given new emphasis by the post-UNCED process in the Community. A lot of problems remain to be solved but the Community member states, following public

21. See footnote 7.
22. See footnote 8.

opinion which has called for environment policies and for improvements to the quality of life, have recognized that in working together to develop a common policy they stand a better chance of resolving them than if they tried to do so nationally.

The obligations of the European Community and its member states in the area of environmental protection are spelt out in the treaties constituting the Community, now updated by the Maastricht Treaty. At the same time there is increasing acceptance of a wider responsibility as one of the leading regional groupings in the world to play a leading role in promoting concerted and effective action at global level, working with other industrialized countries and assisting developing countries to overcome their special difficulties. The Community has recognized that its future depends on its ability to adopt progressive environmental measures for implementation and enforcement by its member states. The internal and external dimensions of Community environment policy are therefore inextricably linked.

11

Harmonization of the EC Environmental Policy After Maastricht

Jan C. Bongaerts

In 1957 the Treaty of Rome was signed and "the Six" formed the EEC. In 1987 the Treaty was amended, and SEA was added in order to enable "the Twelve" to speed up the pace for the completion of the Single Market. During those 30 years, economic welfare increased substantially in the Community. A similar increase occurred, however, also with respect to the use of energy, the consumption of raw materials, and environmental damage.

The SEA established a responsible environmental policy for the Community. From the date of entry into force (July 1, 1987) the SEA provided the Community with a legitimate base for its environmental policy which had been lacking. In fact, the environmental policy of the Community had already started in 1973, but it was based on the Community's economic policy mandate (avoidance of distortions of competition) and on Art. 235 of the Treaty.

The environmental responsibilities of the Community seem to be, on the one hand, very broad and, on the other, rather narrow. In terms of content, they are broad (see Art. 130r of the Treaty). In terms of the area of application, they are bound by the principle of subsidiarity. According to this principle, only those measures should be taken which contribute to an environmental issue in a better way than the measures taken at the level of the member states. Subsidiarity, therefore, seems to suggest that the environmental policy of the member states comes first and that the Community policy comes second. This is, however, a misleading conclusion. This chapter intends to explain why this was the case in the past and why it will become inappropriate in the future. I start with a review of the SEA. I then describe the recent evolution of environmental policy of the Community after the Maastricht Conference. I conclude with a look into the future.

1. The Single European Act

Art. 130r, 130s and 130t of the Treaty contain the basic principles of the Community's environmental policy as they were adopted in 1987. At the Maastricht Conference on December 9 and 10, 1991 some important amendments were added. The most important one deals with the rules for decision making (see Table 11.1).

2. Changes After the Maastricht Conference

During the Maastricht Conference, some important changes and additions to Art. 130r were made:

1. Goals: promote measures at international level to deal with regional and worldwide environmental problems;
2. Principles: a safeguard clause allowing member states to take provisional measures for noneconomic environmental reasons, subject to a Community inspection procedure;
3. Constraints: economic and social development of the Community as a whole and the balanced development of its regions.

Originally, decision making by the Council of Ministers was by unanimous rule (Art. 130s). But in practice, matters were more complex. With the adoption of the Single Act, Art. 100a created a decision rule by qualified majority which includes the participation of the European parliament (Art. 130s merely allowed for a hearing by the Parliament). Art. 100a, however, only relates to issues dealing with the completion of the Single Market, as defined in Art. 8a.

In this context it has to be pointed out that high environmental standards must be maintained (Section 3 of Art. 100a). The Commission, which solely disposes of the right to propose issues for legislation to the Council, interpreted this formulation as an opportunity for adopting environmental legislation on the basis of Art. 100a instead of Art. 130s. The Commission justified this procedure on the grounds that any environmental regulation constituted a precondition for the completion of the Single Market. The Commission also held that environmental policy had to be integrated in other policy areas of the Community.

TABLE 11.1

Environmental Policy in the Single European Act

Art. 130r, 130s, 130t
Also Art. 100a especially (4) (in connection with Art. 8a and Art. 100b)

1. **Goals 130r(1)**
    o   Protect the environment.
    o   Protect human health.
    o   Promote a prudent and rational use of resources.

2. **Principles 130r(2)**
    o   Precaution (prevention).
    o   Abatement at source.
    o   Polluter-Pays-Principle (PPP).
    o   "Integration" of environmental policy in other policy areas.

3. **Constraints 130r(3)**
    o   Science and technology development.
    o   Environmental conditions in member states.
    o   Costs and benefits of measures (taken or not taken).
    o   Economic and social developments in member states.

4. **Competences of the Community**
    o   Subsidiarity 130r(4).
    o   International environmental relations
        (eco-ambassador) 130r(5).

How are decisions made?
Unanimity with exceptions: 130s.
Member states' independent measures: 130t.

Source: IEUP summary of the SEA.

Hence, virtually all proposals for environmental directives prepared by DG XI were sent to the council with the suggestion that Art. 100a be used. However, the Council refused to make a decision on this basis and preferred Art. 130s instead. As a result of these procedural disagreements, many delays occurred.

In 1989, the Council was taken to the European Court of Justice which decided in favor of the Commission.[1] Initially, this decision led to the conviction that "majority" would henceforth dominate "unanimity". In fact, at the Maastricht Conference "majority" was selected as the "standard" procedure. But some years later, the Court decided in favor of Art. 130s (in its pre-Maastricht fashion) i.e., for unanimity.[2] As a result, matters have become rather complex. As the Maastricht Conference was in the planning stage, European environmental organizations stressed the need for a uniform solution, favoring some type of majority rule. This would in any case also strengthen the position of the European Parliament.

The issue was not completely resolved at the Maastricht Conference. In fact, according to the amended Art. 130s legislation will now be decided by majority decision making, which will become the "standard procedure" with three exceptions, to which the previous standard rule of unanimous decision making still applies:

— provisions of a fiscal nature;
— town and country planning; land-use measures (with the exception of waste management); so-called measures of a general nature and management of water resources;
— measures significantly affecting a member state's choice between different energy sources and the general structure of its energy supply.

It is generally expected that this change of procedure with respect to decision making will affect the way in which environmental standards will be set. Since the need for compromise is less strong, tighter standards may result than those that would have been obtained under a unanimous rule which includes a veto right. But it is equally possible that a member state or a (small) group of member states favoring tight environmental standards may find themselves outvoted in the Council. Hence, more negotiations seem to be expected in some cases.

However, Art. 130s now contains a new compromise clause allowing for temporary derogations to measures taken by a majority decision rule or to

---

1. Court Decision C-300/89, June 11, 1991. The Commission used Directive 89/428/EEC on the Harmonization of Programmes for the Reduction and Elimination of Pollution by Wastes of the Titarium Dioxide Industry as a case at hand. Due to the Court's decision, this directive has been withdrawn.

2. See Court Decision C-155/91, which was decided on March 17, 1993. The European Parliament had asked the Court for a decision with respect to the legal base of the Framework Directive on waste 75/442/EEC as amended by Directive 91/156/EEC. Cf. Europe Environment Service (EIS) no. 407, March 30, 1993.

offer financial support from the Cohesion Fund (see Art. 130d) if the costs seem disproportionate to the public authorities of a member state. This is an important addition to the process of decision making since it allows for the economically weaker member states to lag behind and to obtain financial aid. The Council acted swiftly and the Cohesion Fund is already operational. For 1993, the Fund has been earmarked 1.5 billion European Currency Unit (ECU). Until 1999 some 15 billion ECU will be spent on projects in the four poorest member states (Greece, Ireland, Portugal and Spain).

The intended 50-50 balance between transport related and environment related projects is very unlikely to be met. For Spain, the ratio for 1993 stands at 3 to 1 (66.4 million ECU for roads, 22.9 million ECU for environment related projects, including the restoration of natural resources in national parks and an assessment of the damage inflicted upon rivers). For Ireland, the ratio is similar (30 million ECU for roads and 9 million ECU for sewerage systems and municipal waste water treatment plants).

Another important issue deals with the duty to integrate the environmental policy of the Community into other policy areas. In the wording of the SEA, this integration is acknowledged as if it were a fact. In view of the Maastricht Conference, proposals for rewording were formulated in which the stress would be put on the duties. According to some, this would force the Commission to reformulate its transport policy and, obviously, its Common Agricultural Policy.

These proposals were accepted at the Maastricht Conference, and section 2 of Art. 130r now reads: "Environmental protection requirements must be integrated into the definitions and requirements of other Community policies."

Hence, one may expect more intense cooperation between DG XI and the other directorates with respect to policy making. In general, the importance of the environment has been increased because the words "continued balanced expansion" of the Community (Art. 2) have been replaced by "to promote economic and social progress which is balanced and sustainable."

Finally, the principle of subsidiarity is not seriously threatened. Originally, the environmental policy of the Community was based on the need to avoid distortion of competition. Hence, environmental legislation was often subject to economic considerations. With the adoption of the SEA, the subordination of "ecology" to "economy" could no longer be maintained and the principle of subsidiarity was defined in order to set some limits to the competences of the Community.

The Commission has, however, adopted a broad interpretation of its competence. It would be wrong to assume that the environmental regulations of the Community solely deal with transboundary issues. In fact, the Commission has an interest in expanding the impact of its environmental policy.

Examples are urban ecology as described in the green paper on the urban environment, the protection of natural habitats (through an appropriate directive), eco-labeling of products, environmental auditing, and, lastly a combined CO_2 and energy tax.

Hence, subsidiarity does not mean that the environmental policy of the Community ranks behind the environmental policies of the member states. It also does not mean that its importance at Community level will be reduced. Controversies exist with respect to the degree of detail which would be appropriate for environmental laws, such as directives and regulations. In particular, the Fifth Environmental Action Programme calls for more cooperation between the public administrations and the affected parties, such as industry sectors. This may imply less detailed laws, which set the goals and leave the ways of implementation to governments and other affected parties. Another development relates to the inclusion of the economic instruments which would reduce the need for detailed "prescriptive" laws. Both developments can also be registered at the level of the member states. They seem to refer to a change of policy practice, not of policy formulation. Hence, the environmental policy of the Community is, in fact, becoming more and more important. Interestingly enough, the citizens of the Community agree with this development, as shown in Table 11.2.

A proposal was made at the Maastricht Conference to drop the reference to the subsidiarity principle in Art. 130r and to reintroduce the principle at a more general level in the text of the Treaty. In fact, a new article on subsidiarity was proposed and adopted. It reformulates in more detail the basics of this principle. It is not yet clear to what extent this new article may lead to a conflict with Art. 100b, which applies to all issues for which no harmonization is needed in the realm of the Single Market.

According to Art. 100b, the Council may decide with respect to these issues that either it will proceed and adopt some form of Community regulation or that it will allow member states to adopt their own policies. In the latter case, each policy must be accepted by the other member states. Hence, according to this principle of mutual recognition of standards, different "environmental qualities" might coexist and cause problems for member states with high environmental protection aspirations. These states would have strong incentives to restrict products from entering their territory which meet lower standards than their own products and create a trade barrier.

The Treaty is very clear on this point. In case no Community regulation exists, member states introducing certain national regulations that might complicate the completion of the Single Market must "notify" the Commission before they act. This means that the Commission has the right to in-

TABLE 11.2

Do You Think that Member States Should Cooperate in the Area of Environmental Protection?

	Together	Separate	No Opinion
Netherlands	91.0	7.2	1.8
Luxembourg	83.7	11.6	4.7
Italy	83.3	7.7	9.0
Germany	83.2	5.7	11.1
France	80.6	15.9	3.5
United Kingdom	78.0	16.5	5.5
Denmark	70.4	12.0	17.6
Greece	69.0	18.4	12.6
Portugal	62.3	10.2	27.5
Belgium	61.0	8.6	30.5
Spain	60.5	19.0	20.5
EURO 12	77.0	12.2	10.6

Source: Eurobaromètre été 1989, Rapport Zeus 1990.

vestigate such a regulation and, if deemed appropriate, to take action. The Dutch proposal to the Maastricht Conference interpreted this principle of mutual recognition as inappropriate and pleaded for a deletion of Art. 100b; however, no decision was made at the Conference.

3. New Policy Instruments

The Maastricht Conference helped to resolve a number of formal issues with respect to the decision making rules of environmental policy and the future relationships among institutions. Some years earlier, however, the environmental policy of the Community was already subject to criticism — both from within and outside. Several issues were raised:

1. *Implementation:* member states are seen as being slow in transposing EC environmental directives into national law, and the Commission loses a good deal of time and effort in the European Court of Justice.

2. *Administration:* one of the implications of the traditional policy results
   in the need for competent authorities. Their task consists in designing
   administrative arrangements enabling the actual "trans-mission" of
   Community environmental regulations at the level of decision making
   by industry, commerce and trade, and the public at large. With the
   growing complexity of this policy, the competence of these authorities
   does not increase appropriately in all member states. Not all member
   states can afford administrations at the capacity required.
3. *Technology:* traditional regulatory policy includes the innovation of
   end-of-pipe technologies, which adsorb, filter, or remove pollutants
   from exhaust gases, effluents, and wastes and transform them into
   another state (e.g., from liquid to solid). These technologies do not
   reduce emissions, they often consume extra energy, and they require
   substantial investments. Hence, they constitute a burden on the
   economy even if the residuals are recycled.
4. *Costs:* as suggested in points 1 to 3, this type of environmental policy is
   costly both for governments and for industry. Since end-of-pipe technologies do not tend to reduce the volume of materials handled, recycling is necessary. This implies that markets for products made from
   such recycled materials must be created. Hence, this policy also implies costs of opening up new markets.

Experience with this type of policy has largely confirmed these points. It
has also shown that the potential for its adoption is limited, both administra-
tively and technically. With the growing impact — i.e., the increase in the
number of emission sources (or the number of regulated industries) — the
cost of monitoring by the authorities has increased, the time for administrative checks of reported emission data has become restrictive, and law violations have gone undetected. With respect to technologies, costs per unit of
removed pollutant increased more than proportionally with the degree of
abatement. (Every additional percentage of pollutant removed added ex-
ceedingly more to the total cost.) Hence, even if very high rates of removal
may be technically possible, they may be economically infeasible.

As these developments became more and more obvious, new approaches
towards environmental policy entered the discussion. The Commission contributed to this discussion by presenting several proposals for Directives to
the Council. Table 11.3 contains an overview of these instruments.

TABLE 11.3

New Policy Instruments

* Green Taxes
* Community Budget for the Environment
* Eco-labeling
* Environmental Auditing
* Environmental Liability
* Access to Environmental Information

Source: Jan Bongaerts, own compilation from Institute for European Environmental Policy (IEED), Bonn 1993.

3.1 Green Taxes

With respect to this instrument, the Commission has proposed a combined tax on CO_2 emissions and on energy consumption. As seen by the Commission, this tax should yield the following effects listed in Table 11.4.

TABLE 11.4

Expected Effects Resulting from a Combined CO_2 and Energy Tax

Type of Effect	Results
Catalyst	More effective activities in the fields of research, regulation, etc.
Global	All actors (business firms, consumers, etc.) are affected.
Continuous	Permanent stimulation.
Market oriented	Contribution to coherence between environmental targets and market signals.
Substitution	Incentives to explore the potential of other energy sources and low CO_2 emission technologies.

Source: Statement by the Commission, September 26, 1991.

Half of the tax yield is designed to be raised from a tax on CO_2, the other half will come from an energy tax. The tax rates by type of fuel are supposed to apply, as given in Table 11.5.

The estimated reduction of energy consumption is rather small. See Table 11.6 for the pattern that DG XVII predicts.

TABLE 11.5

CO_2 and Energy Tax Rates by Type of Fuel
(ECU per ton of oil equivalent)

	Initial Stage	Final Stage
Gasoline	17.3	57.5
Diesel	17.5	58.3
Heavy fuel	18.0	59.9
Natural Gas	15.4	51.3
Coal	19.9	66.2
Lignite Coal	21.1	70.5

Source: DG XVII, February 1993.

TABLE 11.6

Primary Energy Consumption Around 2000
(million tons of oil equivalent)

	Without CO_2 and Energy tax	With Tax	Percentage Change
Solid Fuels	279	268	-3.8
Mineral oil	576	555	-3.6
Natural gas	314	308	-2.0
Nuclear Power	172	172	-0.2
Other	29	28	-1.5
Total	1370	1331	-2.8

Source: DG XVII, February 1993.

TABLE 11.7

**Weighted Indices of CO_2 Emissions
Per Capita and GNP Per Capita – EC = 100[a]**

Portugal	40
Greece	59
Spain	66
Ireland	83
Italy	92
France	95
United Kingdom	105
Netherlands	111
Belgium	117
Germany	129
Denmark	129
Luxembourg	250

a   The calculating system proposed by the Commission is based on two yardsticks (split 50%–50%), firstly the average level of CO_2 emissions per inhabitant and, secondly, GDP per inhabitant. If the national result of these two combined measurements is below 85% (the Community average in 1990 is used as the reference index = 100) the member state in question will not have to introduce a CO_2/energy tax.

Source: Europe Environment Information Service (EIS), no. 418, Brussels, October 12, 1993.

Meanwhile, the Belgian Presidency has proposed a compromise version which would exempt those member states from an immediate introduction of the tax, whose weighted GNP per capita and CO_2 emissions per capita are below 85 percent of the Community's average. As Table 11.7 shows, the four Cohesion Fund States happen to be very surprising.

3.2 Community Budget

The European Parliament and the Commission have proposed to integrate a number of environmental programs (including the Community Action for the Environment Program – ACE) into a single program, entitled LIFE which should be considered a first step toward establishing a Community budget for the environment. Table 11.8 presents an overview of this scheme.

TABLE 11.8

LIFE: The Community's Instrument for the Environment

Legal basis: Art. 130s of the Treaty.

Purpose: financial instrument for the development and the implementation of the Community's environmental policy (including international conventions and the commitments made under the Community Action for the Protection of the Environment in the Mediterranean [MEDSPA] and Specific Action on the Protection of the Environment in the Coastal Areas and the Coastal Waters of the Irish Sea, the North Sea, the Baltic Sea and the North-East Atlantic Ocean [NORSPA] programs).

Financing: partly from the Community budget.

Priorities: set by the Commission:

— annual objectives;
— pluri-annual projects;
— performance indicators;
— criteria for the selection of individual measures.

At the Maastricht Conference, the decision was made to create this fund for a period of three years. For the coming year, LIFE will contribute some 65 million ECU to more than 120 projects with a total cost of 244 million ECU. About 100 of these deal with the development in clean technologies in various sectors, such as surface treatment, textiles, leather tanning, paper manufacturing, food processing, recycling technologies, reclamation of contaminated sites, landscape amenity, transport, river management, information and monitoring.

Twenty projects deal with habitats and nature. In addition, a new Cohesion Fund was created. As mentioned above, this resulted from an amendment added to Art. 130r which "involves costs deemed disproportionate for the public authorities of a Member State." In such cases, the Council has the choice of granting temporary derogations or awarding financial support. Hence, a fund had to be created. The Cohesion Fund will lead to a center-periphery or a north-south transfer of funds since it will support environmental projects in poorer member states. It will also support so-called trans-European networks which have a per capita gross national product of less than 90 percent of the Community average. Besides Greece, Portugal, and Spain, Ireland will benefit from this fund.

FIGURE 11.1

Eco-Label Procedure

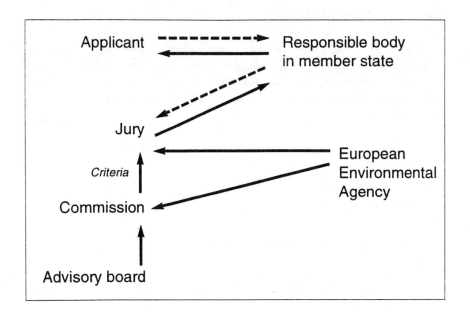

Source: Jan Bongaerts 1993.

3.3 Eco-Labeling

After many years of discussion the Council of Ministers reached an agreement at the December 1991 Council Meeting on the establishment of a Community-wide eco-label for environmentally sound products which do not violate existing EC regulations on health and safety, which are not dangerous according to Directive 67/548/EEC, and which are made in production processes meeting EC regulations. The procedure for awarding the eco-label is very cumbersome, as seen in Figure 11.1.

The applicant sends in an application to the national authority. This authority monitors the use of the label through a user contract. The labels are awarded by a jury, composed of eighteen representatives of the member states and of important interest groups. The jury decides on the basis of criteria set by the Commission, which in turn uses the expertise of an advisory board and of the European Environmental Agency.

3.4 Environmental Auditing

Initially, the Commission planned to have a mandatory scheme applicable to defined industrial sites. This, however, was opposed by a sufficiently large number of member states, so the Commission proposed a voluntary scheme. It was adopted in the Council on June 28 and 29, 1993. The essential elements include:

— industry;
— sites not companies;
— voluntary scheme registration;
— once registered rules must be followed.

Once a company has registered, it must observe all the rules of the scheme which are as follows:

— any industrial enterprise may register;
— applies to sites *not* companies;
— registration is voluntary *but*;
— once registered — rules must be followed and the company must act on the results.

Once a company has chosen to register one, or more, of its sites into the scheme, it must then observe all the rules of the scheme which are as follows:

— conduct an initial environmental review;
— introduce an internal company environmental protection system including:
   o an environmental policy document defining company's overall aims with respect to the environment (i.e., not restricted to a single site);
   o environmental objectives and targets;
   o environmental programme;
   o environmental management system including an environmental audit programme;
   o conduct internal environmental audits which must be examined at the highest level;
— prepare an environmental statement;
— external validation of environmental statement;
— validated statement is submitted to competent authority and published.

3.5 Access to Environmental Data

The purpose of this instrument is to enable citizens to learn about the state of their environment. For this purpose the Commission has proposed a directive on access to environmental data. The Council adopted this directive in 1990 (Dir. 90/313/EEC). The directive constitutes a compromise, as it entitles citizens to obtain this information without expressing any specific interest.

But it also specifies that member states may stipulate the conditions under which access to environmental data is awarded. In this way states may decide to withhold information in the possession of competent authorities which is considered proprietary.

The directive does not contain rules for classifying nor for determining what is supposed to be proprietary. As a result, a certain practice may be developed in a member state which prevents harmonization and therefore may create unequal rights across the Community. Obviously, this may cause some competitive distortions. The directive also fails to link the proposal for a regulation with environmental auditing which intends to establish Community-wide rules for publishing the so-called environmental statement. This must be considered a first step in communicating environmental data to the governments of the member states and the public at large.

3.6 Liability for Environmental Damages

The Commission has sent a proposal for a directive to the Council on civil liability for damages resulting from wastes (COM (91) 219). The proposal intends to establish a strict liability (i.e., a liability without a fault rule) for damages caused by any generator of wastes. In addition, member states must create rights for victims, i.e., determine under what conditions they are awarded. These rights include:

— access to courts;
— claims to seize and desist;
— recovery and compensation;
— reclamation and restoration.

The proposal also states that plaintiffs must bring evidence on causality, that reclamation and restoration may be replaced by appropriate alternative measures if exorbitant costs prevent the former, and that nature conservation interest groups have access to courts either as principal plaintiffs or as joint plaintiffs with victims. However, the proposal has been withdrawn, ever since the Commission prepared and published a green paper on environmental liability in more general terms. The green paper on compensation of environmental damages takes up the issue of environmental liability at a broad level. It discusses the following issues:

— strict versus fault liability;
— limited versus unlimited liability;
— joint (and several) versus single liability;
— the concept of environmental damages;
— the issue of compulsory insurance for environmental liability;
— the issue of an environmental damages compensation fund.

4. Conclusions

The Commission has introduced a variety of new instruments for environmental policy. They all have one element in common: they set incentives to force the polluter to become aware of the environmental impacts of his activities and to internalize them in his cost calculations. This also holds for the Cohesion Fund.

With respect to future development, two questions can be asked:

1. To what extent will these instruments be implemented? This question is not trivial. With respect to the CO_2 and energy tax one may ask whether the rates will be high enough to provide incentives to influence decisions or whether they will merely lead to additional income for the governments of the member states. Similarly, by limiting the group of potential victims having access to the European Court, liability rules may have only nominal functions. With respect to the eco-label, the awarding procedure seems too cumbersome to be convincing.

2. To which extent will the new instruments become complements to or substitutes for existing regulatory instruments? From the outset, the new instruments are seen as substitutes for the existing traditional approaches. Whether they will actually replace them seems, however, questionable from a practical point of view. This is because, whenever a policy is applied, administrative structures are involved; these administrative structures may have difficulty adapting to new policy concepts. Indeed, it is more comfortable to add functions (such as raising energy taxes) to a given administrative structure than to delete some of them to the benefit of others.

Obviously, it is too early to assess the impact of these new instruments on environmental policy and environmental management in business and the actual state of the environment. In view of this, it is important to notice the role of the Fifth Environmental Action Programme of the Community, which was adopted in 1992. One important change in policy making is seen in the introduction of the principle of shared responsibility which allocates tasks to be performed by specific actors with respect to specific environmental policy goals. In this sense, an attempt is made to set incentives to those actors to take appropriate measures who are most capable of doing so. Whether this new principle — which may be interpreted as DG XI's "answer" to the question of the subsidiarity principle — will be put to practice is to be seen in the near future.

References

Community Documents:

COM(91)37 on a Regulation with Respect to a Community Eco-Label, O.J., C 75, 20 Mar. 1991.

COM(91)219 on a Directive with Respect to the Liability for Damages Caused by Wastes, O.J., C 792, 23. Jul. 1991.

Directive 90/313/EEC on Public Access to Environmental Data, O.J., L 158, 23. Jun. 1990.

Commission of the European Communities: Communication on a Combined CO_2 and Energy Tax, Sept. 1991.

Other Sources:

Haigh, Nigel, Environmental Auditing, Developments in the EC and Internationally, NAO Seminar, September 25, 1991, London.

12

East Central European Policy Making: The Case of the Environment

Peter Hardi

1. Introduction

In their development towards democracy and market economies the East Central European countries are experiencing their greatest change in more than 40 years. Both the state institutions and the social structure are in a dynamic state of flux, but the collapse of Communist political power has not changed economic patterns, civil service and administration or social connections with one stroke. The evolution of a functioning open society with participation from citizens' organizations is still in its early stages, and the process is being hindered by economic and political insecurities.

The present paucity of reliable information requires rapid amelioration in order to make rational environmental decisions. Great deficiencies exist in the present environmental protection infrastructures; in addition there is a severe lack of environmental management skills. Environmental administrations need to be strengthened to avoid the sidelining of environmental policy. Such efforts will also help to deal with the serious shortage of resources for environmental protection and to integrate environmental policy into other areas. The public needs to be made more aware of environmental problems and attendant health risks in order to overcome the existing preoccupation with economic hardship and push environmental issues to the top of the political agenda.

This is a shorter and altered version of a policy paper written during the summer of 1991 at the Institute of International Studies, University of California, Berkeley.

In spite of the importance of environmental issues in East Central Europe, since the revolutions there has been a diminution in the priority given to environmental issues and very little progress in environmental improvement. Environmental problems such as air and water pollution persist, with only a few isolated examples of improvement. Transboundary environmental problems remain pressing and the region continues to share problems brought about by mismanagement in the past. The need for regional cooperation is also evident for achieving economic progress and political stability. A major challenge facing organizations concerned with the promotion of environmental improvement and civic societies is to find long-term processes that will help societies face pressing short-term problems.

In this chapter I analyze the factors which impede the making of a coherent and sound environmental policy in most of the newly democratizing countries (NDCs) of East Central Europe, and if such a policy were to exist, I discuss the implementation of it. The emphasis of the analysis is on the determinants of policy making, using the environmental issue as a case in point; the findings are applicable to almost any type of policy making, including industrial, agricultural, and educational.

Such an analysis, however, runs into several difficulties. Though there are informative and sometimes thorough analyses of specific environmental problems in the region, by both local and Western experts,[1] a systematic

---

1. Hilary F. French, "Green revolutions: Environmental Reconstruction in Eastern Europe and the Soviet Union," *Worldwatch Paper* 99, November 1990, pp. 5–62; Jeremy Russell, *Environmental Issues in Eastern Europe: Setting an agenda,* Royal Institute of International Affairs-World Conservation Union, London (1990), pp. iii–34; Helmut Schreiber, "The Threat from Environmental Destruction in Eastern Europe," *Journal of International Affairs,* vol. 44, no. 2 (Winter 1991), pp. 359–391; and Robert Livernash, "Central and Eastern Europe," *World Resources 1992–1993,* World Resources Institute, Washington, D.C. (1991), Chapter 5, (under publication).
    General surveys on individual countries: Bulgaria — Vera Gavrilov, "Environmental Damage Creates Serious Problem for Government," *Report on Eastern Europe,* RFE, May 25, 1990, pp. 4–11; Delcho Vichev, *The Ecological Catastrophe in Bulgaria* (manuscript), Ecoglasnost, Sophia (1990), pp. 1–13; Czechoslovakia — *The State and development of human environment in Czechoslovakia,* Czech Association of Nature Protectors, Prague (1990), (original in Czech); Josef Vavrousek et al., *The Environment in Czechoslovakia,* Federal Committee for the Environment, Prague (1990), pp. 1–105; Hungary — *The State of the Environment,* Hungarian Academy of Sciences, Budapest (1990); Tamas Fleischer and Janos Vargha, "Hungary and Pollution," *FORUM for applied research and public policy,* Winter 1991, pp. 1–5; *Hungary: Environmental Issues,* World Bank Background Paper, Washington, D.C., November 1990; Poland — *The State of the Environment in Poland: Damage and Remedy,*

analysis of environmental politics and policy is still lacking. The adequate analytical framework has been slowly developed in the West and an overview of the scholarly literature from the late 1970s up to the late 1980s demonstrates that the disparate studies still have to be synthesized and related to the general literature on policy making.[2] In order to understand environmental policy making and its implementation, attention must be directed toward the adequacy of national and subnational institutions as well as forward an evaluation of alternative designs; this is no easy task even in countries where these institutions and designs are more developed.[3]

Such an analysis should focus on factors that explain why the expectations about sound environmental policies after the fall of Communist regimes are false or premature rather than on the substance of those policies. A cautious approach and a careful analysis of both the visible and the often hidden legacy of the past is quite important because of the widespread expectations that the countries of the region are in an excellent situation to start with something completely new, to learn from all the mistakes of the West and to create a sounder and more effective environmental policy. Many observers consider the region a *tabula rasa* which is "not buried under the morass of government rules, court rulings, and entrenched political forces that makes environmental regulation so cumbersome in the United States" and where "starting from almost nothing gives ... much freedom to create" a good system.[4]

Unfortunately, these expectations and presumptions are false and based on a misunderstanding of the present situation in Central and Eastern Europe. One cannot analyze environmental politics and policy out of the gen-

Ministry of Environmental Protection, Natural Resources and Forestry, Warsaw (1991), pp. 1–72; Baruch Fischhoff, "Report from Poland," *Environment*, vol. 33, no. 2 (March 1991), pp. 12–37; *Poland Environment Strategy Study*. The World Bank, Washington, D.C. (1990); Janusz Zurek and Krysztof Kacprzyk (eds.), *Quality of the environment in Poland*. Institute of Environmental Protection, Warsaw (1990); Romania — almost no publication is available in English; see E. Nyvelt, *Tanulmany Romania ökologiai helyzeteröl* (Study on the State of Ecology in Romania), manuscript, Regional Environmental Center, Budapest (1991), pp. 1–14.

2.   Paul A. Sabatier and Geoffrey Wandesforde-Smith, "Major Sources on Environmental Politics, 1974–1977: The Maturing of a Literature," *Policy Studies Journal*, vol. 7 (1979), pp. 592–604, see p. 600; John S. Dryzek and James P. Lester, "Alternative views of the environmental problematic," in J.P. Lester (ed.), *Environmental Politics and Policy: Theories and Evidence*, Durham and London (1989), pp. 314–330.

3.   Lester, op. cit. (footnote 2), p. 6.

4.   Fischhoff, op. cit. (footnote 1), p. 37.

eral political context which also raises another question: Can these countries "simply shed a yoke" of the past and start a new democratic development, or does the legacy of "the old system" determine their future?[5] And even giving (unacceptably) a positive answer to the first question one would face a legacy of a longer historical past determining present possibilities and options instead of offering a tabula rasa start.[6]

2. Economic Impediments

Experts usually agree that a switch from heavy industry to more service-oriented industries, changes in energy generation and energy use, and changes in agricultural methods are all critical elements to prevent the further degradation of the environment in Central and Eastern Europe and to improve it in the long run. It is a commonplace that the restructuring of the entire economy in each country in the region is a *sine qua non* of any sound and effective environmental policy.[7]

All economic difficulties which hinder the creation and implementation of a proper and effective environmental policy have to be considered in the context of a major structural change: the transition from a centrally planned economy to a market economy. This process is not simply a domestic affair; it is closely related to the extinction of Council of Mutual Economic Assistance (COMECON) and the collapse of the East Bloc market. Beyond this fundamental issue, environmental policy making has to face specific structural economic problems which have determined the present structure of the industry and the energy sector. In addition to the transition-related and structural problems, there are the issues of scarcity of resources (both financial and technical), international debt, and the foreseeable problems of structural changes and transitions in employment policy. All these points are reviewed in order to reach a better understanding of the environmental policy making context.

5. See editor's foreword in "East Central Europe: After the Revolution," *Journal of International Affairs,* vol. 45, no. 1 (Summer 1991), p. ii.

6. Charles Gati, "East-Central Europe: The Morning After," *Foreign Affairs,* vol. 69, no. 5 (Winter 1990/91), pp. 129–145.

7. Helmut Schreiber and Ulrich Weissenburge, "European Plan of Action on Cooperation for an Environmental Reconstruction in Central- and Eastern Europe," in Deutsches Institut für Wirtschaftsforschung and Institut für Europaeische Umweltpolitk, *Environmental Action Plan for Europe,* Bonn (1991), pp. 10–13.

2.1 Problems of Economic Transition

Economic restructuring, combined with all the political changes happening ever since fall 1989, means a complete departure from past practices, i.e., from the centrally planned economy. This change means a fundamental transformation in each country's economic life, including not only the introduction of market regulations and market institutions but also large-scale privatization, new legislation, and a complete reorientation in trade patterns. The substantial difficulties of this transition have already been addressed in the literature, but they are possibly still not fully foreseen or understood.[8]

The structure of the economy and economic hardships are possibly the most obvious and easily comprehensible examples of the legacy of the past. Yet all the difficulties inherent in a transition have not been anticipated, and in many cases political factors play a crucial role in the slowing down of the processes and in the unexpected outcomes. The political controversies over the policy of economic transition were already present during the first free-election campaigns in the NDCs, even if economic issues were mostly irrelevant during these campaigns.[9] The basic difference in economic programs of the main rivals of the opposition was the issue of timing and comprehensive-

---

8. Guillermo A. Calvo and Jacob A. Frenkel, "From Centrally Planned to Market Economy: The Road from CPE to PCPE," *Staff Papers,* International Monetary Fund, vol. 38, no. 2 (June 1991), pp. 268–299; Ellen Comisso, "Political Coalitions, Economic Choices," *Journal of International Affairs,* vol. 45, no. 1 (Summer 1991), pp. 1–29; Deborah Milenkovitch, "The Politics of Economic Transformation," *Journal of International Affairs,* vol. 45, no. 1 (Summer 1991), pp. 151–164. See also Janos Kornai, *The Road to a Free Economy, Shifting from a Socialist System: The Example of Hungary,* New York (1990). Concerning specific countries, see O. Blanchard and R. Layard, *Economic change in Poland,* Discussion Paper no. 424, Centre for Economic Policy Research, London (1990); Stanislaw Wellisz, "The Lessons of Economic Reform: The Polish Case," *Journal of International Affairs,* vol. 45, no. 1 (Summer 1991), pp. 165–179; Joshua Charap and Karel Dyba, "Transition to a Market Economy: The Case of Czechoslovakia," *European Economic Review,* vol. 35, no. 2/3 (April 1991), pp. 581–590; Vaclav Klaus and Tomaz Jezek, "Social Criticism, False Liberalism, and Recent Changes in Czechoslovakia," *East European Politics and Societies,* vol. 5, no. 1, pp. 26–40; Jan Svejnar, "A Framework for the Economic Transformation of Czechoslovakia," *Eastern European Economics,* vol. 29, no. 2 (Winter 1990–1991), pp. 5–28; Janos Kornai, "Surgery for stabilization," *The New Hungarian Quarterly,* vol. 31, no. 117 (Spring 1990), pp. 84–89; Ivan Szelenyi, "Alternative Futures for Eastern Europe: The Case of Hungary," *East European Politics and Societies,* vol. 4, no. 2 (Spring 1990), pp. 231–254.

9. Comisso, op. cit. (footnote 8), pp. 13–15.

ness of radical reforms.[10] After the elections, this controversy has become a main issue of conflict between government and opposition (as in Hungary) or between government and population (as in Poland) or between rival political groups in power (as in former Czechoslovakia).

The basic dilemma of the new governments is that they won elections by promising not only a democratic and free society, but also a better future and an improvement in the overall standards of living. The West is attractive to NDCs not only because it has an open and democratic society, but because it has a high standard of living. Governments of NDCs have an electoral obligation to fulfill their promises; moreover, they don't feel comfortable (in other words, they are weak) about introducing highly unpopular measures which, in the short run, are contrary to their campaign promises. So the basic political reason for not introducing sweeping measures and for not completing the economic transformation as soon as possible is the fear of its social-political consequences.

The basic economic reason for postponing sweeping reforms is that these governments have to face extensive immediate economic problems. Their short-term, and in many cases medium-term preoccupation is a desperate attempt at economic survival. In other words, the hands of the new governments seem to be tied, making them incapable of action. The extent of their limitation is a heritage of the past which has not been anticipated.

A comparison between the NDCs and the former German Democratic Republic (GDR) demonstrates that the lack of resources really limits the scope of possible actions in completing economic restructuring. But even in the eastern part of Germany, having all available resources of West Germany and being legally integrated into the West by a political act, the process of transformation will take much more time than anticipated, as is already evident in labor and employment policy. It is additionally proved that even if governments can overcome their political fears and have access to necessary financial means, the process of economic transition is going to be lengthy and complicated, with a delay between decision making and actual implementation.[11]

2.2 Difficulties in Industrial Restructuring

The greatest structural problem is the heritage of an oversized, extremely energy inefficient, and in most cases completely obsolete heavy industry, the

---

10. Cf. Mihaly Laki, "Economic Programs of the Exopposition Parties in Hungary," *East European Politics and Societies,* vol. 5, no. 1 (Winter 1991), pp. 73–91.

11. Calvo and Frenkel, op. cit. (footnote 8), p. 269.

operation of which is usually deeply in the red. Restructuring requires not simply privatization and the closing of inefficient factories, but a whole-scale modernization program. The backward industrial structure, together with the irresponsible policy of planned economies, is mainly responsible for the ecological destruction in the region. Yet, beyond vague privatization plans governments have no comprehensive industrial or modernization policies.[12] The kinds of problems that would be generated by the collapse of the arms industry (particularly in Bulgaria and Czechoslovakia), by the radical decline in Soviet oil deliveries or by the disintegration of the COMECON market had not been foreseen. Because of these difficulties, further industrial cutbacks and closings have been much more difficult to make than previously envisioned.

In the beginning of the transition period, there were hopes to eliminate the products of Communist ideology like huge steelmills and aluminum works. These plants were created by an underlying philosophy according to which socialism had to be based on heavy industry and on a working class closely related to that industry. In many cases the creation of huge heavy industry installations was based on the idea of substituting local intelligentsia or peasantry for heavy industry workers (see the steelworks at Nowa Huta near Krakow in Poland or the aluminum works at Ziar nad Hronom in Slovakia). According to conventional wisdom these highly polluting symbols of Communist industrialization should have been among the very first plants to close down during industrial restructuring. Yet the legacy of the past seems to be stronger than had been anticipated.

Because of the lack of comprehensive industrial policy and transition plans, as well as the pressure of immediate liquidity problems, the influence of large, monopolistic industrial structures and the bargaining power of their lobbies have not yet disappeared.[13] At the same time, social tensions aggravate the situation. Even nationality issues play a role in maintaining highly polluting industrial structures.

The second structural problem is posed by the energy sector itself. In the former Communist countries energy needs for the production of US$ 1 equivalent national product are the highest, while energy efficiency is the lowest in an international comparison.[14] At the same time, in most countries

12. Milenkovitch, op. cit. (footnote 8), pp. 159–160.

13. Cf. the consequences drawn by analyzing privatization procedures in Central and Eastern Europe, Eduardo Borensztein and Manmohan S. Kumar, "Proposals for Privatization in Eastern Europe," *Staff Papers,* International Monetary Fund, vol. 38, no. 2 (June 1991), pp. 300–326.

14. Mark D. Levine et al., *Energy Efficiency, Developing nations, and Eastern Europe,* a report to the US working group on global energy efficiency, International In-

of the region, the main source of energy is highly polluting brown coal and/or low quality soft coal or lignite.[15] It means that an inefficient and very polluting energy sector provides the basis of an obsolete and extensively polluting heavy industry. Though energy efficiency and conservation slogans appear in the programs of the new governments, long-term energy programs deal with the creation of new huge power plants. Despite the fact that actual energy consumption has significantly declined since 1990 due to higher energy prices and industrial recession,[16] and despite the recommendations of all relevant international studies demonstrating huge reserves in energy savings[17] (even showing significant energy export potentials[18]), the alternative is not a choice between the present trend and a serious reduction in energy consumption, but a choice between the different methods of increasing energy output. In Hungary, for example, the choice presented by the government is between a huge new lignite-based power station and an extension (doubling) of the existing nuclear power station. The underlying logic is almost identical with the one during the Communist regime: future industrial recovery and expansion will demand more and more energy. The lack of understanding even a sustainable development policy on behalf of the political leaders, and the vested interest of the technocrats in the energy sector (though sometimes rivals for resources but not different in approach) must also be considered part of the legacy of the past, making a shift to a new, environmentally oriented, conservationist energy policy even more difficult.

The past logic of energy dependency is also prevalent in the well-known controversy between the Hungarian and Slovak government over a hydroelectric power station, the Gabcikovo-Nagymaros barrage system (GNB), under construction on the Danube. This is an extremely relevant example of the hidden heritage of the past.

The GNB has been a symbol of Communist industrial mismanagement and secretive decision making. It mobilized environmentalists who consid-

stitute for Energy Conservation, June 1991, pp. 1–60; "Closing Remarks," Planning Workshop on specific IEA activities to address energy-efficient technology and environment problems in Eastern European countries, Budapest, November 1990.

15. Cf. French, op. cit. (footnote 1), p. 11 ff.; Russell, op. cit. (footnote 1), pp. 23–28.

16. Energy consumption decreased by 6.2 percent in Hungary alone, cf. publications of the Central Statistical Office, April 1991.

17. Levine, op. cit. (footnote 14), p. 26; *The Energy Policies of Hungary,* Survey of the International Energy Agency, Budapest, July 1991, pp. 1–6; Schreiber and Weissenburge, op. cit. (footnote 7), p. 12.

18. Marian Radetzki, "Energy Exports from Centrally Planned Economies," *Energy Policy,* vol. 18, no. 9 (November 1990), pp. 806–808.

ered the GNB a major threat to the environment to stage the first major street demonstration (of about 60,000 people) since 1956 in still Communist Hungary. This issue also played a major role in the defeat of the Communist leadership in the fall of 1989 in Hungary.[19] In Czechoslovakia, opponents of the GNB were harassed, and the cancellation of the project was supported by all major opposition groups. Yet, even after the collapse of the Communist system, the new Slovak government has decided to complete the project and has maintained a controversial position *vis a vis* the Hungarian government. Conventional wisdom has predicted an immediate halt to the project which has been a symbol of gigantic Communist industrial policy totally indifferent to environmental considerations and repressive to all public opposition. However, just the contrary has happened. Slovak leaders and technocrats have downgraded the ecological dangers and consider energy production increase a top priority and an important part of a more independent national economy; here nationalistic considerations have also had a role in insisting on the completion of the plant.

The issue of nuclear power, again, provides other examples of the hidden legacy of the past, even if from a different perspective. Environmentalists usually oppose nuclear power in Central and Eastern Europe partly for safety reasons and partly because of the unsolved issue of nuclear waste. In Hungary, for example, one of the most celebrated cases which united the then opposition groups was a protest movement against a proposed low-radiation nuclear waste disposal site at Ofalu (mid-southern Hungary).

Opposition to nuclear power has increased since the Chernobyl accident and since operational problems were recognized in Kozloduy (Bulgaria) and in Bohunice (Czechoslovakia).[20] All the operating reactors in the former East Bloc countries are of Soviet design; up to now Bulgaria, the former Czechoslovakia, and Hungary have had arrangements with the former Soviet Union according to which the Soviets had to handle high-radiation nuclear wastes from these reactors. Bulgaria and Hungary are heavily dependent on nuclear power in the generation of their electricity supply (close to 40 percent in Bulgaria and already more than 50 percent in Hungary).

At the same time, these countries are seriously short of electricity-generating capacity. In addition, a higher reliance on fossil-fuel plants, especially

---

19. Cf. Peter Hardi et al., *The Hardi Report*, Budapest (1990).

20. See *Arguments of Ecoglasnost Against Building a Nuclear Power Station Near the Towns of Belene and Svishtov*, Ecoglasnost, Sofia 1990; Österreichische Expertenkommission für Bohunice, *Bewertung der Sicherheit des Kernkraftwerks Jaslovska Bohunice Block VI*, Band 2, Studie erstellt im Auftrag des Bundeskanzlers, Vienna, January 1991; Steve Thomas, "Comecon Nuclear Power Plant Performance," *Energy Policy*, vol. 18, no. 6 (July/August 1990), pp. 506–524.

those which use lignite, would significantly worsen air quality, increasing CO_2 and SO_2 emissions in a region which is already the most polluted in Europe.

The countries which are now trying to reduce their dependency on the former Soviet Union cannot make a simple switch from Soviet technology to Western technology, although some Western companies are more than ready to participate in nuclear power station constructions and have even exerted pressure on governments (see especially the case of Electricité de France).

Decision makers are trapped by an environmental and a political dilemma: which kind of power generation technology to choose — a potentially hazardous one or a presently polluting one; and how to reduce dependency on the former Soviet Union without significantly increasing Western indebtedness. Financing any investment in nuclear technology demands resources which are unavailable in the region. Yet governments are considering this option because they are unable to get away from the logic which is based on the necessity of increasing the electricity output. They do not seriously evaluate declining demands from a long recession period, from restructuring and new market conditions, or from modernization and switching to more energy efficient technologies and products. It is also questionable whether such an investment is the best use of Western assistance and scarce resources.[21]

2.3 Lack of Resources and Indebtedness

To achieve radical changes in the present environmental situation, governments should follow the radical path in restructuring the entire economy, not simply industry. Here, however, governments run into serious difficulties not only because they lack the necessary financial and technological resources to implement a policy of radical change but also because issues like economic survival and immediate- and short-term budget allocations, increases in export revenues, and a formidable international debt-servicing requirement push environmental consideration down on the priority list.

The lack of sufficient financial resources also means the postponement of clean-up activities and actions for improving the situation. Governments take action only in clear cases of imminent danger or strong local protest, or when a case is highly publicized, without adopting a comprehensive action plan.

International indebtedness, hitting Poland, Hungary, and recently Bulgaria, particularly hard, is another major factor influencing environmental policy. (Although it managed to repay its international debt during Ceaus-

21. Thomas, op. cit. (footnote 20), pp. 507–508.

escu's dictatorship, Romania is rapidly piling up a significant new debt which was estimated to be as high as US$ 5 billion in late 1991.) Just servicing Hungary's debt consumed 57 percent of its export revenues in 1990. From time to time, these countries struggle with servicing the debt on schedule. Poland failed on a few occasions and asked for rescheduling; Bulgaria declared a moratorium on debt servicing in 1990; while Hungary managed to survive and preserve her first-class debtor status but at a price of devoting every available resource to earn hard currency. During the Communist regime the government offered special subsidies and created tax havens for hard currency export, but did not regularly consider efficiency or profitability criteria and definitely did not observe environmental conditions.

The indebtedness is an obvious legacy of the past, a result of Communist policy of the mid-1970s and mid-1980s. Poland, "in exchange" of democratization, got a special relief from the debt burden by a US initiative to forgive half of her government's debts. Hungary, however, could not rely on such relief, having the overwhelming majority of her debt originated in commercial lending banks. The country, however, has been eligible for further credits throughout the years. The hidden legacy of indebtedness is the prevailing policy context in which this issue is handled and which is almost identical with the context of the previous regime; the present leadership inherited an enormous debt which makes timely servicing mandatory in order to be eligible for new credits, without which immediate economic collapse seems to be inevitable. The strict insistence on non-rescheduling debt services, paired with a government austerity program required by major lending institutions (especially by the International Monetary Fund — IMF) to secure eligibility for new loans, ties up all available liquid resources in the economy, and makes major investments in environmental protection or prevention impossible.

2.4 Employment Policy Considerations

Industrial restructuring is delayed also because of leadership fears of social-political consequences. The closure of heavily polluting factories which cause serious health risks is a highly controversial issue because of rising unemployment. Neither the political leadership nor the population is prepared to deal with the consequences of a foreseeable unemployment rate of 5 to 10 percent (which might be considered insignificant or normal in the West). Job security and at least a minimum level of stability was guaranteed by the Communist regime, and during 40 years of Communist rule generations became accustomed to these conditions. Massive unemployment and the ever-decreasing capability of the state (and local governments) to provide social security services are new menaces which, paired with a rapidly increasing impoverishment of large sections of these societies, may create conditions for serious social dissatisfaction. This situation, of course, is a new development, and though it was not fully unexpected, the way people react shows a lasting effect of the past, in both social actions and psychological patterns.

In the NDCs today there is no possibility of significant retraining. Geographic mobility is extremely low; and there is no alternative strategy for future actions. Social tensions could easily be turned into political actions (for example, the so-called taxiblockade was an act of civil disobedience in reaction to a huge increase in gasoline prices without previous negotiations in Hungary in the fall of 1990) which would jeopardize the present leaderships' chances for survival. The fall of the Mazoviecki government in Poland, after the introduction of a severe austerity program, is a good illustration of this point. As a consequence, political leaders are reluctant to take radical steps, at least not for mere environmental consideration. The conventional wisdom expectation, that the legitimation of governments elected by democratic method is strong enough to secure popular support even if they take measures which temporarily reduce welfare,[22] proves to be wrong. It is just the contrary: when the security of many jobs is at stake, the government always yields to local or sectoral pressure not to close down factories even if they pose significant environmental or health hazards.

In almost all NDCs public health issues are of secondary importance in comparison with job and social security. In addition, in certain cases, like in Romania, the amount of and access to information is very limited. This lack of information on public health issues, as well as the low level of concern for environmental risks, is another heritage of the past which influences environmental policy making in a negative way.

These major problems make the transition to a cleaner and conservation-oriented production system extremely slow and difficult. The immediate goal of political leaders is to survive the severe economic crisis and to launch a recovery program as soon as possible. This goal cannot give priority to environmental considerations and does not leave much maneuvering room for environmental expenditure. The long-term perspective is also not encouraging.

The strategic goal is to ensure a strong economic development, combined with a thorough modernization program. Government leaders must create prosperous and competitive economies similar to those of the developed nations, and they must integrate their economies into the Western market sys-

---

22. Michael Kaser, "The Technology of Decontrol: Some Macroeconomic Issues," *Economic Journal,* vol. 100, no. 401 (June 1990), pp. 596–615; see p. 610.

tem.[23] They have no alternative development pattern in mind; even a strategy of sustainable development is considered an impediment. Policy makers must be forced to face environmental considerations either by domestic pressure or by external pressure.

3. Political Impediments

Beyond the economic factors, there are significant non-economic impediments on a sound environmental policy. They can be grouped into political and policy-oriented type of impediments, including party politics, division of power, privatization, legislation, institutional and legal issues, and expertise and managerial impediments. In this section I provide an overview of the political conditions within which environmental policy has to be formulated.

The general starting point when people speak about the political conditions of an improved environmental policy in the NDCs is the underlying premise that a democratic society provides a better framework for environmental actions in both the governmental and the nongovernmental fields than authoritarian regimes. Analysts usually take this point for granted (for example, in Latin America, Asia, or Eastern and Central Europe.[24]) Generally speaking, this premise is true, yet the practical implementation of a better environmental policy is not granted by the change of government or even by the very change of the political system. Here, again, we can discover the heritage of the past and the hidden legacy of the Communist system. However, the analyst cannot rely on such a variety of academic literature as in the case of the problems of economic transformation. This is probably an indication that East European studies on economics and economic policy bear more relevance to the present situation than any of the studies on politics and policy making. The lack of scientific analyses of the present political atmosphere, or past traditions, is even more striking; references regarding the issues in this study are made primarily to the remarks of prominent local observers.

---

23. Cf. Laszlo Csaba, "Gearing up for the Economic Future," *New Hungarian Quarterly*, vol. 31, no. 119 (Autumn 1990), pp. 66–72.

24. Dean E. Mann, "Environmental Learning in a Decentralized Political World," *Journal of International Affairs*, vol. 44, no. 2, pp. 301–337; see p. 311.

3.1 Traditions of the Previous System

The traditions of the past system are still very strong, and it is not clear for how long they will prevail. In countries like Romania, and even Poland, there is a firm conviction that "a strong hand steering the government is a desirable solution." It clearly demonstrates that "though institutions can be established rather quickly, but political mentalities change very slowly,"[25] and this is true despite the expectations of observers who put too much emphasis on institutions and institutionalized processes which can assure liberties and responsible economies.[26]

Other expectations emphasize the changing character of the state in NDCs. The state in Communist regimes had the paternalistic function of generating goods and services for the populace. A transition to the Western model would put forward a very different function of the state in this regard: Protection of the vital interests of its citizens by regulating any excesses which result from the production of goods and services.[27] Giving up paternalistic functions, however, is no easy task, and the new governments, realizing the "sweet taste of power," are reluctant to reduce their own role in society. This is obviously the case in Romania and Bulgaria where authoritarian regimes and dominant authoritarian party systems emerged,[28] but it is also prevalent in the presidential power in the basically one-party-dominated Poland and easy to track in Hungarian government attitudes despite the truly multiparty system of the country (for example, the influential role in privatization of the government-controlled State Property Agency, the interventionist policy of the government as majority shareholder determining commercial bank strategies, and the government's insistence upon initiating all legislation).

The insistence on maintaining more power than necessary in a central government in a democratic regime impedes the spread of local and non-

---

25. "The Road to Democracy and Pluralism in Poland," interview with B. Geremek, *Journal of International Affairs,* vol. 45, no. 1 (Summer) 1991, pp. 67–70; see p. 69.

26. Cf. Walter C. Neale, "Society, State, and Market: A Polanian View of Current Change and Turmoil in Eastern Europe," *Journal of Economic Issues,* vol. 25, no. 2 (June 1991), pp. 467–473; esp. p. 472.

27. Ruth Bell, "Privatization and the Environment in Eastern and Central Europe," unpublished manuscript, Warsaw, July 1991.

28. Andras Körössenyi, "Revival of the Past or New Beginning? The Nature of Post-Communist Politics," *The Political Quarterly,* vol. 62, no. 1 (Jan.–March 1991), pp. 52–74; see p. 53.

governmental organizations' initiatives in environmental policy making and implementation. Waiting for environmental regulations from the central government when its priorities are in other fields slows down the establishment of necessary environmental policy actions. This government mentality is also an unforeseen influence of past indoctrination, that is, a belief in a central solution.

3.2 Public Participation

There is no tradition of public involvement in environmental decision making, policy implementation, and enforcement. A fundamental tenet of Communist power was to prevent all kinds of independent, nongovernmental, or party-controlled initiatives in the society. Previous nonpolitical institutions (such as social, professional, residential, and religious groups, including private clubs) were banned and dissolved. It was a policy systematically and very successfully carried out over the decades; it deprived Central and East European societies from a dimension usually referred to as the "civil society."[29] As a consequence, people were detached from civic obligations, their concern for ideological and societal goals was strongly reduced, and they retreated into private or family affairs.[30]

Grassroots, environmental organizations have no experience in political involvement, and have little knowledge of their rights and their right to information. Environmental groups which were emerging spontaneously during the Communist regimes, in most cases without official approval, were protest groups fighting against local or central authorities or state-owned factory management to achieve certain environmental goals.[31] Most of these groups were single-issue organizations, focusing on one specific problem (for example, the Danube Circle was concerned with the dam). Their basic attitude was mistrust in everything that was official; they challenged the validity of all available or published data, and were unwilling to negotiate with industry leaders. The main form of their activities was organizing local or (in a few cases) national resistance, mobilizing affected people in order to press deci-

---

29. Gail Kligman, "Reclaiming the Public: A Reflection on Recreating Civil Society in Romania," *East European Politics and Societies,* vol. 4, no. 3 (Fall 1990), pp. 393–427.

30. David S. Mason, Daniel N. Nelson, and Bohdan M. Szklarski, "Apathy and the Birth of Democracy: The Polish Struggle," *East European Politics and Societies,* vol. 5, no. 2 (Spring 1991), pp. 205–233; esp. p. 210.

31. Janos Vargha, "Green Revolutions in Eastern Europe," *Panoscope,* May 1990.

sion makers. Yet they had an important role in helping radical changes and promoting collective actions.

A very remarkable legacy of the Communist past is visible in the general attitude of environmentalist and nature conservationist groups in NDCs. Despite the fact that now legitimately elected central and local governments are in power, the prevailing attitude of these groups is still mistrust in everything which is government-related. Environmental groups did not share even the temporary raise in public trust in newly elected non-Communist governments. Their basic approach is still that of a protest group which is reluctant to negotiate or to participate in decision making and/or policy implementation. Environmental groups in the region are not accustomed to receiving financial assistance from governments or governmental institutions — a form of financing accepted by many Western nongovernmental organizations — and these reservations have roots in the history of these movements.[32]

Here again everyday practice refutes many expectations. It seemed to be reasonable to believe that, at the dawn of political changes and the emergence of new governments, environmentalists and their friends and allies in opposition would be able to frame new environmental policies that assist each other in obtaining basically identical goals. Yet, environmental and conservation groups and movements maintain their protest mentality, as it was expressed at national meetings in Hungary and Poland in early 1991 or at an international meeting in Czechoslovakia in mid-1991.[33] This may be less surprising, as one of the activities of environmental organizations in the West is to protest existing practices, both governmental and business; the unexpected element of their behavior in the NDCs is that their present approach toward authorities is almost identical with their approach in the past. Even the environmental programs of new parties which ascended to power have protest characteristics,[34] and environmentalists inside the party attack their own leaders with executive power for not implementing the party strategy into government actions.

This is partly a result of a suspicion built up over the decades, which made a lasting impact on people's attitudes, and partly a result of the very slow changes in official organizations and behavior. The slowness of devel-

---

32. Vesna Terselic, Zagreb Green Club, August 1991, personal communication.

33. See the documents of the Tata Meeting, February 3, 1991 (in Hungarian), the summary of the Brwinow Meeting, February 10, 1991 (in Polish), and the press release and the "Address to the Conference of European Environmental Ministers," Working Together Meeting, Prestavlky, June 1991.

34. Eva Hajba, "Social-political Components of Environmental Issues" (in Hungarian), in *Környezetgazdalkodasi kutatasok* (Environmental Management Research) no. 7, GIO Budapest, December 1990, pp. 67–93.

oping administrative structures and the unsolved organizational problems within the governments, environmental authorities and ministries distracted policy makers from actual environmental policy making (e.g., the reorganization of the Hungarian Ministry of Environmental Protection took literally a whole year). Finally, it is a consequence of the governments' overall economic policies, their efforts to secure a Western-type, free market and to create an affluent society, sacrificing environmental priorities for economic growth.

It is also important to notice that there is some public pressure on governments to address environmental issues on a priority base. Public awareness of environmental issues is very low. There is still no right to an information law enacted, and the rights of citizens' groups are yet to be codified.[35] People are usually unaware of the health risks of environmental degradation and/or pollutants.[36] In addition, national environmental education programs are almost nonexistent.

It has become clear that the emergence of environmental civic consciousness will take much longer than many people had thought. But even the slow evolvement of consciousness has led to the creation of several new and important ecological institutions which will be able to work effectively only in a new political and legal environment.

3.3 Political Cleavages and Environmental Movements

The analyst of the environmental politics in Central and Eastern Europe has to explain the following paradox. Environmentalists were instrumental in organizing and provoking opposition against previous Communist regimes; in certain cases they were the focal points of political opposition. Environmental issues, like the dam on the Danube in Hungary and Czechoslovakia or the Ruse controversy in Bulgaria, were key issues in attacks against Communist power. On the other side, opposition leaders were backed by environmentalists, they were comrades in arms. Since the power takeover, many prominent environmental figures have been elected to high political offices, while their immediate comrades in opposition have become national leaders. Yet envi-

---

35. Some of this problem is addressed by Laszlo Solyom, "Data Protection and Freedom of Information," *The New Hungarian Quarterly*, vol. 31, no. 117 (Spring 1990), pp. 45–49.

36. Clyde Hertzman, *Hungary Report: Environment and Health,* World Bank, Washington, D.C., August 1990, pp. 1–53; Clyde Hertzman, "Poland: Health and Environment in the Context of Socioeconomic Decline," Discussion Paper Series, University of British Columbia, Vancouver, January 1990, pp. 1–19.

ronmentalists now have declining or no political influence and in many cases they have little or no impact on economic and environmental policy making. Why is this the case?

During the transition period when different opposition movements emerged, through the partial decrease of repressive politics, environmental-conservation movements were somewhat better tolerated than direct political- or human-rights groups. Environmentalism opened up an almost legal channel for political and opposition activity, and it attracted many people who were interested in political change but did not want to risk the hardship of direct political confrontation or who believed that the best strategy was to use all available means to attract public support for opposition politics and to weaken the Communist regime. As a consequence, the support for environmental issues came only from those who were concerned about the environment. As soon as legal channels opened up for opposition politics (such as the reform-Communist government in Hungary from 1989 to early 1990) and for genuine political pluralism (such as in Czechoslovakia after the revolution and in Poland in 1990), those who were primarily interested in bringing down the Communist regime or in politics quickly left the environmental groups and movements and began creating political movements or parties of their own; they became preoccupied with politics in general.[37] And now, when they have finally ascended to power, they have found environmental issues burdensome and contrary to their economic and political goals.

Neither the once opposition movements nor the current political society could avoid cleavages. In countries where the opposition was organized around one major movement — like Solidarity in Poland or the Civic Forum in the Czech Republic — political cleavages have taken place within the movement. In countries where the opposition itself was organized around parties — like in Hungary — political cleavages have taken place between parties, and have divided the leaders of the movements or have influenced elite adversaries between the parties on the priorities of environmental issues.[38] As soon as a controversy becomes a crucial element within the party — during election campaigns and especially after free elections when previously allied opposition groups are transformed into genuine political adversaries between government and new opposition and a partisan pattern of

---

37. Cf. Piotr Glinski, "Environmentalism in Poland" (English translation in manuscript), in Przemyslaw Czajkowski (ed.), *The Ecological Movements and Organizations in Poland,* Warsaw (1990).

38. Cf. Comisso, op. cit. (footnote 8), p. 3; and Körössenyi, op. cit. (footnote 28), p. 73–74.

authoritative behavior has been established[39] — nonpartisan groups become caught in party infights and are placed on the periphery of political life.[40] In certain cases, most noticeably in Bulgaria, where the most influential environmental movement, Ecoglasnost, has split into two movements, the once comrades-in-arms have turned against each other.

Environmentalists who remain in the center of political life, especially when they have been elevated to party and/or political positions, are often caught between party loyalty and government loyalty. This is true especially for those government or parliamentary figures who have been in charge of environmental policy making on a party ticket. In the government, either the peer pressure or the stronger position of economic-financial portfolios work against the promotion of environmental interests especially when the so-called hard evidences of economic realities are presented to cabinet members. Finally, environmentally minded politicians, either in government or in legislation, sometimes are overwhelmed by the daily routine and they simply have no time to deal with the business of environmental affairs.

These movements have lost their popularity and political support, and it has become increasingly clear that their strength had been rooted not in environmental issues as much as in political opposition.

The decline of the influence of environmental groups is again part of the legacies of the past, in the sense that the relative strength of environmental opposition in the previous period was a misleading factor. Had there not been a Communist past, these political figures who originally supported environmental causes would possibly have never become part of those movements. The overestimation of the influence of environmental issues in public policy, a misleading facet of these societies in transition, can be considered an overlooked legacy of the past.

3.4 Decentralization

The next issue in the analysis of the heritage of the past is the division of power. One of the basic arguments for democratization emphasized that Communism had excessively centralized power and in a democratic society authority and power should be decentralized and transferred in significant

39. Ken Jowitt, "Post-Communist Eastern Europe: A Survey of Opinion," *East European Politics and Societies,* vol. 4, no. 2 (Spring 1990), p. 195.

40. Mate Szabo, "Changing Patterns of Mobilization in Hungary within New Social Movements: The Case of Ecology," in György Szoboszlai (ed.), *Democracy and Political Transformation: Theories and East-Central European realities,* Hungarian Political Science Association, Budapest (1991), pp. 310–319.

dimensions to local governments and institutions. This claim, together with the human-rights demands, was on the top of the agenda of opposition groups during the last period of Communist rule.

Human-rights issues are now more or less solved in the "four more hopeful" countries. Devolution of power, however, is still an unfinished process. There is still no clear division of power and authority between central and local governments or between governments and institutions. This problem is aggravated by the federal vs. individual republic state controversy in the Czech and Slovak Federal Republic. In most countries of the region, the state is still trying to preserve too many prerogatives, and has limited local autonomy. For consistent regulations and actions, however, it is important to make the division of power very clear, even if it means severe limitation of central authorities. The delay in accomplishing this task is a consequence of both the lasting impact of the previous regime and the predominance of political rivalry within groups or parties now competing for power. Let me illustrate this point with the example of the Hungarian bill for specifying the rights and duties of local governments.

Soon after the elections in 1990, when the coalition government in Hungary had already established its power, it presented a bill to the parliament on the legal status, rights, and duties of local governments. According to election promises, it addressed the central issue of decentralization and intended to provide a relatively large degree of autonomy to local authorities. In September 1990, local elections were held, and, surprisingly, the great majority of the governing coalition's candidates was defeated either by opposition or by independent candidates who in many cases were incumbent local leaders from the previous period. The governing coalition, hoping for a sweeping victory at the time it presented the bill to the parliament, realized that a great degree of autonomy for local authorities would jeopardize its influence in the cities and in the countryside, and started to amend its own bill in order to achieve a legislation that would be less favorable for local power.

From environmental policy making perspective, the real problem at that juncture was not whether more or less power would be allocated to local authorities but the delay and the controversies involved in the discussion and passage of the bill. Without the law, without defining the rights and limits of local power, it was impossible to set up an adequate framework for environmental regulation. Some of the unresolved issues included financial power (the size of budget local authorities would control, the amount of resources they could allocate, etc.), taxing power, and enforcement power. Due to the year-long delay authorities could not address fundamental issues of environmental regulation such as reliance on market instruments (permit fees, fines, levies, taxes), enforcement agencies, monitoring and data collection during a transition period when spontaneous privatization and marketization had uncovered dubious enterprises either paying no attention to environmental protection or deliberately trying to elude environmental regulations. And what is a problem of local authorities vs. central government in Hungary, is a problem of national vs. federal authorities in Czechoslovakia.

4. Policy Impediments

This section focuses on noneconomic policy issues. In the discussion, it is important to consider a separate problem which provides an excellent illustration of environmental policy impediments as part of the hidden legacy of the past. This is the mixture of economic, legal, and political problems; it is the issue of privatization.

4.1 Privatization and Re-privatization

Privatization is usually discussed together with the general issue of economic transformation, as the creation of a predominantly private ownership structure seems to be one of the most important preconditions of a transfer to a market economy. In long-term economic strategy and in macroeconomic terms, the privatization of large state-owned enterprises is the crucial issue. The economic-structural dimension of this type of privatization is well covered in the literature.[41]

Whether the issue is privatization or re-privatization, industrial and agricultural units will be traded and new owners will manage operations and handle property. Both the liability for previous environmental damages and the obligation to clean up are crucial issues for developing environmental policies. Because of the lack of uniform regulations, the uncertainty of own-

---

41. Blanchard and Layard, op. cit. (footnote 8); Borensztein and Kumar, op. cit. (footnote 13); Paul G. Hare, "From Central Planning to Market Economy: Some Microeconomic Issues," *Economic Journal*, vol. 100, no. 401 (June 1990), pp. 581–595; Zoltan Halasz, "A Round-Table on Privatization," *The New Hungarian Quarterly*, vol. 31, no. 117 (Spring 1990), pp. 90–95; Janos Kornai, "Socialist Transformation and Privatization: Shifting from a Socialist System," *East-European Politics and Societies*, vol. 4, no. 2 (Spring 1990), pp. 255–304; David M. Newbery, op. cit.; David Stark, "Privatization in Hungary: From Plan to Market or from Plan to Clan?" *East European Politics and Societies*, vol. 4, no. 3 (Fall 1990), pp. 351–392; Christopher Wellisz, "Privatization in Poland: The Problem of Valuation," *Journal of International Affairs*, vol. 35, no. 1 (Summer 1991), pp. 247–270.

ership terms makes it impossible to develop such policies even in cases when there is no change in ownership. None of the privatization bills or any of their provisions were written with environmental considerations, costs, or specific requirements in mind. Western investors, however, who have experiences in countries where property transfers are strongly influenced and regulated by laws imposing liability for remedy and where lawsuits by affected individuals or public groups can also be anticipated, are reluctant to invest in Central and East European enterprises.[42]

Governments, which want to promote privatization and Western investment, should be compelled to clarify the environmental dimensions of privatization legislation. However, they are reluctant to adopt environmental regulations that are too stringent because of their fear of deterring Western investors. A further factor which will obscure an effective environmental impact of privatization is that a dual economy will exist in the NDCs for quite a long period. This will result in conflicts and frictions, because the coexistence of the state and the private sector will remain inescapable.[43]

4.2 Environmental Legislation

There is a lack of a consistent, comprehensive legal and institutional regulatory framework for the environment in the region. Moreover, NDCs are in transition to a new legal and constitutional system.[44] Each country of the region is in the process of drafting environmental legislation in a situation where the overall legal structure itself is in a transition. Without having an adequate and modern regulatory framework, it is almost hopeless to work out individual solutions to specific problems. Furthermore, privatization has not been completed, and its legal framework has not yet created clarification of liability issues and ownership conditions are still missing.

Environmental legislation offers other important examples for proving my thesis. The constitutions of NDCs do not include articles to ensure a right to information, which would make environmental protection information, especially data on health hazards, risks, and government policy, easily available and mandatory.[45] There is no codification yet for the activity framework of

---

42. Bell, op. cit. (footnote 27), p. 7.

43. Kornai, *The Road to a Free Economy,* op. cit. (footnote 8), p. 304.

44. For a general overview, see Herman Schwartz, "Constitutional Developments in East Central Europe," *Journal of International Affairs,* vol. 45, no. 1 (Summer 1991), pp. 71–89.

45. Cf. Stefan Kyutchoukov, "The Bulgarian Approach to the Problem of Access to

citizens' groups.[46] The elements of a transparent and democratic environmental policy making and its implementation are missing because of the heritage of the previous system in which nonaccountability of the leaders was paired with secrecy of undesirable economic policies.

The change to a market economy also poses new problems on environmental legislation. Up to now the countries of the region were relying exclusively on direct, standard-based regulation which, however, did not include the best available technology (BAT) because of the backward technological state of the industry.[47] Now market incentives are being introduced into the legislative framework, creating a new subject of controversy.[48] Even environmental groups are afraid of giving up the direct command-type legislative approaches — being suspicious of central government and state power — to the rule of law. The fundamental problem of the new democracies, however, is the issue of creating a society in which the rule of law is unquestionable and above dispute; the new democracies must also have adequate means and institutions to enforce the rule of law.

This debate reflects another heritage of the past: the understanding of the relationship between the state and the individual citizen. In most cases, citizens of NDCs expect the state to enact legislation and bring about regulations for citizens' activities while there is no expectation, but among a hand-

Information," *Environmental Legislation Task Force Papers,* Regional Environmental Center (REC), Budapest (1991).

46. Cf. Jane L. Bloom, "Opportunities for Public Involvement in Environmental Policy Making," *Environmental Legislation Task Force.* REC, Budapest, March 1991; *Public Participation in Environmental Regulation,* Environmental Law Institute, Washington, D.C., January 1991.

47. Cf. *Environmental Law-Drafting in Czechoslovakia,* Environmental Law Institute, Washington, D.C. (1991); Gordana Milicevic, "Implications of European Community Laws on Yugoslav Legislation Concerning the Environment," *Environmental Legislation Task Force Papers,* REC, Budapest 1991; R. Stewart, "Comments on Czechoslovak and Hungarian Environmental Law Drafts," personal communication, Budapest, March 1991.

48. Daniel J. Dudek, Richard B. Stewart, and Jonathan B. Wiener, "Environmental Policy for Eastern Europe: Technology-based Versus Market-based Approaches," *Environmental Legislation Task Force, ELTF Papers,* REC, Budapest 1991; E. Donald Elliott, Jane Bloom, and Susan Swift, "An Institutional Perspective on Environmental Law in the US," *ELTF Papers,* REC, Budapest, 1991; Lothar Gündling, "Some Observations on the Proposed Environmental Protection Acts for Hungary, CSFR, Bulgaria, and Poland," *ELTF Papers,* REC, Budapest, 1991; L. Kramer, "Defining the Environment," *ELTF Papers,* REC, Budapest, 1991; US EPA, "Review of Eastern European Environmental Laws," *ELTF Papers,* REC, Budapest, 1991; *Setting Standards: The Best Available Technology Option,* Environmental Law Institute, Washington, D.C., January 1991.

ful of people, that the law should also reflect the interest of the citizens and
protect them against state practices.

There is a lack of adequate enforcement practices and a complete lack of
judicial processes and court procedures enforcing environmental legislation
in these countries. There is no history of citizens' lawsuits, and there has
been no authority to take over citizens' lawsuits. This means that, first, legislation is needed to create the possibility for citizens' to sue; then a public
awareness campaign is needed to educate citizens' groups about their rights;
third, there is a need to train lawyers and judges on how to handle environmental law cases. In more general terms, it means the establishment of a new
judicial review process which is still missing from the legal structure of the
NDCs.

Environmental law drafting has not been on the top of the legislative priority list of the new governments and legislation. In Hungary, for example,
the parliamentary discussion of a draft has been postponed twice. Legislators
are overwhelmed by other pressing issues of the political and economic
transformation, and the changed schedule reflects the priorities of the government. Though most of the environmental groups severely criticize the
delay in passing a comprehensive environmental law, in my opinion the delay
has certain advantages because it opens up the possibilities of input from international organizations and NGOs. As a legacy of the past, politicians in
power still consider legislative initiatives a government prerogative; government officials, however, have no experience in environmental legislation; in
many cases they even lack necessary language skills; and they are preoccupied with day-to-day management and administrative regulatory tasks. Each
NDC wants to catch up to the European Community standard, ultimately
they want to be a member of the community of Western, developed nations,
so they need an international perspective of the legislative process. The delay
time factor helps in this case.

There is another overlooked aspect of the legacy of Communist past. It is
not enough to train experts and adapt different techniques. Both the transformation of the civil service and its bureaucratic structure and the creation
of a social network are necessary in which both the experts and their techniques can operate. It means the establishment of different institutions and
their integration into society and government. This, however, is the more
general problem of re-creating civil society, civic duties and responsibilities,
and a responsible and interested democratic public — a task which includes
all aspects of overcoming the inherited burden of attitudes of social disintegration. As an analyst of the Polish society stated, the passive, apathetic society will have to struggle against itself to overcome the legacy of Communist

rule and build up consciousness to revitalize a larger, abstract concept of common good.[49]

5. Conclusion

The combined impact of all these factors presents a formidable challenge — the tasks must be prioritized and then implemented. This challenge is almost impossible to meet in the short run. At the same time, my findings suggest that the principal impediments are structural-institutional and policy related, rather than technical, and policy changes are more important than resources and capital investments to improve the state of the environment. In the NDCs, the environment is seen as a part of the broader issue of economic transition, industrial restructuring, and infrastructure development, on the one hand, and as a part of a broader issue of democratization and the creation of a civil society based on the rule of law, on the other hand.

My analysis demonstrates that the compelling issues of immediate economic survival prevent political leaders and governments from focusing on a long-term vision. As a consequence, there is no actual discussion of a more essential question: What type of development pattern should these countries follow? Will they just simply imitate the West (of course, necessarily not as effectively endorsing a development economy path)? Will they be confined to the periphery of Western countries? Or, especially in the light of the latest developments in the region (including ethnic wars), might they become Third World societies? From the environmental politics point of view, the relevant question to discuss would be the one of sustainable development (whatever vague meaning this term might have) or the one of a reversed logic: How is economic transition, industrial restructuring, and long-term development policy a part of a broader issue of environment and conservation? Policy making circles do not have these issues on their agenda yet.

---

49. Mason et al., op. cit. (footnote 30), p. 233.

13

The Central European Initiative

Georg Potyka

1. Introduction

In the wake of the fundamental changes in Europe starting in 1989, the end of the Cold War, and in particular the breakdown of communist regimes in Central and Eastern Europe, new forms of regional cooperation were considered. After the fall of the Berlin Wall four Central European states — Austria, Hungary, Italy, and former Yugoslavia — were the first countries that formed an informal agreement on cooperation.

The Central European Initiative (CEI — originally Quadrangulare, then Pentagonale, then Hexagonale) was set up on 11 and 12 November 1989, by foreign ministers and the deputy prime ministers of Austria, Hungary, Italy, and former Yugoslavia in Budapest. The former CSFR joined on May 20, 1990, Poland on July 27, 1991, Croatia, Slovenia, and Bosnia-Herzegovina on July 18, 1992, the Czech Republic and Slovakia on January 1, 1993, and Macedonia on July 17, 1993. Moldavia and Albania have applied for membership. Belarus, Bulgaria, Romania and Ukraine are cooperating in a pragmatic way in various working groups. Russia has shown interest in a casual cooperation with the CEI (an exploratory meeting to this effect has taken place on October 4, 1993).

The CEI has no charter, constitution, or formal constitutive agreement. According to the joint declaration issued by the foreign ministers in Budapest on November 10, 1989, the purpose of the CEI consists in improving the political climate in Europe, especially in Central and East Central Europe, and in strengthening the CSCE.

2. The Activity Profile of the CEI

The CEI operates according to the principle "no transfer of funds," which means that every member state pays for its own projects. It has, however, developed a flexible and adaptable political structure.

Every year, in alphabetical order, one member state is assigned the duty of the presidency of the CEI (November 1989–July 1990, Hungary; July 1990–July 1991, Italy; July 1991–December 1991, Yugoslavia; 1992, Austria; 1993, Hungary; 1994, Italy) and hosts a meeting of the heads of government. Meetings of the deputy heads of government are held during the year whenever required; meetings of the foreign ministers take place twice every year.

Each member state appoints one national coordinator for its entire activities within the CEI; these national coordinators meet to prepare the meetings at the governmental level or to discuss regional cooperation. The project-oriented work of the CEI is carried out by working groups of experts from the member states. Each working group is coordinated by one member state; thus, in addition to the national coordinators, there are the coordinators of the working groups who organize subject-oriented international tasks.

A liaison office of the CEI with the European Bank for Reconstruction and Development (EBRD) in London has been set up. This office is staffed and paid for by Italy.

Due to the informality of the cooperation within the CEI, it is not necessary that all member states take part in all projects. However, outside states may well be admitted as observers or even as full members to certain working groups or projects, if all member states so agree. Thus, Poland participated in the working group on environmental issues before being admitted to the CEI. However, the member states agree that only sovereign states, and not autonomous regions, should be members. It may be pointed out that several working groups of autonomous regions exist within the territory covered by the CEI (like Alpen-Adria, Arbeitsgemeinschaft [ARGE] Alp, ARGE Donauländer). Duplication of work between these working groups and the CEI is prevented by consultations with representation of the various working groups at CEI meetings. Besides the cooperation between the governments and administrations of the member states, regular contacts exist between the Parliament and trade unions.

TABLE 13.1

Working Groups in the CEI

Topic	Coordinator
Production and transport of energy	Czech Republic
Telecommunications	Croatia
Agriculture	Poland
Environmental questions	Austria
Disaster relief	Italy
Small and medium enterprises	Hungary
Science and technology	Italy
Culture, education and youth exchange	Slovakia
Media	Austria
Migration	Hungary
Tourism	Croatia
Statistics	Austria
Transport	Italy

Source: Federal Ministry for Foreign Affairs, Vienna (1993).

The activities of the CEI are twofold:

1. It serves as a forum for the coordination of political initiatives of the member states. This happened during the preparations for the UNCED. At this conference the CEI tried to present a common project for the prevention and settlement of international disputes in environmental matters.
2. It initiates various political cooperations among its member countries, through the working groups (see Table 13.1).

3. The Working Group on the Environment

The Working Group on environmental issues comprises six subgroups:

Subgroup I — Harmonization of Environmental Monitoring and Data Systems. The main task is the establishment of an initiative-wide monitoring network that will be compatible with the monitoring network of the European Communities. This subgroup has set up several task forces, namely: on air pollution, ambient air pollution (groundlevel concentration) and deposition (precipitation), water pollution, soil pollution, forestry, and data exchange and standardization.

So far, several results have been achieved. In cooperation with the IIASA a methodology for the establishment of a common inventory of emissions has been agreed upon. This inventory was finalized by the end of 1992. A working session has been held to determine compatible methods for ambient air pollution and deposition. Technical standards for the exchange of environmental data have been agreed upon. These standards are compatible with ECE standards. A company to run the Central European Data Request Facility (CEDAR) in Vienna has been founded. CEDAR serves as a clearing agency for environmental data. It has been established in cooperation with the Regional Environmental Center for Central and Eastern Europe (REC) in Budapest, a nongovernmental organization which has been set up by participants from the USA, Hungary, and Austria. CEDAR supplies REC with environmental data.

Subgroup II — Waste Management. The main task is to facilitate the creation of a common disposal system for dangerous waste. An exchange of information on several items has taken place. Activities of this group include designation of a list of wastes, discussions of stricter regulations on waste imports and exports, and encouragement of replacement of dangerous substances and removal of wastes. In 1992, three seminars were held: 17 to 19 February 1992 legislation on wastes, ÖNORM S 2100 Abfallkatalog (waste catalogue), and European standardization; 25 to 27 May 1991 waste analysis, ÖNORM S 2101, and ÖNORM S 2110; 19 to 21 October 1992 requirements for waste disposal. In 1993, a glossary on waste management terminology in German, English, Czech, Slovak, Polish, Serbo-Croat, Slovenian, Hungarian and Russian was started to be worked out. Two further seminars are scheduled for fall, 1993.

Subgroup III — Nuclear Safety. This subgroup is working to establish a common early warning system on ionizing radiation.

Subgroup IV — Energy and Environment. This subgroup deals with the promotion of energy saving and environmentally sound energy production. In February 1991, a seminar was held entitled "Energy from Biomass." In June 1991, a seminar entitled "Transboundary Energy Partnerships" was held. As a follow-up to this meeting attempts have been made to transfer the Austrian system of self-building communities for solar heat collectors to other member states. Efforts have been initiated between Slovenia and the Austrian province of Styria. A program for training technicians in the Czech and Slovak Republics began in May 1992 and was completed successfully in summer, 1993.

Subgroup V — National Parks. This subgroup deals with the establishment of transboundary national parks. The establishment of the Neusiedlersee park in Austria and Hungary has been completed; national parks in the Tarvis Alps and Danube Basin have been considered; however, due to the bilateral character of these projects, this subgroup was dissolved in 1993.

Subgroup VI — Environmental Peace Keeping. This subgroup has elaborated two resolutions on the prevention and settlement of international disputes concerning the environment. These two drafts were discussed at the 4th session of the Preparatory Committee of the United Nations Conference on Environment and Development in New York in March 1992.

The structure of the working group on environmental questions shows that it does not work according to a comprehensive strategy. Rather it attempts to achieve cooperation between the member states in fields which are not yet covered by formally established international processes. The activity of the working group may thus be described as patchwork.

This is not surprising, since there are no environmental problems that are specific to the territory of the CEI countries. Environmental problems are either global or regional and thus under the authority of the UN or of its regional commission for Europe, the ECE, or of the Council of Europe. They are also sometimes subregional, like the protection of special areas, such as the Alps or the Danube; these areas are best protected by bilateral or subregional arrangements among the countries concerned. Due to the geographic variety of the CEI territory, no such geographic formation and no regional environmental problem seems to extend throughout the whole of it.

As far as global environmental problems are concerned, the Initiative thus serves as a forum for coordinating the policies of the member states on a global scale. This task has been undertaken by subgroup VI with regard to the environmental peacekeeping proposal that was discussed within UNCED.

Local and subregional problems will continue to be discussed by the environmental working group, but any measures recommended by the working group may often be broken up into several projects, like the program of subgroup IV on solar heat collectors (this program has been broken up into two separate projects). The most impressive project of the environmental working groups is CEDAR, set up according to an agreement between Austria and the Regional Environmental Center (REC) in Budapest to supply the REC with environmental data.

The environmental working groups anticipated the admission of Poland into the CEI. Since its admission Poland has cooperated as a full member of the working group. Its admission on July 27, 1991, transformed the Pentagonal Initiative to the Hexagonal Initiative. Bulgaria, Rumania, and Ukraine have participated as observers in the working group, but are not members of the Initiative. It would be wrong, however, to conclude from the Polish experience any particular importance of the working group as a political trendsetter for the Initiative as a whole: the casual cooperation of nonmember states in the working group is easily possible just because of the nonpolitical character of these activities.

4. Summary

The Initiative has successfully coordinated the participation of its member states within larger institutions and has tackled transboundary problems among its member states.

In the latter respect, however, the competence of the CEI is subsidiary to any other institutionalized international process as well as to bilateral processes where the bilateral approach seems to be preferable because of the purely bilateral nature of the problem. Thus, the problem of the quality of the Danube water is dealt within the framework of the ECE, the problem of the environment of the Danube basin as a whole is under discussion equally outside the CEI. However, the CEI remains a suitable forum for informal cooperation among its member states wherever such cooperation is needed or might be needed in the future.

14

Regional Environmental Policies
in Europe: Baltic/Nordic Cooperation

Tapani Kohonen

1. Basic Character of the Baltic Sea

The Baltic Sea is the world's largest basin of brackish water. Three characteristics make the Baltic Sea unique: the horizontal and vertical differences in salinity, the temperature differences (these first two characteristics combine to create strong stratification of the water), and the varied geological development during the past 10,000 years.

The thresholds of the Danish sounds regulate the exchange of water between the Baltic Sea and the North Sea, a fact that increases the sensitivity of the Baltic Sea to pollution.

The Baltic Sea is relatively shallow: the average depth of this semi-closed sea is 55 meters, and the maximum depth 459 meters. The total surface area of the Baltic Sea is some 372,000 square kilometers, which is one-thousandth of the total area of all seas and oceans. However, almost one-hundredth of the world's population lives in the catchment area of this enclosed sea. The gross domestic product of the population amounts to one-tenth of the global GDP. Fish catches in the Baltic Sea have been one percent of total catches, which is much more than its size warrants. The volume of water lies around 22,000 cubic kilometers, of which some five pro mille annually streams into the North Sea and to the Atlantic Ocean. It has been calculated that the circulation time for all this water is some twenty to thirty years. This means that environmental poisons which do not disperse easily and other water-polluting substances remain in the Baltic Sea for a long period of time.

The special character of the Baltic Sea also comes out in its ecosystems. The number of plant and animal species in the Baltic Sea is smaller than the number in lakes or oceans. The organisms include both inland and saltwater species, even containing a few species specially adapted to brackish water. Marine animals in the Baltic Sea are definitely smaller than in the oceans. The species that have been capable of adapting to the unusual conditions in the Baltic Sea exist near their tolerance limits, which makes them extremely sensitive to all detrimental changes in their living environment.

2. Present International Cooperation

2.1 Cooperation Around the Gulf of Finland

Hydrologists in the Baltic countries began arranging joint congresses in 1926, and this cooperation forms the basis for all later activities. Information about the worsening of the state of the Baltic eventually resulted in unofficial cooperation between Finnish and Soviet scientists in 1965. As soon as 1968, a Convention on the Protection of the Gulf of Finland and its marine environment was signed under the auspices of the Scientific and Technical Joint Commission between Finland and the Soviet Union. This epoch-making work has continued ever since in the Gulf of Finland Working Group under the Joint Commission for Environmental Cooperation. In April 1992 the Agreement between the Government of Finland and the Government of the Russian Federation on Cooperation in the Field of Environmental Protection was signed. In addition to this environmental agreement an Action Program for Water Pollution Control was signed in May 1992. This program includes also cooperation for protection of the Gulf of Finland.

The experience gained in this working group had a favorable influence on the signing, in 1974, of the Convention on the Protection of the Marine Environment of the Baltic Sea Area. Prevailing conditions and the situation in the Gulf of Finland affect the whole of the Baltic Sea, and vice versa. The bilateral cooperation for the protection of the Gulf of Finland was also significant insofar as it provided the impetus for cooperation between Sweden and Finland in the form of the Gulf of Bothnia Committee.

2.2 Cooperation Around the Gulf of Bothnia

At a recommendation by the Nordic Council of Ministers, Finland and Sweden established the Gulf of Bothnia Committee in 1972 to coordinate research on the marine environment of the Gulf of Bothnia. The Committee's intention is to promote cooperation between Finnish and Swedish research institutions and researchers studying the Gulf of Bothnia. Reports on the pollution load have been published, and seminars discussing research results have been organized.

In 1991, the Gulf of Bothnia Committee decided to concentrate all available research resources in both countries on a joint multidisciplinary effort to obtain a comprehensive description of the condition of the Gulf of Bothnia and to create an extensive and representative data base as a reference for future studies.

Recently, the Nordic Council of Ministers through the Ministers of the Environment have commissioned studies and reports on the pollution load in the Gulf of Bothnia and especially in its northernmost part, which have been conducted by Finland and Sweden conjointly.

2.3 The Helsinki Convention

The Convention on the Protection of the Marine Environment of the Baltic Sea Area, also called the Helsinki Convention, which was signed in 1974, entered into force in 1980. Finland took this initiative during the UN Conference in Stockholm in 1972. Finland also acts as the depository government for this Convention. The permanent international secretariat of the Helsinki Commission is located in Helsinki.

The present Helsinki Convention covers the entire area of the Baltic Sea. The internal waters of the parties, however, are not part of the actual Convention area. However, according to the Convention the parties undertake to ensure that the aims of the Convention will be obtained in their internal waters as well.

The Helsinki Convention was the first and is still the only overriding Convention for the protection of the marine environment which covers land-based and airborne pollution as well as pollution from ships, and which forbids dumping (with the exception of marine accidents). Dumping includes incineration of waste at sea. The Convention calls for cooperation in research and in combatting oil and chemical damages. There are tight restrictions on discharges from ships; prohibition against discharges and emissions of DDT (1.1.1-trichloro-2.2-bis-(chlorophenyl)-ethane) and its derivatives, PCB's (polychlorinated biphenyls), and PCT's (polychlorinated terphenyls) from land-based sources; and an exhortation to strictly limit pollution with harmful substances such as heavy metals and oil into the sea, in the form of both land-based pollution and as airborne pollution.

3. Activities Within the Helsinki Commission

3.1 Monitoring the State of the Baltic Sea

According to the Convention, the Helsinki Commission is charged with collecting scientific, technological and economic information on the Baltic Sea to provide a basis for proposals geared to reduce pollution. The monitoring of the state of the Baltic was started by the Interim Commission in 1979. All parties to the Convention pursue hydrographic, chemical, and biological research throughout the year.

The first pilot study on the state of the Baltic Sea dates back to 1977. A joint follow-up program was based on this study. A second thorough study was made in 1980. The first periodic assessment on the state of the Baltic Sea covers the years from 1980 to 1985. Regular studies provide an overall picture and display current trends. The estimates are made at five-year intervals according to the follow-up program and the results of other studies. The most recent report is for the years from 1984 to 1988.

Because the effects of direct or indirect riverborne and land-based pollution are first visible in coastal sea areas, the 10th meeting of the Commission in February 1989 decided that the parties will regularly present estimates of the state of their coastal waters. The first of these reports will be published in 1994.

3.2 Pollution Load in the Baltic

The state of the Baltic Sea is mainly influenced by the pollution load in the sea; consequently the Helsinki Commission initiated, in 1980, a long-term program to collect information on the pollution load. The first estimate was published in 1986; however, information was still deficient. Some estimates were also given on airborne pollution. According to this report, the total nitrogen load (from land-based sources) amounted to 530,000 metric tons per year; the total phosphorus load, to 42,000 metric tons per year; the total cadmium load, to 60 metric tons per year; the total zinc load, to 9,000 metric tons per year; and the total copper load, to 4,200 metric tons per year.

The share of airborne nitrogen pollution in the sea varies considerably, it is particularly significant that over half of the nitrogen load in the central parts of the Gulf of Bothnia is airborne. According to the second pollution load compilation in 1993 including data of 1990 the corresponding figures are

661,855 metric tons per year for nitrogen and 45,827 metric tons per year for phosphorus. A presentation of a summary review on the basis of the other determinants was impossible due to several reasons. On the one hand, the list of obligatory parameters by pollution source was not unified, and on the other hand data on heavy metals, submitted by the countries were not complete. Despite the adopted guidelines, the monitoring program was not fulfilled in all parts and the data about all substances were therefore not complete. However, even with all the shortages, the second report was a progress in the evaluation of the pollution load of the Baltic Sea and serves as a new step to the long-term comparable monitoring and reporting system. In spite of that the second report is more complete and precise than the first one, information should be used with care in order to avoid misinterpretation.

3.3 Recommendations of the Commission

The Helsinki Convention, as such, does not tangibly promote the protection of the Baltic Sea, yet it provides the framework within which the contracting parties may improve the protection of the Baltic Sea in relation to political will and preparedness and economic resources. In practice, activities are based on Article 13, section b in the present Convention, according to which the Commission should recommend actions forwarding the aims of the Convention.

To date, the Helsinki Commission has approved more than 100 recommendations, some of which supersede earlier ones. More than 40 of these recommendations deal with reduction of the load in the Baltic Sea. These recommendations are not legally binding; nevertheless being unanimously adopted by the Commission, they constitute a moral and political obligation for the contracting parties to meet them or at least to take action to fulfill them. The Commission has agreed on a regular reporting system to implement the recommendations. These reports will also be published regularly.

3.4 Ministerial Declaration in 1988

The state of the Baltic Sea, and in particular the volume of land-based pollution, caused the ministers responsible for environmental matters to issue, at the 9th meeting of the Commission in February 1988, a declaration on reduction of discharges and emissions and more efficient action in other fields of protection of the marine environment. According to the declaration, by 1995 land-based pollution from nutrients, heavy metals, and poisonous or chemically persistent pollutants should be reduced by some 50 percent as compared with the 1987 levels.

Yet the Scientific and Technological Committee of the Commission stated at its meeting in autumn 1988 that a 50 percent reduction was impossible to achieve in the sectors where the best available technology is already in use.

So far, the work of the Helsinki Commission has been based on decisions and equal obligations jointly approved by all parties. Implementing the recommendations and the declaration on reducing pollution, again, are based on the specific situation in each country. The reporting on the progress toward the 50 percent goal is simultaneous with the reporting on the implementation of the recommendations.

3.5 Baltic Sea Declaration by Prime Ministers

In Ronneby, Sweden, in September 1990, the Baltic Sea Conference was attended by the prime ministers of the Baltic Sea riparian countries, Norway, and the Czech and Slovak Federal Republics and by representatives of the Commission of the European Communities, the World Bank, the European Investment Bank, the European Bank for Reconstruction and Development, and the Nordic Investment Bank. At this Conference the Baltic Sea Declaration was approved to speed up the work in the Helsinki Commission and to improve the prerequisites to implement the goals of the Helsinki Convention. The Conference stressed the importance of implementing the goals of the ministerial Declaration (a 50 percent reduction in pollution) and the recommendations of the Helsinki Commission on reducing the load in the Baltic Sea.

The Baltic Sea Declaration states that the required protective measures expressly concern the Baltic marine area and actually initiated a new era in the protection of the Baltic Sea. In practice, specifying the worst problems and finding solutions to them as well as implementing the measures required will demand enormous financial sacrifices, and the problems can hardly be solved even by means of international assistance. At the Conference it was decided to establish, in conjunction with the Helsinki Commission, a high-level task force, which was instructed to present, by the end of 1991, a Baltic Sea Joint Comprehensive Environmental Action Program, taking into account the special needs in various subregions of the Baltic Sea and the steps needed for ecological restoration. The most urgent and important steps were to be taken by 1993 at the latest. The selection of means should be based on maximizing the improvement of the state of the Baltic Sea in relation to required financial input. However, only a draft action program was presented at the annual meeting of the Commission in February 1992. The final version was accepted by the ministers of the environment in the diplomatic conference in Helsinki on April 9, 1992.

The conference in 1990 also called for an inventory of ways and means of cooperation between the Helsinki Commission and the International Baltic Sea Fishery Commission (the Gdansk Commission). To this end, an expert meeting was arranged in Poland in September 1991 to study the state of the Baltic Sea and factors influencing it in relation to the living conditions for marine organisms.

3.6 Diplomatic Conference 1992

At its meeting in February 1991, the Helsinki Commission discussed, on the basis of proposals from a legal working group supplemented with experts on research and technology, ways to tighten the Helsinki Convention and its annexes and their binding force.

The Helsinki Commission requested at its meeting in February 1992 the Government of Finland to convene a Diplomatic Conference on the protection of the marine environment of the Baltic Sea area. The Conference was held in Helsinki on April 9, 1992.

The conference adopted

— a new Convention on the Protection of the Marine Environment of the Baltic Sea, 1992, and the related Resolutions, and
— the Baltic Sea Environmental Declaration, 1992, which approves the strategic approach and principles reflected in the Baltic Sea Joint Comprehensive Environmental Action Program as the result of the work of the ad hoc high level task force, established by the conference on prime ministerial level, held in Ronneby 1990.

3.7 Helsinki Convention 1992

All nine coastal governments, Denmark, Estonia, Finland, Germany, Latvia, Lithuania, Poland, Sweden, Russia and the European Economic Community signed the new convention. The European Economic Community will be later on a contracting party to both the 1974 and 1992 Helsinki Conventions. The new convention is proposed to enter into force after ratifications by all coastal states of the Baltic Sea.

Both Estonia and Lithuania acceded to the 1974 Helsinki Convention in 1992, Latvia so far being an observer to the Helsinki Commission.

The new convention contains new provisions dealing with the use of "best available technology," "best environmental practice" and "precautionary principle," and the necessary definitions of these terms, environmental impact assessment, prohibition of incineration at sea, notification and consultation on pollution incidents, nature conservation and biodiversity, reporting and exchange of information, information to the public, protection of information, and detailed provisions on prevention of pollution from exploration and exploitation of oil and gas.

The convention area is extended to cover the internal waters of the contracting parties, which are excluded from the coverage of the 1974 convention. Although the structure of the 1974 convention has been preserved in the new convention most of the substantive provisions have undergone major changes that are intended to strengthen the obligations to protect the marine environment of the Baltic Sea area. The institutional articles, however, are basically the same as in the 1974 convention. Some amendments have been necessitated by the expected participation of the European Community and possible other economic integration organizations. The existing Commission will continue to function also under the new convention.

The fundamental principles and obligations have been strengthened to the formulation "the contracting parties shall individually or jointly take all appropriate legislative, administrative or other relevant measures to prevent and eliminate pollution in order to promote the ecological restoration of the Baltic Sea area and the preservation of its ecological balance. Implementation of this convention does not cause transboundary pollution in areas outside the Baltic Sea area. Furthermore, the relevant measures shall not lead either to unacceptable environmental strains on air quality and the atmosphere or on waters, soil and ground water, to unacceptably harmful or increasing waste disposal, or to increased risks to human health."

Most stringent demands have been expressed by the wording "the contracting parties undertake to prevent and eliminate pollution of the marine environment of the Baltic Sea area caused by harmful substances from all sources, according to the provisions of this convention and, to this end, to implement the procedures and measures of Annex I." This annex contains criteria on the allocation of substances and priority groups of harmful substances which are totally banned or banned for certain applications.

3.8 Joint Comprehensive Environmental Action Program

The diplomatic conference 1992 signaled the launching of a concrete effort to "assure the ecological restoration of the Baltic Sea, ensuring the possibility of self-restoration of the marine environment and preservation of its ecological balance."

That effort is the Baltic Sea Joint Comprehensive Environmental Action Program. The program is coordinated by the Helsinki Commission Program Implementation Task Force (HELCOM PITF), which is a joint endeavour of the Baltic Sea States (Denmark, Estonia, Finland, Germany, Latvia, Lithuania, Poland, Russia and Sweden), other countries of the catchment area (Belarus, Czech Republic, Norway, Slovak Republic and Ukraine), the Commission of the European Communities, and four international financial institutions (European Investment Bank, European Bank for Reconstruction and Development, Nordic Investment Bank and World Bank), as well as the International Baltic Sea Fisheries Commission. PITF also includes organizations which act as observers: several intergovernmental and nongovernmental organizations — the Coalition Clean Baltic, Greenpeace International and the World Wide Fund for Nature.

Following the Baltic Sea Conference of 1990, eight pre-feasibility studies were carried out in:

— Karelia, St. Petersburg, St. Petersburg region and Estonia;
— western coast of Estonia;
— Gulf of Riga and Daugava River basin;
— Kaliningrad region and Pregel River basin;
— Vistula River basin and Baltic coast of Poland;
— Oder/Odra River basin, and
— Mecklenburg-Vorpommern catchment area.

These studies investigated point and non-point source pollution in the eastern and southern areas of the Baltic Sea catchment area. Three topical studies were also undertaken concerning wetlands, agricultural run-off and atmospheric deposition of pollutants.

The program has identified 132 "hot spots," 47 of which have been assigned a high priority. Investment actions of the program will focus on controlling pollution at these hot spots. Formulation of specific actions and approaches is based on a set of key principles.

Key principles of the program are:

— recognizing the importance of a long-term perspective as the cornerstone of program strategy:
— taking account of the important role of natural factors;
— harmonization of economic and environmental objectives;
— harmonization of national development with regional environmental objectives;
— undertaking preventive and curative actions;
— controlling pollution at the source;

— establishing conditions for private sector participation, and
— taking action to overcome constraints and build local capacity.

The long-term program of specific actions consists of six components:

— policy, legal and regulatory measures;
— institutional strengthening and human resources development;
— investment activities;
— management programs for coastal lagoons and wetlands;
— applied research, and
— public awareness and environmental education.

The Baltic Sea Joint Comprehensive Environmental Action Program will be implemented in two phases. The first phase (1993–1997) is estimated to cost 5.0 billion ECU and the second phase (1988–2012) will call for an additional 13.0 billion ECU. It is clear that implementation of the program will require a multiplicity of funding sources.

In order to provide for the broadest possible financial support, an international conference on resource mobilization took place on March 24–25, 1993, in Gdansk, Poland. In addition to bilateral and multilateral financing institutions, various groups, including private, semi-public, and public merchant banks, export credit agencies, and risk capital financiers participated in the conference.

The program, when implemented, is expected to have major economic and environmentally beneficial impacts on the rivers of the Baltic Sea catchment area. The coastal waters as well can be expected to improve rapidly. A reduction in nutrient loads and heavy metals will also help to restore the ecological balance of the open sea as well as coastal lagoons and wetlands.

Finally, the strengthening of environmental management capacity at all levels throughout the Baltic Sea region will be the most important action to ensure the achievement of the long-term goal of the program — the ecological restoration of the Baltic Sea.

When the goal of a recovery of the ecological balance of the Baltic Sea, or possibly even a recovery of its natural state, was set in Ronneby, in September 1990, it was not possible to specify goals in terms of the state of the Baltic Sea or in target years. Yet it is important to remember that even though it may be possible to minimize the load in the sea within a reasonable period of time, it still will take many years before the substances which have already polluted the Baltic Sea, and which still exist there, disappear. It is apparent that a lowering of the nutrient content of the Baltic Sea would also affect fish catches and render fishing in its present volume impossible.

4. The Future Outlook

4.1 The State of the Baltic Today

In the period from 1984 to 1988 there was some improvement in the state of the marine environment. Protective measures in the states around the Baltic Sea have, for instance, reduced DDT and PCB concentrations in fish and waterfowl. The concentrations of heavy metals, especially mercury, in fish in open sea areas approach the so-called natural concentrations in fish in the North Sea and the northern Atlantic. The lead concentrations in the Kattegat and the Belts have diminished as a consequence of increased use of unleaded petrol. The strong increase in nutrients, phosphorus, and nitrogen, in several sea areas in the 1970s, has now come to a halt, with the exception of the Kattegat and the Bight of Riga. Nevertheless, the concentrations still remain so high that biological production damaging the ecosystem is still possible.

In recent years the increase in environmentally harmful organic substances has been a cause of alarm. The concentrations of organic chlorine compounds in fish in the Baltic proper are between three and ten times higher than corresponding values in the southern Atlantic. In the Kattegat and Belt areas, algal blooms have occurred with increasing frequency, and the primary production has doubled during the past 25 years. In the southern Baltic Sea low oxygen contents have impeded life for bottom organisms, also affecting fishing. During the past 10 years the salinity of the Baltic Sea has decreased because swells of saline waters from the North Sea to the Baltic Sea have not occurred. This is the longest observed period of the century with practically no exchange of water. In the Gotland depths the incidences of the disappearance of oxygen and the occurrence of hydrogen sulfide are among the worst ever. For the Baltic Sea as a whole oxygen deficiencies have varied but not increased. The number and quality of saline water swells into the Baltic Sea have a major influence on the state of both the Danish Sounds and the depth areas of the Baltic Sea and subsequently on the state of the Gulf of Finland and the Gulf of Bothnia. Thus protective measures in the North Sea and the north-western Atlantic are very important for the future of the Baltic Sea and vice versa.

4.2 Education and Attitudes

It is very important to point out that no investment in the environment is effective if the public has not accepted the need for environmentally sound thinking and measures. A key element for policy makers should therefore be to invest in professional education and training that encourages positive environmental thinking. Even a totally new type of education focusing on integrated environmental understanding in all sectors of life might be necessary, starting in grade school and ending at the university level.

4.3 Independent Baltic Republics and Former Socialist Countries

The responsibilities of decision makers often lie at a very practical level. An important problem to be solved is the status and the capacity of the countries with economies in transition (Estonia, Latvia, Lithuania, Poland, and Russia) in the present family of the Baltic countries.

In the Nordic countries investments to change and improve the technology used in industrial plants are common and routine, depending mainly on economic possibilities of the companies concerned and the policy of the government. In contrast to these countries, from an environmental priority point of view, in the former Socialist countries all problems should be solved at the same time — now. Economically and most often politically, even in the new free atmosphere, this is unrealistic. Consequently, the only real practical solution is to consider a realistic timetable and to decide on the list of priority action for each problem area. This was accepted as Baltic Sea Joint Comprehensive Environmental Action Program by the ministers of the environment on April 9, 1992, together with the revised Convention on the Protection of the Marine Environment of the Baltic Sea Area.

Bilateral agreements between the republics of the former USSR (Estonia, Latvia, Lithuania, and Russia) and the Nordic countries (Denmark, Finland, Norway, and Sweden), already signed, will intensify the implementation of the joint decisions made in the framework of the Helsinki Commission.

4.4 Responsibilities of the Baltic States

Realistic actions to protect the Baltic environment are not possible based only on governmental funding in the countries with economies in transition.

During the coming years substantial financial investments must be channelled to these nations from international sources. The international financial institutions such as the European Bank for Reconstruction and Development, the European Investment Bank, the Nordic Investment Bank, and the World Bank will have a very important role, particularly in implementing the Baltic Sea Joint Comprehensive Environmental Action Program. In addition, in many cases the special bilateral and multilateral aid of the Western countries is the prerequisite for the success of any priority action program in Eastern countries. However, the main responsibility still is in each country itself. Cooperation and joint efforts are necessary, but, in all cases, the responsibility is that of the political decision makers of each country.

4.5 Nordic Cooperation

Environmental cooperation between the Nordic countries is based on the additional articles in 1974 of the so-called Helsinki Agreement (articles 1 and 30–32), which was signed in 1962. Decisions of the council of ministers (ministers of the environment) of the Nordic countries, which are made on a consensus basis, are binding on the governments involved.

Treaties between the Nordic countries, however, must be considered and ratified by the parliaments of the Nordic countries, e.g., the 1976 Nordic countries' treaty on environmental protection and the agreement to set up the Nordic countries' environmental fund (NEFCO) in 1990.

The committee for the environment (previously the committee for the environment and social affairs) of the Nordic Council (a joint body for parliamentarians) deals with issues such as transport problems in addition to the environment. Cooperation between the council of ministers and the Nordic Council takes place primarily in conjunction with sessions of the Nordic Council, and at meetings between the ministers and the members on the committee. The Nordic Council issues statements on proposals from the council of ministers, as well as introducing motions.

Nordic cooperation covers almost every sector of society. This is a valuable asset from the standpoint of a unified environmental policy.

References

HELCOM 1981, Assessment of the Effects of Pollution on the Natural Resources of the Baltic Sea, 1980. Part A-1: Overall Conclusions. Balt. Sea Environ. Proc. No. 5A.

HELCOM 1981, Assessment of the Effects of Pollution on the Natural Resources of the Baltic Sea, 1980. Part A–1: Overall Conclusions, Part A–2: Summary of Results, Part B: Scientific Material. Balt. Sea Environ. Proc. No. 5B.

HELCOM 1986, First Periodic Assessment of the State of the Marine Environment of the Baltic Sea Area, 1980–1985; General Conclusions. Balt. Sea Environ. Proc. No. 17A.

HELCOM 1987, First Periodic Assessment of the State of the Marine Environment of the Baltic Sea Area, 1980–1985; Background Document. Balt. Sea Environ. Proc. No. 17B.

HELCOM 1987, First Baltic Sea Pollution Load Compilation. Balt. Sea Environ. Proc. No. 20.

HELCOM 1989, Deposition of Airborne Pollutants to the Sea Area 1983–1986 and 1986. Balt. Sea Environ. Proc. No. 32.

HELCOM 1990, Second Period Assessment of the State of the Marine Environment of the Baltic Sea, 1984–1988; General Conclusions. Balt. Sea Environ. Proc. No. 35A.

HELCOM 1990, Second Period Assessment of the State of the Marine Environment of the Baltic Sea, 1984–1988; Background Document. Balt. Sea Environ. Proc. No. 35B.

HELCOM 1991, Airborne Pollution Load to the Baltic Sea 1986–1990. Balt. Sea Environ. Proc. No. 39.

HELCOM 1993, Second Baltic Sea Pollution Load Compilation. Balt. Sea Environ. Proc. No. 44.

HELCOM 1993, Summaries of the Pre-feasibility Studies. Prepared for the Baltic Sea Joint Comprehensive Environmental Action Program. Balt. Sea Environ. Proc. No. 45.

HELCOM 1993, High Level Conference on Resource Mobilization. Gdansk, Poland, March 24–25, 1993; Compilation of Presentations and Statements. Balt. Sea Environ. Proc. No. 47.

HELCOM 1993, The Baltic Sea Joint Comprehensive Environmental Action Program. Balt. Sea Environ. Proc. No. 48.

Kohonen, J.T., "Protection of the Marine Environment of the Baltic Sea — An Example on Multilateral Cooperation," *Marine Pollution Bulletin* vol. 23(1991), EMECS — 90, pp. 541–544.

15

Comments on the Baltic/Nordic Cooperation

Markus Amann

1. The Nordic Council

Dr. Kohonen's chapter gives a valuable overview of activities within the Baltic cooperation, which are important examples of a cooperation among countries with different economic and political systems. However, the Nordic Council is a second forum of cooperation in Scandinavia worth mentioning. The Nordic Council, founded in 1971, is a collaboration of Denmark, Finland, Iceland, Norway, and Sweden and focuses on problems common to all Northern European countries. Environment plays a prominent role in the Nordic cooperation. The Nordic Council maintains, *inter alia*, a coordinated research policy including ecological research, which proved to be a major driving force for stimulating environmental science in the whole of Europe.

The Nordic Council of Ministers puts forward motions at the sessions of the Nordic Council, carries out the recommendations of the Council, and is ultimately responsible for the work within the various sectors. Regular meetings of the Nordic Council of Ministers has led to a joint environmental policy of the countries involved, materializing, for example, in the "Nordic Convention on Environmental Protection" (1976) and the "Common Nordic Action Plan on Environmental Protection" in the fields of air pollution, marine pollution, and technological cooperation. Again, these common action plans not only had impacts on environmental policy in Scandinavia, but also were strong driving forces on a Europe-wide scale.

2. The Critical-Loads Approach

The propagation of the so-called critical-loads approach by the Nordic countries is a recent example of the Nordic Council initiating a Europe-wide reconsideration of environmental policies. In the 1980s most European countries signed the "Convention on Long-Range Transboundary Air Pollution" and, as part of the convention, the so-called Helsinki-Protocol, in which all signatories committed themselves to reduce their SO_2 emissions by 1993 by at least 30 percent compared to the levels in 1980. This early agreement reflects the initial phase of international environmental negotiations in Europe and has to be considered a rather simple attempt to manage the international equality problem (all countries reduce their emissions by the same extent). In the meantime it has been recognized that such "flat-rate" approaches usually do not result in a cost-effective international allocation of (limited) resources. Major differences among countries occur in environmental sensitivities, in the present pollution load, and in the potential and costs of reducing emissions, which could be considered reasons for differences in national reduction requirements. Consequently, guidelines to determine country-specific requirements to reduce national emissions have been sought.

Based on results of environmental research coordinated by the Nordic Council, the Nordic countries have developed and have advocated the critical-loads approach. According to this concept the extent of emission reductions should ultimately be oriented toward the elimination of negative environmental impacts of emissions.[1] The approach consists of three steps:

1. The determination of critical loads for all ecosystems in a particular region. Critical loads reflect the maximum exposure to one or several pollutants below which, according to current knowledge, no damage occurs to ecosystems;

2. As interim goals for the environmental policy so-called target loads should be specified. These target loads should take into account the current level of pollution, the critical load as the ultimate exposure level to eliminate environmental damage, and the feasibility and costs of emission reductions necessary to achieve the target exposure levels;

3. Finally, the country-specific emission reductions should be identified to achieve deposition below target loads.

---

1.   J. Nilsson and P. Grennfelt, *Critical loads for Sulphur and Nitrogen*, Miljørapport 1988:16, Nordic Council of Ministers, Denmark (1988).

This procedure to quantify reduction requirements is rather complex and data intensive; however, it aims at an efficient use of resources. The practicality of implementing such a concept is definitely debatable. However, the change in the basic perception of international environmental policy toward effect-oriented approaches as advocated by the critical-loads concept is remarkable: emission reduction strategies should no longer be exclusively oriented along their technical feasibility and associated costs; for the first time, the requirements for maintaining an undamaged environment have been established as long-term targets.

Common action of the Nordic countries succeeded in getting this concept accepted as a major guideline for specifying emission reduction requirements in the future. The critical-loads approach has been introduced to the Sofia-Protocol of the Convention on Long-Range Transboundary Air Pollution (aiming at the reduction of emissions of nitrogen oxides) and will most likely form the basis for the revised sulfur protocols of the convention.

3. Equity in International Agreements in Nordic Countries

A major problem in most international environmental agreements concerns the equal distribution of commitments or burdens on the signatories. Traditionally, flat-rate commitments, in which all parties are required to reduce their emissions by an equal percentage compared to the level of a common base year, try to mimic international equity. For example, the early protocols of the Convention on Long-Range Transboundary Air Pollution call for fixed percentage reduction of national emissions; also the Baltic Sea declaration requests all countries to cut their emission releases by 50 percent.

It has been demonstrated that in many cases such approaches do not result in a cost-efficient use of resources.[2] Still, it could be argued that, if such approaches would achieve real equity among the parties of the treaties, a violation of the cost-effectiveness might be justified. However, there are serious doubts whether such flat-rate strategies do really help to establish international equity. If they do not, the question arises whether well-functioning forms of international cooperation, for example, in Northern Europe, have created other mechanisms to facilitate the implementing commitments which put different burdens on countries.

2. M. Amann, G. Klaassen, and W. Schöpp, *UN/ECE Workshop on Exploring European Sulfur Abatement Strategies,* SR-91-03, International Institute for Applied Systems Analysis, Laxenburg (1990).

As an example Table 15.1 lists the costs of a 50 percent cut of SO_2 emissions for countries in Northern Europe expressed as percentage of GDP. These data have been estimated with the RAINS model. The RAINS model has been developed at the International Institute for Applied Systems Analysis as a tool for the integrated assessment of alternative strategies to reduce acidification in Europe. The model combines information on energy consumption, emission generation, the control potential and costs, atmospheric transport, and the environmental impacts of acidic emissions. It is currently used as a major analytical tool in international negotiations on further reductions of SO_2 emissions in Europe.[3]

The table demonstrates that, according to estimates made using the RAINS model, the burden of a 50 percent cut of the SO_2 emissions as suggested by the Baltic Sea declaration (expressed as the percentage of GDP required for emission control measures) is typically between 0.02 and 0.10

TABLE 15.1

Costs to Reduce SO_2 Emissions by 50 Percent, Expressed as a Percentage of the GDP

Country/Region	Costs in % of GDP
Finland	0.10
Sweden	0.07
Norway	0.04
Denmark	0.02
West Germany	0.09
Poland	0.20
Estonia	0.58
Latvia	0.10
Lithuania	0.23
St. Petersburg	0.07
Kola	0.47

Source: IIASA 1992.

3.   J. Alcamo, R. Shaw, and L. Hordijk (eds.), *The RAINS Model of Acidification: Science and Strategies in Europe,* Dordrecht (1990).

percent in Western European countries, whereas equal percentage reductions in Eastern European countries require between 0.07 and 0.58 percent of the GDP. Whereas some Western European countries consider emission reductions requiring some 0.1 percent of their GDP as too expensive (compare, for example, the reconsideration of the committed NO_x reduction of Finland), they apparently have no problems in requesting considerably larger relative efforts from other countries.

An obvious solution to trigger necessary environmental measures in countries with less economic power would be a transfer of funds from economically wealthy countries. However, such a transfer faces many theoretical and practical difficulties and not many examples for actual implementation have been reported. Since such burden-sharing approaches seem important for the rapid improvement of environmental quality not only in Northern Europe, but also in large areas in Central Europe, the long historical experience in international cooperation gained around the Baltic is therefore of extreme value to all of Europe.

PART FIVE

Domestic Environmental Politics in a Comparative Perspective

16

Domestic Environmental Politics in a Comparative Perspective: The Nordic Countries

Christer Ågren

This chapter gives a brief description of environmental protection activities in the Nordic countries (Denmark, Finland, Norway, and Sweden); it does not provide a critical analysis of whether or not the decisions made are being fully implemented, or if the environmental policy described is satisfactory.

1. Nordic Cooperation

The Nordic countries have some common features, such as history, language, and climate. The Nordic countries have been addressing issues of environmental protection since the early 1970s. For example, a Nordic convention on environmental protection was agreed upon in 1976. Even though efforts have been made to harmonize and standardize various rules and procedures related to environmental protection, differences between the Nordic countries still exist. For example, Denmark is a member of the EC, while the other Nordic countries are members of the European Free Trade Association (EFTA).

Through the Nordic Council and the Nordic Council of Ministers, representatives of the parliaments and governments of the Nordic countries meet regularly. In recent years several Nordic action plans on environmental protection have been adopted, such as the Nordic Action Plan Against Air Pollution; the Nordic Action Plan on Pollution of the Seas; and the Nordic Action Program on Cleaner Technology, Waste, and Recycling.

2. Environmental Problems

In urban areas air pollution is a large problem, and emissions from motor vehicles are the main source of this pollution. Sweden and Norway introduced obligatory US 1987-standards for passenger cars beginning with the 1989 models. Denmark introduced similar standards in October 1990, despite objections from the EC, and Finland introduced mandatory US standards in November 1990. Lead-free petrol is widely available in all four countries. All four countries have also instituted emission standards on heavy-duty vehicles and buses. The emissions of air pollutants from domestic heating have gradually decreased during the 1970s and 1980s as a result of, among other factors, an expansion of district heating systems and a lowering of the highest permissible sulfur content in fuel oil.

In the period from 1980 to 1989 the emissions of sulfur dioxide in the Nordic countries were reduced by more than 50 percent, while those of nitrogen oxides remained about the same. Sweden and Finland have officially declared their intention to reduce emissions of sulfur dioxide by at least 80 percent between 1980 and 2000.

Water pollution has been controlled through expansion of sewage treatment plants combined with purification of industrial effluents. In Sweden, more than two-thirds of all the urban population is connected to sewage treatment plants with chemical and biological purification. Examples of remaining water pollution problems are emissions of chlorinated organic substances from the pulp and paper industry, leaching of heavy metals from mining activities, and eutrophication of coastal waters.

A common problem for the Nordic countries, and also for most of Europe, is transboundary air pollution, resulting in acidification of soil, groundwater and surface water contamination and damage to vegetation and materials. The main pollutants contributing to acidification, nitrogen saturation, and the formation of photochemical oxidants such as ozone are sulfur dioxide, nitrogen oxides, volatile organic compounds, and ammonia.

Of Sweden's 85,000 lakes (those with a surface area of more than one hectare), about 15,000 are acidified to the extent that sensitive species in the lakes have been damaged or wiped out completely. In south Norway, fish are virtually depleted in lakes and rivers covering an area of 18,000 square kilometers, and in another 18,000 square kilometers fish populations have been strongly affected.

An estimated area of 650,000 hectares of forest soil in Sweden is acidified to pH values below 4.4. At this level of acidity, mineral nutrients such as calcium, magnesium, and potassium are leached out of the soil, and potentially harmful metals such as aluminum and various heavy metals become more mobile. Losses of vitality of forest trees, measured as crown defoliation, are widespread in all four Nordic countries. In Sweden, the increased levels of ozone have been estimated to cause reductions in harvest yields, costing a total of about 1.5 billion Swedish Krona (SEK) every year.

Norway and Sweden were leaders in the international negotiating process that in 1979 resulted in the UN ECE Convention on Long Range Transboundary Air Pollution (LRTAP). Furthermore, the Nordic countries to a large extent were the architects of the so-called Thirty Percent Club, that in 1985 resulted in the addition of the sulfur protocol to the LRTAP convention.

It was also the Nordic countries that introduced the so-called critical loads approach to the international negotiations under the LRTAP convention.

In recent years Nordic countries have provided economic and technical support to Eastern European countries. This is in addition to the bilateral support and exchange activities carried out by each Nordic country to help Eastern Europe. One example of a joint activity is the measures planned for reducing emissions of air pollutants at the Russian metal smelter industries on the Kola peninsula.

Some examples of other common Nordic environmental problem areas are agriculture, forestry, chemicals, and waste.

3. Environmental Protection in Sweden

In 1967 the Swedish Environmental Protection Agency was established. This is a state authority, responsible for the protection of land, water, and the air. The Environmental Protection Act, restricting water and air pollution, and noise pollution from industrial plants and other permanent installations, was introduced in 1969. According to this act, a license is required for the construction of certain types of industries and other establishments. A special authority, the Franchise Board for Environmental Protection, and the county administrations are responsible for licensing. The government, however, must grant licenses for activities that entail very great nuisances.

The Environmental Protection Agency is responsible for central supervision, that is, it coordinates supervisory activities and provides advice and guidance. Detailed supervision is handled by the county administration and the local environment and health protection boards.

In 1986 the Act on Chemical Products was introduced, administered by the National Chemicals Inspectorate, who has the power to regulate any chemical, for instance, through restriction in its uses. Disposal of chemicals is regulated by the Ordinance on Hazardous Waste (1986). The Act and the Ordinance on Sulfur Content of Fuel Oils was enacted in 1976. Today these limits are set at a maximum sulfur content of 0.8 percent in heavy fuel oil, and 0.2 percent in light fuel oil and diesel. As from July 1, 1993, the sulfur content of diesel was lowered to 0.05 percent.

The Natural Resources Act (1987) contains basic regulations on the conservation of natural resources, and it sets out the responsibilities of the state and local governments for land and water use.

Since the 1980s, Sweden has introduced a number of economic incentives, such as environmental taxes and charges, to protect the environment. In 1984 an environmental charge on artificial fertilizers and pesticides was introduced. On January 1, 1991, an environmental tax on emissions of carbon dioxide was introduced, amounting to SEK 0.25 per kilogram of CO_2 (equal to SEK 0.58 per liter of petrol). For comparison, the Swedish CO_2 tax equals US\$ 18 per barrel of oil. Furthermore, as from 1991 Sweden introduced an emission tax on emissions of sulphur dioxide (SEK 30 per kilogram of sulfur). Since 1989 domestic air traffic has been taxed on its emissions of nitrogen oxides and hydrocarbons, and since 1991 it has been taxed on its emissions of CO_2.

Since January 1, 1992, emissions of nitrogen oxides from heat and power generation plants have been charged at a rate of SEK 40 per kilogram (as NO_2). Most of these taxes and charges payed to the state are simply added to the state's finances, but others are earmarked for environmental purposes, such as research, landscape protection, and liming activities. The NO_x charge, however, is planned to be re-distributed to the generating plants in relation to the electricity or heat produced.

Recently it has been decided to introduce a so-called environmental classification system for diesel fuels, passenger cars, and heavy-duty vehicles and buses. In each category, three classes will be used: very low emissions; low emissions; only meeting the standards. Various economic incentives will be used to promote the sale of cleaner vehicles and fuels.

At the governmental level, responsibility is largely vested in the Ministry of Environment. The Environmental Protection Agency is the central administrative authority that executes the decisions of the parliament and the government, and also proposes new measures to protect the environment.

The main responsibility for environmental protection at the regional level rests with the county administrators, who have special environmental protection units for that purpose. Local responsibility rests with the environmental and health protection boards of the local communities.

4. Public Concern and Priorities

In Swedish opinion polls, environmental issues are given a very high priority among the public. This was especially the case in the late 1980s, when the environment was generally considered *the* most important issue, more important than, for example, unemployment, health care, taxes, and military defense. In 1988 the public concern for the environment seemed to peak, when more than 60 percent of the population said it was the most important issue. This figure can be compared with the level of 4 percent in 1968 and 37 percent in 1990.

In recent years the priorities seem to have changed slightly, and the environment has in some polls fallen from first to third or even fourth place. Higher priority has instead been given to issues such as health care and unemployment. Some polls, however, carried out in the summer of 1991, show that the public is still giving the environment the highest priority.

Environmental issues of most concern to the public in Sweden in 1990 were, according to one opinion poll:

— the dumping of industrial wastes at sea;
— industrial air pollution from other countries and industrial emissions of chemicals;
— the destruction of rain forests;
— destruction of the ozone layer;
— eutrophication of rivers and coastal waters.

"Green" environmental issues, such as landscape and species conservation, were not included in this poll.

The public seems to have great difficulties in realizing the importance of the environmental problems that they themselves contribute to directly by their personal activities and choices, such as car emissions, domestic waste, and pollutants resulting from energy use.

Opinion polls have been carried out to investigate which groups of the society have the highest credibility in the eyes of the public, as regards environmental issues. The results show that environmental organizations have the highest credibility, followed by scientists at universities. Industry and journalists have the lowest credibility, while authorities and political parties end up in the middle.

5. Environmental Organizations

The support to environmental organizations, expressed as number of members or supporters, increased substantially in the 1980s, even though that increase has been slowing down recently. In Sweden, the largest organization is the Swedish Society for Nature Conservation (Naturskyddsföreningen), with more than 200,000 members, organized in some 260 local groups. Greenpeace Sweden has some 150,000 supporting members, and Worldwide Fund for Nature (WWF) Sweden also has about 150,000. Much smaller (in number of members or supporting members) but still active and influential environmental organizations include the Environment Federation (Miljöförbundet) and the Swedish Youth Association for Environmental Studies and Conservation (Fältbiologerna).

In Denmark the dominant organization is the Danish Society for Nature Conservation (Naturfredningsforeningen), with some 250,000 members; in Norway the Norwegian Society for Nature Conservation (Naturvernforbundet) has about 60,000 members.

As compared with many other European countries, a relatively large proportion of the population in the Nordic countries are supporting environmental organizations.

6. Political Parties

In Sweden, the Green Party was elected to the national parliament in 1988, the year of peak environmental concern among the public; it was already represented at a number of local and regional parliaments. However, in the September 1991 election, it did not receive the four percent of votes necessary to be represented in the national parliament. Instead two "new" parties — the Christian Democrats and the New Democracy, both oriented toward the "right wing" — were voted into the parliament.

Since 1982 there has been a Social Democratic minority government, and as a result of the September 1991 election, Sweden now has a four-party "non socialist" minority government. From having had a comparably stable parliamentary situation, Sweden has now entered into a situation resembling one which has existed for a number of years in Denmark and Norway. It remains to be seen if this will result in any major changes in environmental policies.

The political parties that have so far been trying to build a profile, at least partly on their environmental policy, are primarily the Green Party, the Left Party, and the Center Party. The Liberal Party has tended to focus its green profile primarily on "green" environmental issues, such as landscape and species conservation. The two biggest parties, the Social Democrats and the Conservatives, are often seen as less radical as regards environmental issues.

7. Decision Making and the Influence of Environmental Organizations

Sweden has a long tradition of developing policies and making decisions by some form of consensus, that is to involve the principal interested parties in discussions and negotiations until a solution, acceptable to most of the actors, has been reached. This means that politics in Sweden usually is less confrontational than in many other European countries.

As regards environmental issues, most proposals from authorities and government are submitted to various "interest groups," such as industry or environmental organizations, and these groups are invited to present their views on the proposals. This provides some opportunities for influencing decisions at an early stage, and for considering public opinion in the decision making process.

Environmental organizations, especially the bigger ones, quite often meet with representatives of the Ministry of Environment, the Environmental Protection Agency, etc., for discussion and consultation. These procedures do not, however, prevent major differences in views. For example recent important environmental issues with elements of conflict and confrontation include:

— energy policy, especially the phasing out of nuclear power;
— transport policy, especially the agreement between Denmark and Sweden to build a bridge between Copenhagen and Malmö;
— forestry practices, especially the clear-cutting of forests in the mountainous region in northern Sweden.

Another example of an issue of concern and of potentially large environmental controversy is the expected agreement between the EC and EFTA on the so-called European Economic Area (this agreement was recently signed, but has yet to be ratified). The next step is likely to be when Sweden, and also Finland and Norway, joins the EC. Exactly what the environmental consequences of those changes may be are largely uncertain, and the debate has just begun. For example, the effects on energy and transport policies, including emission standards for motor vehicles, are issues of concern in this context, as is the issue of labeling and banning of certain chemicals.

Another issue of concern in this context is the important function of some countries, or regions of countries, as "forerunners" or "examples." This, of course, is not only applicable to the Nordic countries. It also relates to, for example, the Netherlands or Germany. With increasing harmonization, the possibilities of acting nationally, or regionally in groups of countries, diminishes. The potential for forerunners lies especially in rich, technically skilled, and environmentally aware countries. Of the European countries fulfilling these criteria, all may within the next few years be tied up by the driving force of harmonization in the European Community. This could reduce the speed of international negotiations on environmental issues and reduce incentives for development of alternative solutions.

References

National Swedish Environmental Protection Board, *Pollution Control in Sweden*, Stockholm (1988).

Swedish Ministry of the Environment, *Sweden: National Report to UNCED 1992*, Stockholm (1991).

Nordic Council of Ministers, *Nordic Action Plan against Air Pollution*, Stockholm (1990).

Swedish Environmental Protection Agency, *Air Pollution '90*, Stockholm (1990).

Swedish Environmental Protection Agency, *Acid Magazine and Enviro Magazine*, Stockholm (1984–1991).

Swedish NGO Secretariat on Acid Rain, *Acid News*, Stockholm (1982–1991).

17

Drifting Countries:
Politics and Environment
in East Central Europe

János Vargha

1. Technology, Politics, and Environment

The evolution of technology in East Central Europe was slowed down by the economically unreasonable operation of the totalitarian political system based on state property, central "planning," and central redistribution. This resulted in the development and extension of industrial and agricultural systems consuming more resources and causing more serious environmental impacts than the technological systems in the Western Hemisphere. This process had been accomplished in a similar way in all East Central European countries, due to the strong political and economic control by the Soviet Union. The Czech *Blue Book* (Moldan) divides the history of the totalitarian era into three parts. The first period (1948–1960) is characterized by rapid economic development, accompanied by practically no attention toward ecological problems. The second (1961–1970) is the slowdown period of economic development, with the first signals of serious — though still only local — disturbances of the ecological stability, a dramatic impairment of water quality. The third period (1971–1990) is described by alternating intervals of economic growth and stagnation, accompanied by the efforts to maintain an acceptable living standard — because of the extensive devastation of the environment and inadequate exploitation of natural resources.

The development of technological monopolies (mining, energy, metallurgy, machine industry, military industry, etc.) in the East Central European economies was directed by oligarchies which gained extremely strong political influence. These groups, in cooperation with a stale administration, controlled almost all parts of society. In spite of their inability to operate the economy effectively, they were able to maintain power for a long time. Thus, the periodically emerging economic and political crises were solved without changes in the system itself, but by strengthening the system at a price of increased exploitation of resources and deteriorating the environment. During the 1980s, it was only Western credits that made the survival of totalitarian systems possible. (Some of these countries are some of the most indebted countries in the world based on debt per capita.)

The so-called non-productive or service sectors and activities were poorly supported by centrally redistributed financial sources. Environmental protection belongs in this category, and was considered a task of the state according to the ruling ideology. Only in the last years of communist rule did the states allow some strictly controlled public participation (called "societal discussion" in the official terminology), in order to balance the increasing influence of independent movements. But these groups were not recognized and registration of their organizations was hampered by the authorities.

2. The Environmental Movements and Political Changes

Public opinion in Eastern Europe has linked the crisis of the environment with the political system. Among the list of crimes brought about by the political system, low standards of living and polluted air, water, and soil can be linked together. People concerned about the environment fight for their basic human rights — exactly as the politicians in opposition must do. These views of the environment created hope among the public that the change in the political system will solve ecological problems nearly automatically. People in East Central Europe are fascinated by the economic and military success of countries of the Western model. The cleaning of the air in London, improvement of water quality in the Rhine, use of lead-free gasoline and catalytic converters have made a strong impression that basic environmental problems can be solved by market economies.

3. New Political Concepts for Environmental Protection

The dramatic political changes in 1989 terminated one-party political systems. The totalitarian political model lost the armament race and the economic competition in the world market because of the low efficiency of technologies developed within this model. The younger generation of the political elite realized the unavoidable defeat just in time, which allowed for the basically peaceful start of transition. At the beginning of this process, environmental movements seemed to play an important role in the political scene. According to a Western observer,[1] one of the distinguishing features of the East European revolutions of 1989 is their strong environmental component. In numerous instances, the environment in the pre-revolution days served as a rallying point from which broader demands for political change emerged. Initially perceived as relatively benign by the region's Communist governments, environmental movements soon acquired unstoppable momentum. It has been assumed that newly formed political parties, aimed unanimously toward the market economy based on privatization, will incorporate ecological principles into their programs. This assumption is reflected by the environmental programs of the new governments. A brief overview of such programs of the current Hungarian, Polish, and Czech governments illustrates the environmental concepts of new political forces in East Central Europe.

The Hungarian government published its political program in late 1990, in which the environmental program is summarized in Chapter 5. (It is important to note that within the twelve pages of the chapter, two and a half pages are written about the problems of the Danube hydroelectric power plant system. This joint Czechoslovak-Hungarian project, which was built with Austrian participation, initiated a strong environmental movement in Hungary in the last years of the totalitarian system. In 1989, the movement successfully blocked the construction of the project in Hungary.) The most important principles of the program are (in the original order):

— development and operation of the economy in harmony with the environment;
— environment-friendly change of the structure of production;
— establishment of the market economy;
— improvement of the "owner's attitude;"
— change of priorities, increase of environmental consciousness;
— right to a clean, healthy environment;
— general use on environmental impact assessment;
— environmentally oriented credit, tax, and customs policy;
— cooperation with environmental institutions of the European Community;
— separation of the issue of environment from direct interests of production.

---

1. H.F. French, *Green Revolutions: Environmental Reconstruction in Eastern Europe and the Soviet Union*, Worldwatch Paper 99, Washington (1990).

The program of the Polish environmental ministry, published in November 1990, mentions that the new environmental policy departs from what was once a narrow understanding of environmental protection, and now includes a broader goal of sustainable development. The concept of sustainable development is defined by the program as "the attainment of a balance between social, economic, technical, and environmental conditions in the process of development." The basic principles of this policy are listed as follows:

— control at the source (choice of preventive measures);
— a law-abiding principle (no opportunities for circumvention of the law for reasons of "circumstances outside one's control," "public interest," or "impossibility");
— the principle of a common good;
— an economization principle (taking the greatest possible advantage of market mechanisms);
— the "polluter pays" principle;
— principle of regionalization;
— principle of common solution (i.e., international cooperation);
— principle of staging (selection of priorities for each particular stage of a long-term policy).

The "Rainbow Program" of the Ministry of Environment of the Czech Republic, published in 1991, also gives a list of principles and basic approaches:

— the concept of sustainable development and prevention against the various economic growth strategies aimed at a high consumption of natural resources;
— economic, legal, and other social conditions facilitating an ecologically friendly lifestyle in various forms;
— distribution of information concerning ecologically friendly processes in the production sector and among consumers;
— renewal of the people's contact with nature, especially in towns;
— the principle of real effect (i.e., trying to restrict confusion in the systems in planning activities);
— the principle of reasonable consumption;
— the principle of caution;
— the principle of consideration for other;
— the principle of respect for life;
— the principle of citizenship of the planet Earth.

In spite of many objections to these principles and/or other programs, it seems that the governments are looking for effective environmental policies — and finding them — by applying the Western economic model. The new concepts generally accept that the introduction of market mechanisms will also improve environmental conditions, and their undesirable impacts can effectively be limited by legislation and state control.

According to the Polish National Environmental Policy program, there is common ground between a sustainable development policy and the economic interest of the country. Closing the existing gaps between harvesting, processing, and consuming natural resources which lead to waste, high costs, and low-quality products, will open up possibilities for economic gains. The opportunity for receiving such benefits is growing, particularly at a time of economic privatization. Thus, environmental protection, in its broadest sense, will be an ally to a modern, effective, and prudent economy. Authors of the document emphasize that in connection with the transition of the Polish economy to the market system, environmental policy will be, to the maximum extent, subject to the economization principle, which means that the greatest possible advantage will be taken of market mechanisms, with the necessary maintenance through state intervention. Fewer concerns are expressed in the Hungarian document about harmful environmental impacts of a market economy, and most elements of an alternative approach are included in the Rainbow Program of Bohemia. This program accepts that modern society has determined that the free application of market forces is the basis of the modern economy, but these forces tend to underestimate the real value of natural resources. Because this policy does not take long-term goals into consideration, they must be effectively defined with the aid of laws: "The laws must determine the rules and limits of the market system so as not jeopardize one of the basic human rights — the right to a healthy environment."

All of these programs give considerable weight to the practical implementation of the principles mentioned above. The most particular measures are promised by the Hungarian government. Unfortunately a discussion of them would exceed the limits of this paper.

4. Programs and Realities

In winter of 1984, Austrian police attacked people protesting against the construction of the Hainburg Dam on the Danube. This happened in a democracy. Two years later, Hungarian police in Budapest stopped the demonstration walk of Austrian and Hungarian environmentalists protesting against the construction of the Gabcikovo-Nagymaros Dam System with truncheons and tear gas. This happened in a dictatorship.

In the summer of 1990 in Poland, police and anti-terrorist brigades dispersed blockades of environmentalists who tried to stop the construction of the Czorsztyn Dam located in the heart of a nature conservation area. One year later, Slovak police troops brutally attacked environmentalists who occupied a pumping station symbolically protesting against pumping water into the lateral canal of the Gabcikovo hydropower plant under construction. (This water-pumping process was aimed to kill plants which break through the asphalt layer of the canal.) The "realpolitik" of governments seems to be stronger than their programs. According to environmentalists, the chief investor in the Czorsztyn Dam is the Polish Ministry of Environmental Protection, Natural Resources, and Forestry. In Hungary, the commissioner of the Ministry for Environmental Protection and Regional Planning supported the operation of the lateral canal of the Gabcikovo hydropower plant; and the environmental minister of the Czech and Slovak Federal Republic argued for the same during his visit to Budapest. (During the totalitarian era, both persons were well-known opponents of the project.)

Other experiences in Hungary indicate similarly that there are large gaps between the governmental program and the actual activity of the government. In more than three years, the Ministry for Environmental Protection and Regional Planning was not able to work out a draft environmental law. A comprehensive draft law worked out by independent experts for the Environmental Committee of the Parliament was rejected with arguments as "it is too long and complex" or "it would inhibit foreign capital investment in Hungary." Basic laws for the economy have been created without efficient environmental legislation. A number of practical measures promised in the program were not fulfilled. A commissioner of the Ministry said in an interview: In spite of its many efforts, the environmental ministry is not able to represent the medium- and long-term interest of the environment and of citizens effectively. Environmental protection does not serve everyday income, thus it has the lowest priority among sectors in the state budget. It is very difficult to make the difference between lobbies and mafia.[2] This statement would not be a surprise from an environmental activist in 1988. But it was said by a governmental officer in 1991.

---

2.   P.P. Boday, "Környezetvedelem, avagy a demokracia korlatai?" (Environmental Protection or Limits of Democracy?), in *Magyar Hirlap*, August 27, Budapest 1991.

Bochniarz[3] points out that in Poland and other East Central European countries, in spite of the obvious deterioration of the quality of the environment and its consequences, an appropriate response in the form of a comprehensive strategy to deal with the crisis is lacking. Bochniarz explains that this along with the legacy of the communist rule, poses serious problems for these countries, and can be solved only by designing and establishing new institutions (partially by reforming existing ones), as a behavioral framework for a sustainable society. Institutions are social inventions and, for that reason, a relatively long process of establishing new institutions gives more opportunity for a society to recognize and understand their functions (legitimization) and to internalize their practices as their own (socialization). Bochniarz discusses major deficiencies in the existing system of environmental protection in Poland. Theses deficiencies are in the following areas: environmental laws, economic mechanisms, environmental management, public participation, environmental education, environmental awareness, the political system, research and development, environmental technologies, and international collaboration.

5. Drifting Countries

Among domestic deficiencies and other problems Bochniarz mentions on the donor side, there are many cases showing a lack of understanding of basic needs of the Polish environment, and, in some cases, interests of donors are dominant over interests of receiver.

We should pay much more attention to this problem, taking into consideration the role of the external determination in the domestic affairs of the East Central European countries. In the past, external determination resulted in the establishment of Communist systems in these countries which became satellites of Russia. After the breakdown of the Eastern bloc, the former satellites declared their wish to return to "the European Common House." This reproduces the decisive role of external determination, because these countries are not able to transform their economies and political systems without Western assistance.

On the other hand, the adoption (or transplantation) of the Western model of development does not necessarily mean that they will be an inte-

3. Z. Bochniarz, "Overview of the Polish Environmental System: Deficiencies and Constraints," in Richard Bolan and Zbigniew Bochniarz, *Designing Institutions for Sustainable Development: A New Challenge for Poland*, Minneapolis-Bialistok (1991).

grated part of the Western European central unit of this model. These central units (i.e., highly industrialized countries) use most of the resources of the world, which means that the sustainability of the Western model involves the asymmetry of the global order. Specific resource demands of the central units determine a minimal level (and probably a certain pattern) of asymmetry. If the upgrading of East Central European countries changes these conditions too much, their joining the central unit as equal partners will certainly be ruled out. In this case, this region would operate as an outside territory under a strong control, just like many countries of the Third World.

Present tendencies indicate that strong forces have compelled the East Central European countries to drift in this direction. One example is the pressure from Western governments and companies to build power plants — especially nuclear reactor units — in this region with Western assistance and transport electricity to Western Europe. Such actions may have essential impacts inhibiting any efforts to improve domestic environmental politics of East Central European countries. This means that the successful implementation of their new environmental programs depend essentially on the success of the transformation of the global order itself. Therefore the East Central European countries should develop policies and action plans and integrate them into a common strategy of an ecologically sustainable development.[4] Unfortunately, this principle has relatively low priority in political programs as well as in practice at present.

Selected References

A nemzeti megujhodas programja (Program for the Revival of the Nation), Budapest (1990).

Moldan, B. (ed.), *Environment of the Czech Republic*, vol. 1-3, Ministry of Environment of the Czech Republic and the Czechoslovak Academy of Sciences, Prague (1990).

Moldan, B. (ed.), *Rainbow Program*, Environmental Recovery Program for the Czech Republic, Academia Prague and the Ministry of Environment of the Czech Republic, Prague (1991).

Ministry of Environmental Protection, Natural Resources and Forestry, *National Environmental Policy*, Warsaw (1990).

---

4.   J. Vargha, *Environmental Sound Options for the Political and Economic Transition in Central and Eastern Europe*, Discussion paper IEWSS International Conference on Western Assistance to East Central Europe, Bardejov 1991.

18

The Political Infrastructure of Environmental Politics in Western and Eastern Europe

Volkmar Lauber

Environmental politics consists in the struggle between those who strive for sustainable development and those who press for other goals, implicitly or explicitly, and in the management of this struggle by the state and similar institutions. This chapter defines the function of the environmentalist response to industrial destruction and explains why it developed rather late. It describes the special conditions for the formation of this response in Western Europe, its eventual institutionalization, and the adjustments it has brought about in those societies. It then analyzes the factors that distinguish Eastern European societies and which have so far constrained the environmentalist response there. The conclusion points out that, up to now, the impact of the environmentalist response has been quite limited even in Western Europe. It may certainly be the case that sustainable development cannot be achieved by simply continuing on the course that took shape over the past twenty years.

1. Sustainable Development, Society, and Politics

There is much discussion today about what kind of development is sustainable. It seems easier to agree on what is not sustainable, i.e., the pattern of industrial development that tends to deplete the earth's nonrenewable resources (such as fossil fuels which are transformed into CO_2 and other pollutants); to poison the biosphere by its wastes; and to deplete mankind's future by setting up time bombs such as radioactive or chemical pollution, the greenhouse effect, the depletion of the ozone layer, and the reduction of biological diversity.

In most countries some form of resistance to this pattern of development — or at least to its effects — is by now well established. Among the industrial countries, the resistance is particularly strong in the United States and in some of the more developed countries of Western Europe. This is a fairly recent phenomenon which dates back to the 1970s, and which has expanded considerably since then. This resistance led to a certain reorientation of policy toward the environment and modified to some extent the way in which decisions are made. Such developments can be viewed as the first elements of a political infrastructure for sustainable development.

In a living system, destruction will normally cause pain in some form or other. The pain will usually serve to activate certain parts of the system which in turn will attempt a feedback to the headquarters of the system concerned, with a view to modify the behavior which is causing the pain. If all works well, the system should thus be able to minimize the amount of self-inflicted destruction.

With a certain amount of imagination, human communities (local, regional, or worldwide) embedded in their environments may be viewed as such systems. Much industrial development caused (and often still causes) destruction. The destruction affects human life and its outlook, and the more sensitive (or the more perceptive) forms of life may register the pain caused by this destruction; others, in fact, do or did not register the pain because their awareness was focused on other phenomena or was unable to make use of the information provided. If the pain is felt, it may lead to a feedback to the nerve centers of the system (political and economic). This feedback can take on different forms, and may range from a simple retransmission of feelings in their raw state to the elaboration and transmission of proposals for alternative courses of action. In both cases the nerve centers of the system will be under pressure to revise their course, although in the first case the necessary learning process still needs to take place. This represents another important threshold to be overcome.

At a very abstract level, this brief description sums up the basic idea of the political infrastructure necessary for achieving sustainable development. Of course it is but an infrastructure, and as such cannot guarantee that the outcome for the environment will be positive; but it should create conditions favorable to such an outcome. At least that seems to be the lesson of past experience, which is reviewed in section 2.

2. Failure to Develop a Response to Environmental Deterioration

If one holds the above outline of the social-environmental system against past developments, what is most striking is the fact that the response to environmental deterioration failed to evolve for such a long time. This shows that a functioning political infrastructure for sustainable development can by no means be taken for granted. Potential problems emerge at several levels.

First, there is the level of perception. The chief agents (economic and political) of early industrialization tended to ignore the deleterious effects of their activities on the environment. They did so mostly with a good conscience: they were serving the cause of progress by using the forces of nature to create new wealth or power. Those of their adversaries who were viewed as the most radical at that time — the early socialists and the Marxists — shared their basic optimism about the potential of technical progress; their main protest concerned only the way in which the fruits of progress were being distributed.

The social question was not the only issue to divert attention from the emerging environmental problem. The expansion of political participation along the cleavage lines of the nineteenth century and nationalistic passions reflecting the competition between nations which took the shape of several wars (culminating in the two world wars of this century) absorbed undoubtedly the greatest part of attention given to politics. The advances of industrialization and market society were powerful factors changing people's lives; and there was a strong fascination with technical progress.

A second problem relates to the level of the social imagination, i.e., the ability to imagine a different course of socio-economic, technical, or political development. This is a difficult feat under any circumstances if one wants to move beyond the level of generalizations. It also requires faith which may be lacking. History illustrates this; for example there were those in the nineteenth century who did not join in the general enthusiasm for progress because they perceived its damage, but they generally limited themselves to purely negative views or actions. This was the case of the Luddites, but also of many conservatives (often poets) who simply regretted the passing away of an earlier age, a development which they felt could not be changed. Even early societies for the protection of nature were characterized by a similar attitude; they limited themselves to press for the preservation of individual fragments of nature and did not outline an alternative course.

Perception and a minimum of social imagination are the first requirement of an environmental movement on which a feedback to the system can be based. Those who dissented from industrial development in the nineteenth and the first half of the twentieth centuries did not, on the whole, fulfill these requirements; thus they remained isolated and politically ineffectual, apparently destined to be passed over by history.

Even if no environmental movement existed, some of the instruments that were to serve it later were already developed in the liberal societies of the late nineteenth century, with their respect for private property and the rule of law. Individuals could, as property owners, resist various forms of damage imposed on them by emissions from polluting installations. Even if at the time this provision did not seem to have a great impact, an instrument was installed that became important later on. Also, the extension of the suffrage prepared the ground for popular participation and a politically active citizenry.

The most difficult intellectual feat is probably the charting of a credible alternative course of development. It takes a special kind of faith to go against the general trend. In addition, those who prepare an alternative differing from the prevailing model of rationality must overcome special difficulties in arguing their case. It will be difficult for them to muster the expertise necessary to counter technocratic argumentation. Such an enterprise may require a whole counter culture of scientific and technical knowledge, which in turn can only develop on the basis of substantial sympathy and support (organizational, financial, and so on).

Yet this is not all. If alternative paths of development are credibly worked out, this information still needs points of access to the political system in order to alter the course taken by societies. The basic problems are those of legitimacy and power. The rise of the contemporary environmental movement in the West took place between the late 1960s and the 1980s; in fact, the process does not yet seem to be completed, as membership in environmental associations is still substantially on the increase (and the fate of green parties is far from being clear).[1] Why did the movement come into existence just then?

---

1. Katharina Krohberger and Christian Hey, *Die Beteiligungschancen der Umwelt-verbände auf europäischer Ebene,* EURES Discussion Paper 11, Freiburg (1991).

3. The Environmental Movement in Western Europe

3.1 Conditions That Gave Rise to the Western Environmental Movement

The 1950s and 1960s were years of high growth rates in Western Europe. After the disaster of two World Wars, a great depression, and half a century of politics marked by strong ideological conflicts, Western societies welcomed comfort and affluence. The high economic growth rates of this period proved a solvent for all sorts of group conflicts, just as this was originally intended by the technocrats of the Marshall Plan.[2] Political ideas increasingly lost in importance; so did most social antagonisms. At the same time Western European countries were clearly among the world's leaders in prosperity and power, in the context of the Atlantic Alliance. The waning of the traditional political conflicts probably represented an important precondition for the development of the environmental movement; it cleared the way for its emergence.

At the same time, this phase of rapid growth caused considerable environmental damage due to such developments as the widespread use of the automobile (noise, air pollution, urban sprawl), the stepped-up use of energy, and the increase of nondegradable waste. For much of the older generation whose life had been marked by insecurity and often deprivation, this was negligible. For the generation that came of age in the 1960s and early 1970s, things were different. They could take security for granted, and they saw more clearly the costs (environmental, psychological, and otherwise) of the quest for the new way of life. In one of the more important conflicts of that time (the Paris events of May 1968, a time when the environment was hardly a theme), the favorite targets were unsurprisingly the technocrats, symbols of growth, national power, and the triumph of technique over human values.

When it first emerged, environmentalism was not marked by an emphasis on confrontation. In the United States ecology entered the political scene as a "motherhood issue," a theme on which everybody seemed to be in agreement. The first large events were characterized by enthusiasm and not by bitterness: Earth Day in the United States in May 1970 was a joyful event,

---

2. Charles S. Maier, "The Politics of Productivity: Foundations of American International Economic Policy after World War II," in Peter J. Katzenstein (ed.), *Between Power and Plenty,* New York (1977), pp. 23–49; Volkmar Lauber, "From Growth Consensus to Fragmentation in Western Europe," *Comparative Politics,* vol. 15, no. 3 (1983), pp. 329–349.

the Stockholm Conference in 1972 was a meeting which generated hope. European governments (West and East) took up the new course with varying degrees of commitment, as an additional item on their agendas, but one that was not viewed as being particularly controversial.

Confrontation came a few years later. In 1972 the Club of Rome published its famous report *The Limits to Growth*, and the idea began to take hold that expansion could not be continued indefinitely, that a different model of development was required. Things came to a head in 1974. After the oil embargo and the first oil price shock, most European governments began to develop very ambitious nuclear power programs based on extrapolating old growth curves. These programs met with strong resistance not only at the particular sites concerned but also because the whole approach taken to energy policy was viewed with increasing skepticism. While public awareness about the environment was rising, governments tended to give lower priority to this issue because they viewed it as an impediment to growth; in some cases they even came to treat environmentalists as enemies of the established order.[3] At the same time, the traditional parties were still so wedded to the ideology and interests of economic growth that they were in most cases unable to take up the new impulses coming from the environmental movement.

The politics of environmental activism did not always lead to such hostile confrontations as those in the nuclear power area. The new participatory politics extended to many fields; citizen initiatives sprang up in the most diverse areas, and their relationship to state and local bureaucracies was usually one of antagonistic cooperation. This wave of participation in the name of the public interest (rather than private or group interests) represented an important new phenomenon, at least in Europe. It showed that people could organize themselves to change their world without relying on the initiative of established parties or interest groups. This required a great deal of self-confidence, optimism, mutual trust, and, to some extent, idealism, elements that contrast strongly with the often cynical or at least instrumental views of politics that seemed well established in European political culture, and the commonplace assumption that citizens are not prepared to take on the hardships of collective action.

---

3. In the Federal Republic of Germany and in Austria, secret police closely followed the environmentalist scene (particularly but not exclusively the antinuclear movement). French secret agents sank a Greenpeace boat, killing one activist.

3.2 From Protest to Participation: The Institutionalization of the Environmental Movement in Western Europe

When it first began, the environmental movement seemed to view itself as a force of protest, one that would try to put sand into the machine of growth to slow it down even if it could not stop it. Over the years however, the movement increasingly used the potentials for participation offered by democratic societies and managed to bring its influence to bear on the course of economic and technological development, trying to inflect its course rather than simply opposing it. While it has little reason so far to be satisfied, it has clearly made headway.

The process started out with mostly local initiatives, often around specific industrial projects, urban problems, and the like. Despite a frequent distrust for organization, the movement's activities led to a process of cooperation and organization; central institutions were developed for specific functions. Sometimes the traditional conservation societies set up in the late nineteenth century could fulfill such functions after undergoing a process of radicalization which led to an expansion of their goals; in most cases new organizations (sometimes international in scope) were set up for this purpose.

Carried by a strong wave of public sympathy and by an increasingly large social and financial basis (mostly in the middle class), the movement branched out. A process of specialization and a division of labor set in: some organizations specialized in information, protest, and/or lobbying; others, in research (thus the Öko-Institute in Germany and Austria); still others, in legal work (this activity has a long tradition in the United States in the form of public interest litigation). There was also specialization by issues (energy, acid rain, traffic, chemical pollution, and so on). Given the limited economic and career opportunities in this sector of alternative/environmentalist organizations, it was remarkable how well they could recruit talents, who, as a rule, acquired their credentials on the job.

These institutions became closely connected and formed a veritable network that may be viewed as the backbone of the environmental movement, the source of its greatest strength apart from public acceptance. This network gave durability to a cause that otherwise would have been exposed to the fluctuations of media and public opinion.

In most Western European countries this specialization also led to the creation of green political parties, whose fortunes show great variations.[4] It is sometimes assumed that green parties represent the highest stage of organi-

---

4. Sara Parkin, *Green Parties,* London (1989).

zation of the environmental movement.[5] This is not an inevitable conclusion if the task of that movement is seen, at the political level, as consisting in the promotion of ecological priorities in the decision making of governments, bureaucracies and international organizations. Here the so-called German pattern contrasts with what one might call the Scandinavian pattern. In both these cases there is a highly differentiated and strongly institutionalized environmental movement, stronger than in most parts of Western (and particularly Southern) Europe.

In the case of West Germany this led to the creation of political organizations (green/alternative/multicolored lists) early on; they were successful first in local and regional elections, and later in national elections. The Greens moved into the German parliament in 1983 (they had to vacate their seats again in 1991). This was an important step because the established political parties had long been reluctant to take up environmental issues, and also because success at the polls opened the flow of federal funds for party finance. These funds were channelled, by the Greens, to the network of environmental organizations, in order to finance the development of environmentalist expertise in various areas of policy making.

The Scandinavian example shows that setting up a green party is not the only way to make sure that environmental priorities are taken up by the political system. In pluralist democracies this should happen as the result of electoral competition. If other parties or actors effectively take up the green cause the same purpose is achieved by a different method. The Scandinavian experience seems to illustrate this point. Thus Denmark has one of the strongest ecology movements in Europe; the main association, *Nature Preservation Organization,* had more members in 1988 than all Danish parties put together. Denmark's energy policy is a model of how efficiency can be used to stabilize and even reduce energy demand, especially for fossil fuels. Yet most Danish environmental organizations resisted the formation of a green party and the Danish Greens, founded in 1983, contested their first election in 1988 without being able to pass the 2 percent threshold necessary to secure representation (they stood somewhere around 1.5 percent).[6]

In Norway, the first time a green party participated in national elections was in 1989. It received only 0.4 percent of the vote despite the fact that envi-

5. Christopher Williams, "From Iron into Green Curtain: The Environmental Crisis in Central and Eastern Europe and the Emerging Green Movements/Parties, 1989–91," Paper presented at the Conference on New Perspectives for Social Democracy in Central and Eastern Europe, Brussels, October 1991.

6. Jorgen Goul Anderson, "Denmark: Environmental Conflict and the 'Greening' of the Labour Movement," *Scandinavian Political Studies,* vol. 13, no. 2 (1990), pp. 185–209.

ronmental issues ranked very prominently. This was mainly because other parties had already taken up this cause, in particular the Liberal Party founded in 1884, more than a century ago, and "reborn" as a strongly environmental party in 1973.[7]

In Sweden finally, a green party was founded in 1981, but achieved only 1.6 percent of the votes in 1982, and 1.5 percent in 1985. The party succeeded in entering the national parliament only in 1988 (with 5.6 percent of the votes), but failed to pass the necessary threshold in the election of 1991 (in which it fell to 3.4 percent).[8] This does not mean that there was no widespread public concern about environmental issues during this time or that the Swedish government was not among the most innovative in Europe with regard to environmental questions.

In fact, there can be no doubt that the Scandinavian countries are among the most sensitive when it comes to environmental policy.[9] That this happened in the absence of important green parties shows that the presence of such institutions may not be central for environmental politics. The main function of a green party — orienting political competition and policy with environmentalist priorities — can be taken up by other actors as well. This will tend to happen if a network of environmental organizations keeps alive the discussion of alternatives, and if the general public is sufficiently sensitive to the problems.

3.3 Adjustments in Politics, Law, and Business

For the environmental movement to make itself heard and felt within the political system, it is not enough to be institutionalized. Such a development also requires points of access for environmental organizations to the structures of the political, administrative and judicial systems. The parliament or other political institutions can serve as such a point. Proceedings before administrative organs and courts are another such point. In this area liberal democracies had already provided important opportunities for owners of real-estate property who could defend themselves (or rather their property) against polluters.

7.   Bernt Aardal, "Green Politics: A Norwegian Experience," *Scandinavian Political Studies,* vol. 13, no. 2 (1990), pp. 147–164.

8.   Martin Bennulf and Sören Holmberg, "The Green Break-Through in Sweden," *Scandinavian Political Studies,* vol. 13, no. 2 (1990), pp. 165–184; Diane Sainsbury, "The 1991 Swedish Election: Protest, Fragmentation, and a Shift to the Right," *West European Politics,* vol. 15, no. 2 (1992), pp. 160–166.

9.   See Christer Ågren in this volume.

Under the pressure of events some countries considerably increased opportunities for public participation in administrative or judicial proceedings. The purpose was not so much to accommodate the wishes of the environmental movement as to avoid situations in which a permit for a particular installation (e.g., a construction permit) had been granted by a governmental authority, but could not be used because political protest and/or drawn-out court proceedings delayed or even prevented this. The idea was to let the likely protesters take part in the original proceedings in order to secure their (possibly reluctant) consent. This was first practiced in the energy area;[10] it expanded to many other areas as well.

In Western European countries and the United States, there is a great variety of possibilities of public participation in administrative decision making. These possibilities range from a generalized right of standing for every citizen to more restrictive solutions where only certain citizens or groups may participate, perhaps only with regard to certain subject matters and with only limited legal possibilities.[11]

Another important concession to the rise of environmental concern was the creation of governmental agencies, at some point usually ministries, charged with environmental protection.[12] Even though such creations often were only symbolic in character, they quite naturally became a focal point for the lobbying activities of environmental organizations that frequently came to represent their most important political constituency and political ally. The same applies to advisory bodies and related institutions in the environmental area; they all represented points of access to the political system on which pressure could be brought to bear.

The environmental movement also draws strength from its sympathizers, especially in the civil service, in schools and universities, and in the media. Businesses play an important role as well. Once an industry has accepted high environmental standards (even if it may actually have fought them in the first place), it has an interest in seeing these standards enforced on all poten-

10. Volkmar Lauber, "Energy Politics and Public Participation," in Wilfried L. Kohl (ed.), *After the Second Oil Crisis,* Lexington (1982), pp. 271–294; Herbert Gottweis, "Zur Politisierung des Energiesektors. Ein internationaler Vergleich," *Österreichische Zeitschrift für Politikwissenschaft,* vol. 15, no. 1 (1986), pp. 43–59.

11. Volkmar Lauber, "Private Schutzbefugnisse als Instrument der Umweltpolitik," *Österreichische Zeitschrift für Politikwissenschaft,* vol. 20, no. 2 (1991), pp. 177–190; Martin Führ and Gerhard Roller (eds.), *Participation and Litigation Rights of Environmental Associations in Europe,* Frankfurt (1991).

12. Martin Jänicke, "Erfolgsbedingungen von Umweltpolitik im internationalen Vergleich," *Zeitschrift für Umweltpolitik und Umweltrecht,* vol. 13, no. 3 (1990), pp. 213–232.

tial competitors, domestic or foreign (unless the industry plans to benefit from relaxed standards by moving to locations where environmental regulations are less stringent). Achievements in environmental quality may even provide a competitive edge if regulations are designed in a way not to ignore this aspect. "Clean" industries may thus create a momentum of their own in favor of environmental improvement.

So far this section has dealt with developments at the national level; at this level there is great diversity within Western Europe. In the affluent North environmental concern, the environmental movement, and citizen participation are considerably developed; things are markedly different not only in the poorer countries of Southern Europe but also in France, Belgium, and Ireland.

The European Community as a political structure offers substantially fewer opportunities for the environmental movement than the more advanced of its member states. Environmental organizations have no right to information; they have no right to be consulted in advance of a measure taken by Community organs, and no right of standing before the European Court of Justice; they can at best file complaints according to articles 173/175 of the European Community Treaty.[13] According to this treaty, the Commission will hear from, consult with, and draw upon the representatives of economic and social life in formulating its proposals. The only groups that are privileged to consultations with and participation in the Community's legislative process are the official representatives of organized business and labor, and sometimes consumers. This reflects not only the goals of the European Community Treaty (promotion of economic growth), but also its understanding of who the important social and economic groups were and are, an understanding marked by the time at which the Treaty was drawn up (i.e., the late 1950s). Environmental organizations practically did not exist at that time; today, however, their membership in the European Community is estimated at some 10 to 20 million, and it makes little sense to ignore them as if nothing had changed since 1958.[14]

Business, labor, and sometimes consumers do have special rights of participation in certain European Community agencies. In fact, environmental organizations are also consulted, but only on an informal basis and usually only when the Commission seeks information or support for specific projects. Environmental lobbies do of course exist, but they find themselves in a weak position: the "radical" environmental groups are kept out entirely, only "cooperative" groups are privileged with good contacts and funds for research.

---

13. This section relies strongly on Krohberger and Hey, op. cit. (footnote 1).

14. Ibidem, p. 5.

The asymmetry with regard to the economic organizations is quite clear.[15] There is, however, one important European Community contribution to the environmentalist political infrastructure: the directive on environmental impact assessments which came into effect in 1988. According to this directive, all major projects likely to have a significant impact on the environment must be assessed and this assessment must be made available to the public before any authorizations are granted.[16] In many countries this directive should improve the status of information available to the public. Another important step would be the creation (discussed for some time now) of a European Environmental Agency. It would probably create an important point of access for the environmental lobbies to Community institutions. And of course, the EC bureaucracy may, in an indirect way, serve as a point of access to the environmental movement. If this movement achieves a favorable regulation in a powerful member country such as Germany, this regulation may be extended to other countries via an EC directive that Germany manages to get passed.

4. Environmental Politics in Eastern Europe

For the last several centuries, Eastern Europe has been a latecomer in terms of intellectual, economic and political modernization.

Industrialization came to these countries (except for Czechoslovakia) with an important delay, and then it came rather suddenly. This is important because a society's ability to deal with the problems of industrialization can only develop alongside with that process. But even after industrialization set in, the environmental learning process was blocked for a long time. Eastern European societies failed to generate an environmentalist response, partly because they were preoccupied with other matters that were more urgent, and partly because the ruling groups had been successful in impeding the constitution of such a response.

---

15. Ludwig Krämer, "Participation of Environmental Organizations in the Activities of the EEC," in Führ and Roller (eds.), op. cit. (footnote 11), pp. 129–140. On marginal innovations in this respect, see *Ökologische Briefe*, September 30, 1992, p. 5, and December 2, 1992, pp. 8–13.

16. See Robert Hull in this volume.

4.1 The Communist Past and Its Handicaps in the Formation of an Environmental Movement

The fact that Eastern Europe was dominated by a Communist power elite had immediate consequences for the environment. This meant a Stalinist type of industrialization, with an emphasis on heavy industry (plus the development of a loyal Communist working class) and an extensive mode of growth that put a strong emphasis on the input volume of natural resources rather than on the efficiency with which those resources could be used to satisfy consumer demand.[17] Communist hegemony also meant the adoption of the Marxist theory of value, according to which human labor is the source of all value; as a practical consequence, natural resources are free. This view leads to a tendency to overuse these resources in production and enhances the commons problem first outlined by Hardin.[18]

While these effects of Communist rule were in some way intentional, other environmental harmful consequences were unintentional. The low efficiency of the centrally managed economies led to further waste of resources (at the same time that it held down growth rates). The low cost of energy (oil and natural gas were provided by the Soviet Union at low prices) encouraged not only energy-intensive industries, but also careless and inefficient use.[19] Finally, the difficulties of Communist regimes in maintaining legitimacy in the face of declining economic performance — particularly from the 1970s until the late 1980s — led to the *mining* of capital investments and of the natural environment. Costs and deficits accumulated as these regimes favored the maintenance of current consumption levels (financed in most cases by foreign borrowing) over long-term strategies of development.

In the social sphere, the results of Communist hegemony were also highly unfavorable to the development of an environmentalist response. While the continuous economic expansion of the 1950s and the 1960s served to greatly reduce ideological and group conflicts in Western societies, thus clearing the

---

17. Frantisek Valenta, "Framework of Economic Reform in Czechoslovakia," in United Nations Economic Commission for Europe, *Economic Reform in the European Centrally Planned Economies,* New York (1989), pp. 20–27.

18. Garrett Hardin, "The Tragedy of the Commons," *Science* no. 162 (1968), pp. 1243–1248; Garrett Hardin and John Baden, *Managing the Commons,* San Francisco (1977); J.M. Kramer, "Environmental Problems in the USSR: The Divergence of Theory and Practice," *Journal of Politics,* vol. 36, no. 4 (1974), pp. 886–899.

19. John M. Kramer, "Eastern Europe and the Energy Shock' of 1990–1991," *Problems of Communism,* vol. 40, no. 3 (1991), pp. 85–96.

way for the emergence of new political issues, no such development took place in Eastern Europe. Political repression dominated public life; economic growth was not so impressive as to provide regimes with strong political legitimacy. Beginning in 1970, decay (political and economic) and bitterness spread visibly. The waves of political mobilization were directed against the most strongly felt problem, i.e., the political repression by the regime. Totalitarian education and propaganda could mobilize some (especially youth) at first, but in due course led to apathy and withdrawal from the public sphere. Only toward the end of the Communist period did new social movements take shape; they are discussed in section 4.2.

A society preoccupied with such basic problems is not a favorable ground for the growth of an environmentalist response. The restrictions on foreign contacts (travel, media, etc.) contributed to this state of affairs. And when the beginning of such a response set in, the Communist regimes did their best to stifle it. They did so by imposing secrecy on environmental data, by restricting the scope of environmentalist activities, and by tightly controlling and frequently infiltrating the respective associations.

Until the early 1980s most East European countries adhered to the official line according to which environmental damage was the result of the capitalist search for profit and therefore did not exist (or at most exceptionally) in socialist societies. In some countries this meant that a veil of secrecy was spread over basic environmental information. This was the case of the more repressive of the East-Central European countries, i.e., East Germany and Czechoslovakia, where secrecy lasted until 1990. To publish such data was clearly an oppositional or subversive activity; it did happen at times. In East Germany opposition came from the Protestant Church; in Czechoslovakia a secret report on the state of the environment by the Czechoslovak Academy of Sciences was published in 1983).[20] In the Soviet Union a similar publication occurred in the *Samisdat* press in 1978; a first national environmental report appeared only in late 1989.[21]

---

20. On East Germany: Horst Förster, "Umweltprobleme und Umweltpolitik in Osteuropa," *Aus Politik und Zeitgeschichte,* no. 10 (1991), pp. 13–25; Christian Koth, "Und wieder stehen wir im Regen," *Politische Ökologie,* August/September (1991), p. 48. On Czechoslovakia: Catherine Albrecht, "Environmental Policies and Politics in Contemporary Czechoslovakia," *Studies in Comparative Communism,* vol. 20, no. 3/4 (1987), pp. 291–302; Rolf Oschlies, "Es lebe der Genosse Jakes — von 1000 Kronen monatlich!" *Forschungsjournal Neue Soziale Bewegungen,* vol. 3, no 2, (1990), pp. 41–48.

21. Hilary F. French, *Green Revolutions. Environmental Reconstruction in Eastern Europe and the Soviet Union,* World Watch Paper no. 99, Washington (1990), p. 5.

Information has been available in Poland since 1980, when the Polish Ecological Club was set up together with the legalization of Solidarity.[22] In Hungary the government tightly controlled the spread of environmental information until the mid-1980s; even afterward (until 1988) it did not give permission to publish a national environmental periodical and harassed the publications of the more informal associations such as the Danube Circle.[23] In Bulgaria, the government developed environmental protection activities quite early on (this included the founding of one of the first ministries of the environment), and in the press environmental issues were openly and competently discussed in the early 1970s. But even so the exact data on pollution in the case of Ruse — the city was probably the single biggest health risk in the area — were kept an official secret until 1987.[24]

Given the scarce availability of information, it is hard to see how an environmental movement could take shape or set targets for itself that would go beyond the local level. (However, somewhat surprisingly, a study by the Hungarian Communist Youth Organization conducted in 1983 showed a rather high level of environmental consciousness in that country plus a remarkable willingness to contribute to solving the problem[25]).

Political restraints were not limited to the spread of information. In Eastern European countries freedom of association was strongly restricted as well. For a specific purpose only one organization was supposed to exist in each country, usually as part of the National Front, i.e., of an organization designed to support the regime. This facilitated political control by the top and inhibited the formation of an environmental movement that could have served as a vehicle for protest, except to the extent that protest was tolerated by the regime or even considered useful by it. (To minimize repression, independent environmental associations claimed to be apolitical — a claim that most Communist regimes accepted in their own interest.)

---

22. John M. Kramer, "Die Umweltkrise in Polen," in H. Schreiber (ed.), *Umweltprobleme in Mittel- und Osteuropa*, Frankfurt (1989), pp. 197–221; Maria Welfens, "Umweltprobleme und Umweltpolitik im Prozeß der Systemtransformation in Polen," in Sylke Nissen (ed.), *Modernisierung nach dem Sozialismus*, Marburg (1992), pp. 83–99; Michael Waller and Frances Millard, "Environmental Politics in Eastern Europe," *Environmental Politics*, vol. 1, no. 2 (1992), pp. 166–167.

23. Hubertus Knabe, "Umweltschutz in Ungarn — Eine Bestandsaufnahme," *Südosteuropa*, vol. 37, no. 10 (1988), pp. 531–557; Gabor Szabo, "The Main Issues of Environmental Management in Hungary," *Mehrwert*, no. 33 (1991), pp. 86–92.

24. Wolf Oschlies, "Schwefelstaub auf Rosenblüten — Zu Umweltproblemen Bulgariens," *Südosteuropa*, vol. 37, no. 7/8 (1988), pp. 360–376.

25. Knabe, op. cit. (footnote 23), p. 549.

In Hungary in 1972 the Patriotic Popular Front organization was established to deal with environmental concerns, and it developed a modest amount of autonomy due to conflicts within the Communist Party. But only in 1988 did the regime give its permission to set up a national Hungarian environmentalist association outside the Popular Front. Other organizations had sprung up earlier (for example, in 1984 the Danube Circle was concerned with the hydro-electric dam projects on that river), but because their status was on the borderline of legality they were harassed with considerable success.[26] In the Czech Republic, the Society for the Protection of Nature (SOP) was never allowed to be a member of the National Front and was also harassed by the Communist regime.[27] The situation was different in Poland where the independent Polish Ecological Club, established in 1980, could attract a great number of professionals (especially technicians); this facilitated the development of expertise, so the Club could not be ignored by the political system.[28] The Club was suppressed during the martial law period, but was reactivated later.

Other factors inhibited the specialization and institutionalization of the environmental movement. Under the Communist system individuals could not press legal claims against the state, and there was (except for Poland) no system of administrative courts. Most environmental legislation was simply ignored by polluters. No suits could normally be brought against these polluters by private citizens; even if this possibility existed on paper, it was usually ineffective in practice, as in Hungary.[29] In Poland, environmental associations enjoyed extensive legal rights but made little use of them against industrial combines. The reason was partly that the relevant associations were controlled by the regime and partly that the rule of law was simply not taken seriously, not by the authorities nor by citizens and associations. Finally, independent organizations such as the Polish Ecological Club lacked the financial and personal resources to make extensive use of costly legal procedures.[30]

---

26. Ibidem, pp. 548–555.

27. Peter Jehlicka and Tomas Kostelecky, "The Greens in Czechoslovakia," Paper presented at the ECPR Joint Sessions 1991, pp. 4–5.

28. Christopher Williams, "From Iron into Green Curtain: The Environmental Crisis in Central and Eastern Europe and the Emerging Green Movements/Parties, 1989–1991," Paper presented at the Conference on "New Perspectives for Social Democracy in Central and Eastern Europe," Brussels, October 1991, p. 8.

29. Andras Sajo, "Participation Rights of Environmental Associations in Hungary," in Führ and Roller (eds.), op. cit. (footnote 11), pp. 57–60.

30. Jerzy Jendroska and Konrad Nowacki, "The Participation Rights of Environ-

In sum, the environmental movement ran into obstacles at every stage of its formation and institutionalization. Lack of information and of freedom of communication hampered the building up of support and membership; lacking freedom of association served as a further handicap. Public interest legal activities were almost nonexistent for lack of legal opportunities and money. Lobbying was difficult because the regimes made great efforts to control and even infiltrate those movements that they could not prevent. Without a large membership the development of specialized research institutions is difficult to imagine. Green parties in turn were incompatible with the constitutions of people's democracies. The environmental movement enjoyed only one advantage which turned out to be quite ephemeral: even if its claims to be apolitical were not really taken seriously by the regime, they were often accepted to "neutralize" this issue. As a result, it was less risky politically to be an environmentalist than to be a member of an opposition party. For this reason much of the opposition to the regimes in place temporarily assembled under the banner of the environment.

It should not be forgotten that Eastern European regimes also passed many pieces of environmental legislation. Often these were ineffectual. At times of extreme economic difficulties production was given clear priority; the shift to brown coal in the 1970s proved a disaster. But some environmental policy innovations were pioneered in Eastern Europe, in particular the system of economic instruments such as taxes and effluent charges. Most of these laws were simply ignored, as described above, or applied in a highly ineffective way. (Ironically these instruments are, in Western Europe, considered typically market-oriented.[31]) In any case they did not provide opportunities for public involvement and generally did not have much effect.[32]

4.2 Problems of Environmental Politics in Eastern Europe Since 1989

In 1989 when the Communist regimes came down across most countries of Eastern Europe, the euphoria that set in also extended to environmental affairs. It seemed then that there would be rapid improvement in this area as in others. In many countries, former activists of the environmental movement

---

mental Associations and their Possibilities of Taking Legal Action in European Perspective," ibidem, pp. 39–56.

31. OECD, *Economic Instruments of Environmental Protection*, Paris (1989).

32. In the United States, by contrast, effluent fees can be enforced by private persons as well. Laura Bulatao, "Citizen Suits under the United States Clean Water Act," in Führ and Roller (eds.), op. cit. (footnote 11), pp. 121–126.

were now in prominent positions; most of the new political leaders had in the recent past at least proclaimed their attachment to environmental values. This gave rise to a considerable flow of environmentalist rhetoric.[33]

There was every reason to be hopeful. The old restrictions on environmental associations had fallen by the wayside. Information about the environment began to flow freely, in most cases even official information, though there were some notable exceptions.[34] Stunning details on environmental damage were revealed, and it seemed unlikely that the former catastrophic course would be continued by the new governments acting under public scrutiny. Western countries took a lively interest in the situation. In the European Community, the World Bank, the European Bank of Reconstruction and Development, and many governments plans for assistance were drawn up and discussed, pledges of aid formulated and (less frequently) actually carried out.[35]

Happy but dangerous illusions also prevailed with regard to the economy. The replacement of the Stalinist pattern of economic development by affluent market economies as in Western Europe was commonly viewed as imminent, and many appeared to think that in a market economy the environmental problems would disappear by themselves. This reasoning ignored the fact that the environmental situation of the Western European countries reflected decades of struggle and the fact that even the highly incomplete accommodation of environmental priorities had often been granted quite reluctantly. Of course some of the greatest abuses of the earlier industrial model were bound to disappear in a market economy that would be based on world market prices for energy and on the termination of subsidies to heavy industry.

The year 1990 brought a grim awakening. With the crisis in Kuwait, the international conditions became harsher. The economic transition to the market economy began to appear quite traumatic. Old problems reasserted themselves, sometimes in new forms; in most cases they demoted the envi-

33. Jiri Pehe, "The Green Movements in Eastern Europe," *Report on Eastern Europe*, no. 11 (March 16, 1990), pp. 35–37; Williams, op. cit. (footnote 28), pp. 2–5; see also Janos Vargha in this volume.

34. In Hungary and Slovakia the new environmental agencies are positively hostile to making information available to the public. Brian Slocock, "Environmental Policy in Eastern Europe: The Emerging Coordinates," Paper presented at the ECPR Joint Sessions 1991, p. 11.

35. Maria Welfens, "Umweltprobleme und Umweltpolitik im Prozeß der Systemtransformation in Polen," in Silke Nissen (ed.), *Modernisierung nach dem Sozialismus,* Marburg (1992), p. 96; Jiri Kosta, "Strategie für einen ökonomischen und ökologischen Umbau in der Tschechoslowakei," ibidem, p. 111.

ronment to a minor issue. The environmental movement itself was depleted both of its leaders and of its membership, its momentum spent; increasingly it faced a hostile milieu. Eastern Europe seemed to slide back to a phase that looked like a mixture between the Great Depression and the first few years after the Second World War as experienced in Western Europe. There were few signs that the issue of the environment would be given a high rank in the near future.

The transition to a market economy proved much more painful than expected. For years most Eastern European regimes had taken out hard currency credits to finance the standard of living and to maintain their own political legitimacy. This practice was now ended. In East Central Europe a new politics of austerity slashed subsidies and held wage increases below the inflation rates which followed price liberalization. For the first time many firms were confronted with the reality of the market. This situation would have been difficult in any case; it was rendered worse by the rapidly rising cost of imported energy (cheap Soviet sources progressively dried up, and deliveries took place now at world market prices), the collapse of trade within the Council of Mutual Economic Assistance (CMEA), the crisis in Kuwait which reduced Western readiness to grant financial aid,[36] and finally the worldwide economic recession which ensued.

Under these circumstances unemployment increased considerably, reaching about 10 percent in Poland and Bulgaria and about 6 percent in Hungary and the former Czech and Slovak Federative Republic (CSFR) by the end of 1991, with substantial increases yet to come as the traditional labor overhang in state-owned enterprises could be expected to be eliminated as a result of privatization and increasing financial constraints.[37] The market economy surely seemed to take care of the environmental problems caused by the heavy industry typical of Stalinist industrialization: by closing down a large part of it. Under Communist regimes unemployment had been almost non-existent and was not a substantial consideration that could be mobilized against environmental policy measures. This changed with the advent of the market economy. Even if most plant closures occur for economic reasons, it is easy to see why workers threatened by such closures turn against environmentalists. This fits with the reports of environmentalist advocates who in

---

36. Volkmar Lauber, "Ostmitteleuropas schwieriger Übergang zu Marktwirtschaft und Demokratie," *SWS-Rundschau*, vol. 32, no. 1 (1992), pp. 3–18.

37. Hubert Gabrisch, et al., Depression and Inflation: Threats to Political and Social Stability, Research Report by the Vienna Institute for Comparative Economic Studies, Vienna (1992), pp. 5–6.

1991 reported low levels of sympathy — and sometimes outright hostility — to their position.[38]

At the same time some Western firms used the dismal economic situation (unemployment, foreign indebtedness, lack of funds) in Eastern European countries to plan investments in the area which they could not easily have placed at home because of public opposition there. This applied particularly to nuclear power. Despite the fact that energy (and electricity) demand was likely to shrink and later stagnate over the coming decade because of unrealistically low prices and extreme inefficiencies of energy use in the past, the Western nuclear energy lobby made a strong push for expansion into Eastern Europe. In a heavy-handed propaganda campaign it painted the grim picture of an energy gap that in all likelihood (even in the judgment of the World Bank) does not exist.[39] In this effort the Western nuclear lobby benefited from its Eastern European counterpart (often holdovers from the communist past) and from the relative ignorance of the populations (and often policy-makers) who had no knowledge of the energy efficiency potential, but much experience with dirty coal technology and perhaps a strong faith in the superiority of Western technology.

These economic problems created unfavorable conditions for the emergence of the environmental issue; other problems seemed of greater urgency. This takes us to the role played by the Eastern European citizens and societies. Given the economic, political, and social upheavals, it would in any case have been difficult for environmental issues to occupy a top place on the Eastern European agenda for very long. The political and economic constitutions of these countries were and are being worked out; economic interests were unleashed through privatization and the market economy (in this respect the transition resembled a gigantic game of Monopoly); national passions are breaking loose in some cases; old values and practices are crumbling. The most common individual reaction seems to be to limit one's horizon to the private world, to try to salvage or improve one's economic position, and if possible to satisfy the pent-up desire for a Western standard of

---

38. In the heavily polluted Katowice area of Poland environmental activists linked to Solidarity could no longer visit factories because the work force was so hostile to them. A similar situation currently prevails in Slovakia, whose economy is based to a large extent on Stalinist industrialization; anti-environmentalism there combines with nationalism. Slocock, op. cit. (footnote 34), p. 10; Duncan Fisher, "Toward a Pan-European Approach to Environmental Protection," *Ecological Studies Institute/East West Environment Programme,* London (1991), pp. 4–6; and Peter Hardi in this volume.

39. Fisher, op. cit. (footnote 38), pp. 4–7.

living.[40] There are parallels here to Western European societies in the years that followed the two World Wars.

In addition, Eastern Europe had little experience of democratic political life even before World War II. This was reinforced by decades of Communist rule, which left behind an inheritance of public passivity and sometimes distrust, few autonomous associations, and a lack of enterprise in all areas (not just the economy). The faculty of social imagination — the ability to project alternatives, an important precondition of the new social movements — seems to be strangely afflicted. Perhaps it is the exhaustion which follows the excitement of the transition and the disappointment in the face of the economic disaster after such high expectations.

Finally, there are problems specific to the environmental movement. As already mentioned, many of its leaders joined other parties and often took on important positions in government or in bureaucracies unrelated to the environment. Those who stayed placed much effort in setting up green parties which usually fared poorly at the polls. Surprisingly, green parties were relatively successful in some of the poorest countries: in Bulgaria (where an environmental movement had been implanted for some time[41]), and in Romania (in the 1990 elections). The Bulgarian parliament counted 32 green deputies (out of 400) in April 1991, in Romania two green organizations achieved between them 4.2 percent of the votes.[42] In the CSFR by contrast the green vote hovered a little over 3 percent in the June 1990 elections (for the Czech and Slovak national councils and for the federal assembly), but was slashed in half at the local elections in November 1990.[43] In Hungary (elections in March/April 1990), the green vote amounted to only 0.36 percent.[44] In Bulgaria, Czechoslovakia, Hungary, and Poland green themes were frequently

40. Bernd Baumgartl, "Environmental Protest as a Vehicle for Transition: The Case of Eco-Glasnost in Bulgaria," in Pal Kamas and Aanna Vari (eds.), *Environment and Democratic Transition: Policy and Politics in Central and Eastern Europe*, forthcoming; Tom Atlee, "Notes on Czechoslovakian Grassroots Activism," Mimeographed paper, May–July 1991.

41. Baumgartl, op. cit. (footnote 40); Oschlies, op. cit. (footnote 24).

42. Tom Gallagher, "Romania: The Disputed Election of 1990," *Parliamentary Affairs*, vol. 44, no. 1 (1991), pp. 79–93; Williams, op. cit. (footnote 28), pp. 5 and 10.

43. Jehlicka and Kostelecky, op. cit. (footnote 27), pp. 17; Gordon Wightman, "The Collapse of Communist Rule in Czechoslovakia and the June 1990 Parliamentary Elections," *Parliamentary Affairs*, vol. 44, no. 1 (1991), pp. 94–113.

44. Williams, op. cit. (footnote 28), p. 8.

picked up by at least some of the other parties, which may help to explain the relatively poor showing of the greens.[45]

But was it really a poor showing? After all, green parties in Western Europe, where the environmental movement is much more strongly implanted, are not always in greatly different positions. But there is a question of the usefulness of investing so much effort in the building of (often competing) political parties rather than trying to institutionalize the environmental movement outside the electoral arena, or tackling specific issues where environmental improvements are technically within reach and make sense economically. The most obvious example of such an issue is energy policy, where serious improvements in efficiency combined with the phasing out of heavy industry could strongly reduce consumption levels. (Most official policy supported by Western European lobbies seems to prefer a shift to nuclear power.) However, it may be that the environmental movement is simply not sufficiently prepared (in terms of knowledge, penetration, and so on) to take on such issues.

4.3   Environmentalism from Above?

This takes us to a more general point. Environmental politics in Eastern Europe receives its impulses not only or even primarily from civil society and an environmental movement, but also to a large extent from outside the area, in particular from Western Europe. In part this is due to concern there over transboundary pollution (especially airborne). The possibility of European Community membership for Hungary, Poland, and the Czech (perhaps also the Slovak) Republic serves already to orient environmental regulations in those countries. EC labor organizations have a natural interest in harmonizing regulations in order to prevent a massive exodus of certain productions to the East, where labor is much cheaper. For industrial enterprises the situation is less clear: tightening up regulatory standards in Eastern Europe protects against environmental "dumping"; on the other hand, loose regulations also have their advantages for businesses desirous to move there.

Given the financial weakness of Eastern European countries combined with the political weakness of their domestic environmental movement, it may well be that Western governments and industrial enterprises have a decisive influence on the decisions concerning the future of the environment in Eastern Europe.[46]

---

45. Ibidem; Waller and Millard, op. cit. (footnote 22), pp. 168–172.

46. Brian Slocock, "Umweltpolitik und politischer Wandel in Osteuropa," in Nissen (ed.), op. cit. (footnote 35), pp. 60–61.

If environmental policy is initiated from abroad and/or from above, its priorities may not correspond to those of the domestic environmental movements. This may make for even more difficult relationships between governmental bureaucracies and activists and is likely to inhibit the development of points of access to the political system, depriving environmental policy of a considerable source of strength and inspiration.

5. Comparisons and Conclusion

This review of environmental politics in Europe, both West and East, points out important differences. In Western Europe the environmental movement started at a time of great economic and political strength, a time when these countries enjoyed high levels of affluence and security. Environmental discomfort was felt early on because many traditional problems had faded away, thus clearing the deck. The 1974 oil crisis sharpened the issue and furthered the spontaneous development of the environmental movement, at a time of marked expansion of political participation characterized by self-confidence and a new ethics of commitment. Increasing institutionalization led to the formulation of alternative paths to modernization and eventually to significant reforms, which opened the making of environmental policy to a variety of "green" impulses that regularly originate in those societies.

As a result of both the market and environmental politics and policies, Western European societies became much more efficient in their use of natural resources per unit of GDP. However, as their economic expansion continued almost without interruption, the net effect of greater efficiency in resource use was often counterbalanced. Still, as societies became more knowledgeable about the environmental consequences of their activities, this theme was increasingly treated as a serious issue, and there were (and are) efforts — both national and international — to prevent further deterioration. But even though progress was achieved in specific areas, many trends still point in the wrong direction, and there is little political willingness to take decisive action. Western societies may call for environmental improvement, but they also insist on a high level of consumption. The end result of the environmental movement's efforts may well be a pattern of economic development oriented toward increasing personal comfort rather than sustainability.

The situation in Eastern Europe is quite different in many respects. There is no indication that social tensions there decreased in the postwar decades as they did in Western Europe, and the basic problems intensified considerably after 1989. Even though environmental discomfort was and is much more intense in the East than in the West and even takes the form of shortened life expectancies, this did not lead to a significant response from environmental groups. To begin with, information about dangers and damages and knowledge of other possibilities of development were for decades systematically suppressed by the regime, and the constitution of an environmental movement as well as its differentiation severely inhibited. As a result huge problems built up, problems that left their heritage not only on the landscape but also in political institutions and in the very psychology of Eastern European populations. The year 1989 seemed to offer a chance for an environmental break-through; but after a brief euphoria came a very serious setback. The environmental movement, with only a narrow basis of support in civil society, was soon submerged by the political and economic upheaval, and it is hard to predict whether or when it will reemerge. It seems quite likely that East European environmental politics will not be marked for some time by a grassroots movement that could draw on the strength of popular participation. Under current conditions environmentalists in Eastern Europe have little reason for self-confidence; withdrawal and bitterness are more likely. Policy is likely to be initiated from above (and from abroad) and to imitate Western European developments with a certain time lag. Chances are slim for an innovative policy. The environmental movement will not become a powerful actor in the formulation of public policy for some time, and there is no other domestic actor in view to take up the environmental cause.

Eastern Europe is likely to acquire additional environmental problems while moderating those it already has. Undoubtedly Western "mistakes" in the production of affluence will be repeated; in addition, there may be a transfer of polluting industries to the East. On the whole, Eastern European development is likely to follow the example of Western Europe, with considerable delay but with all the environmental problems attached. It is unlikely that these countries will discover a shortcut to the situation now achieved in Western Europe, much less to sustainable development.

Will it be possible to reach sustainable development in societies dedicated, in their economic and political institutions, to the maximization of personal affluence defined as a high level of material per capita consumption? There is reason to remain skeptical. In Western Europe the elements that press for an ecologically sound development are definitely better placed than in the East. But even in Western Europe, current trends do not correspond to a pattern of sustainable development, and the changes currently contemplated as a result of environmental pressure do not seem sufficient to alter this pattern.

19

Domestic Environmental Politics in a Comparative Perspective: The Italian Case

Maria Berrini

It is very difficult to consider Mediterranean countries as a unity, especially from the point of view of environmental policies. All of the Mediterranean countries have long coastlines that face the Mediterranean basin, and they have mild weather, but they also are very different from one another. France and Italy have two opposite institutional systems: the former strong, efficient, and very centralized; the latter inefficient and decentralized. Greece and Spain have economic systems very different from the others, and they are new members of the EC. France has chosen nuclear power as a primary energy source; Italy, through a referendum, has refused nuclear power. In this area, Italy represents a specific "style" of environmental policy in Europe, which is discussed in a comparative perspective in this chapter.

1. The Context

Like other Western European nations in the 1950s, Italy's economic growth accelerated. Industrial development such as chemical, steel, and cement plants was mainly concentrated in the northern part of the country. Large industrial plants and infrastructural projects such as highways, dams, and power plants were promoted by Italy's central government to foster development in specific regions, especially in the southern part of the country. But the large development projects in the south did not promote the spread of economic activities, and southern Italy remained largely undeveloped compared with the rest of the country.

During the 1960s, a large number of small and medium-sized factories, often with fewer than 100 workers, in northern and central Italy experienced the "economic miracle." The speed of the economic transformation was astonishing (Table 19.1).

The "success" of Italy's economic transformation and its total lack of environmental policy in these years has caused a steep, nationwide decline in environmental quality. Pollution has increased from industries, power plants, traffic, tourism, and mechanized agriculture. Some examples are given in the following sections.

1.1 Quality of Water

Many of the industrial plants in Italy are highly polluting. For example, 70 percent of the world's total production of ceramic tile is concentrated in a 50-kilometer area near Modena, which now suffers from serious water (and air) pollution. Numerous leather tanneries in three northern and central regions also contribute to water and air pollution. Heavy industries such as petrochemical and steel production have spoiled the landscape and polluted the water along the coasts where many plants are located. Underground water is heavily polluted by agrochemicals such as nitrates and pesticides (Table 19.2).

TABLE 19.1

Employment in Economic Sectors in Italy
(1952 and 1987)

	Agriculture	Industry	Other Sectors
1952	42%	31%	27%
1987	10%	33%	57%

Source: Statistics Institute Italy, Rome 1988.

TABLE 19.2

**Towns and Residents Affected by Water Pollution
from Herbicide and Nitrate in 1989**

Regions	Herbicide Towns	Habitants	Nitrate Towns
Lombardia	79	309.609	39
Veneto	95	441.066	35
Marche	48	425.157	30
Piemonte	52	257.013	58
Emilia Romagna	23	339.025	0

Source: Ambiente Italia 1991, Rome 1991.

TABLE 19.3

Coastal Water Quality (1991)

Regions	Total Extension of Not Analyzed Coast (km)	Coast Where Bathing Is Not Allowed of Analyzed Coast (km)	(%)
Liguria	25.90	77.60	22.69
Toscana	212.10	24.60	4.30
Lazio	47.80	107.10	32.66
Campania	0.10	181.00	38.11
Calabria	231.80	31.40	4.52
Basilicata	27.10	1.60	2.68
Puglia	108.80	61.30	7.66
Molise	4.50	0.90	2.77
Abruzzo	13.90	10.70	8.09
Marche	9.80	35.40	20.40
Em.Romagna	2.00	34.00	25.47
Veneto	84.00	16.50	8.72
Friuli V.G.	2.20	59.10	55.29
Sicilia	499.30	229.30	22.06
Sardegna	508.30	245.90	15.01
Tot. Italia	1,777.60	1,116.40	16.62

Source: Ministry of Health, Rome 1992.

The coastal waters are too polluted for swimming (Table 19.3) and not well monitored.

1.2 Quality of Life in Urban Areas

Vehicle traffic is one of the most serious contributors to air pollution in urban areas. Table 19.4 lists several economic sectors and their contribution to air pollution in Italy.

The few existing monitoring networks managed by environmental associations have found that pollution often rises well above quality standards, and vehicles contribute the most emissions.

Figure 19.1 shows hydrocarbon and lead concentrations in air in many cities. The data were collected by Treno Verde (Green Train), a monitoring campaign sponsored by Lega per l'Ambiente. Figure 19.2 shows noise levels in urban areas.

TABLE 19.4

Estimated Contributions to Air Pollution in Italy
(by Sector)

Sector	Sulfur Oxides	Nitrogen Oxides	Carbon Monoxide (%)	Parti- culates	Volatile Organic Compounds
Industry	30	12	1.6	12	1.0
Transportation	4	51	90.6	56	87.0
Residential	7	5	4.7	11	5.8
Power plants	58	27	0.4	14	0.9
Agriculture	1	5	2.7	7	5.3
Total contributions (in tons)	2,074	1,569	5,570	412	768

Source: Ministry of Environment, Rome 1989.

FIGURE 19.1

Air Pollution

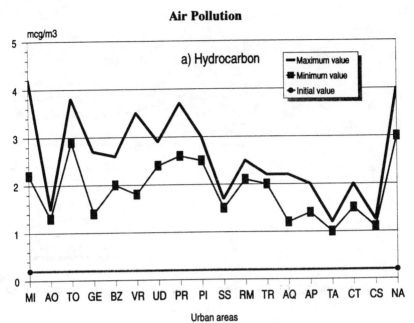

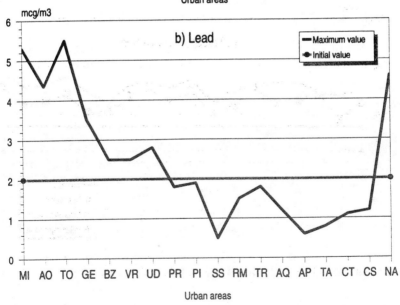

Legend on p. 277.
Source: Ambiente Italia 1991.

276

FIGURE 19.2

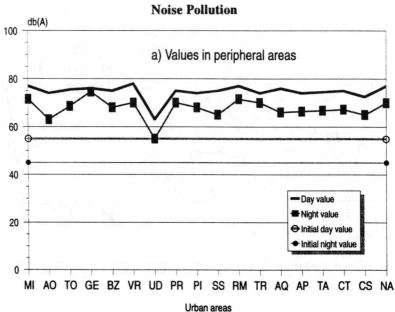

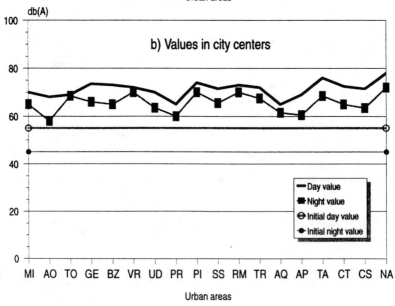

Legend on p. 277.
Source: Ambiente Italia 1991.

Legend for Fig. 19.1 and 19.2:

MI	Milano	UD	Udine	AQ	L'Aquila
AO	Aosta	PR	Parma	AP	Ascoli Pileno
TO	Torino	PI	Pisa	TA	Taormina
GE	Genova	SS	Sassari	CT	Catania
BZ	Bolzano	RM	Roma	CS	Caserta
VR	Varese	TR	Trapani	NA	Napoli

1.3 Conservation of Landscape and Natural Areas

Intensive urbanization has destroyed many important areas. For example, the per capita consumption of cement in Italy is three times higher than that of the United States, West Germany, or Great Britain. Built-up areas increased from 120,000 square kilometers in 1961 to 260,000 in 1986 and now occupy about 9 percent of the national territory. In the Po valley (the most fertile soil in Italy), 0.6 percent of the farmland disappears every year. Soil erosion is severe in many places, and landslides (about 3,000 every year) are caused by poor agricultural management. Construction has increased along the coast because of the tourist industry, especially along the North Adriatic Sea. Since 1960, beaches have been eroded along 50 percent of the 8,000-kilometers Italian coastline, largely because of human activities that have modified sea currents.

2. Environmental Policy

2.1 Delay and Inefficiency

Until 1986, there were no serious efforts to define environmental policies in Italy. More than 20 years were spent trying to establish a good legislative framework. The first law to address the air pollution problem was enacted in the late 1960s; the next law was established in 1976 and dealt with water pollution. In the following years urban wastes, sea protection, and detergent biodegradability were treated. Only recently has Italy enacted legislation on industrial risks, soil protection, national parks, and energy saving.

The Ministry of Environment was established in 1986, and in 1989 and 1992 it published the first and second "Report on Environmental Quality in Italy." Actually Italy does not have any national plan for environment, as suggested by the UNCED Conference in Rio in 1992.

But the main problem in Italy (as in other countries) is political ineffi-
ciency. There are many indicators of this: deficient implementations of environment policy, inefficient laws and standards, and lack of public funds. For
example, Italy is far behind in adopting EC directives; national and regional
governments spend less than half of the money they have on environmental
problems; less than 40 percent of Italy's polluted water is managed properly.
The following section gives reasons for this.

2.2   The Causes

Italy has a regulatory approach based on fixed nationwide emission standards and not on environmental standards and preventive tools. For example,
of the total budget for environmental protection 60 percent is spent on conservation (hydrogeologic protection), 35 percent on emissions reductions
(water treatment), and only 5 percent on prevention (energy conservation).

This is an old approach, exceeded by EC legislative framework. The weak
public structures have to manage a very hard system of "command and control," and it is very difficult to achieve good results. However, evidence shows
that when a decision was made to avoid some pollutants or to change some
technologies, the results were better.

In addition, in many areas with a great concentration of pollutant sources,
emission standards are not enough to protect the quality of life. "End of the
pipe" policies cost more, require more maintenance, and often create conflicts with the local population.

In this way, the government often has to react to "emergencies" (illegal
landfill, eutrophication, pesticides in drinkable water), spending a lot of
money and making bad choices, due to the lack of time for studying better
solutions. Recent political scandals in Italy have shown that many actions,
negative for the environment, were linked to corruption of public administrators (bad realization of roads, landfill, etc.).

Another problem is the lack of a defined role for local and regional authorities. Very often regions do not develop their tasks (regional plans on
water or wastes, for example). In addition, the central government does not
define its programs and guidelines, and it does not exercise strong control
over regions. A verification system is nonexistent: often the central government distributes money without studying the needs of an intervention and
without verifying the results.

Italy has no economic tool for environmental policies: for example, there
are no ecological taxes (the price for petrol is high, but not for environmental

reasons). Water and electricity consumption are not controlled by progressive prices.

Furthermore environmental politics is still separated from main stream politics. There is no expertise to determine other relevant policies as for transportation, agriculture, energy, land use, and so on. For example, while the Italian Minister of Environment attempts to introduce policies to reduce CO_2, the National Energy Plan expects an increase in emissions (Figure 19.3).

Nevertheless, action has been taken, but slowly. The Minister of Environment is working on a ten-year plan that would define some constraints, but its real power is not clear.

FIGURE 19.3

CO_2 Emissions Expected by National Energy Plan 1988

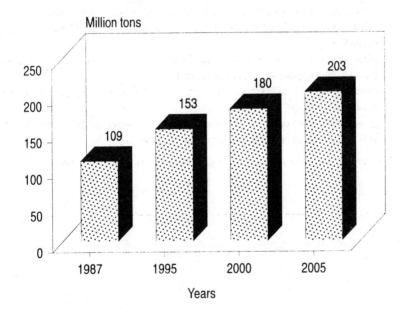

Source: G. Silvestrini, "Effetto Serra," *Ambiente Italia,* Rome 1990.

3. Perspectives

It is difficult to know whether environmental protection is becoming a main issue in Italian policies. The green movement has not received much support in recent elections. Nevertheless, Italy must accept EC regulations, including its environmental constraints. In addition, environmental concerns are felt by the public and there is great opportunity for a new green consumerism.

The main proposals coming from the ecological movement that can contribute environmental policies are:

— move toward a real preventive framework (in laws, budget, plans);
— develop more software and orgware (information system, plans, and management capacities);
— define specific targets (environmental standards or global reduction of pollutants), plan priorities, implement actions, and verify results;
— adopt other tools (ecological taxes, incentives, educational systems, ecolabels);
— give power to new authorities defined by recent laws (river basin authority, metropolitan areas authority);
— develop a control system of "other" policies or implement a real ecodevelopment;
— guarantee participation (Environmental Impact Assessment [EIA] procedure on plans and projects, audit procedure).

And, of course, develop environmental cooperation in Europe.

20

Environmental Policy:
The Case of Austria

Otmar Höll

1. Introduction

The main threats to the global environment requiring international attention and action may conventionally be grouped into the following five problem areas: green house gas induced climatic change; destruction of the stratospheric ozone layer; acidification of terrestrial and aquatic ecosystems; deforestation and degradation of land; pollution and toxification of air and water. They are all linked to one another in a very complex way.

It should be noted that at the time when the concern for the global environment was beginning to be established in the industrialized world, some three decades ago, in Austria this concern was only devoted to some specific areas like local air pollution, water/lake pollution, or soil degradation. Traditionally the protection of nature and the environment has primarily been considered a governmental task in Austria.

Today, the environmental situation of Austria is still rather comfortable compared with most European countries. Austria still possesses relatively intact and extensive environmental resources which include substantial bodies of water and forests. But this environmental richness is highly endangered. The geographical location of Austria in Central Europe, within a moderate and varied climatic zone, means a rich and great variety of fauna

I would like to thank Harald Glatz, Josef Hackl, and Andreas Molin for their fruitful comments. Any shortcomings of the article obviously are my own responsibility.

and flora; however, because of its location Austria also receives an extensive amount of pollution from abroad, which is especially true for its northern and eastern parts (cf. Figure 20.1).

The overall record of Austria's environmental policies is ambiguous. For twenty years, the environmental policy has scarcely progressed beyond fluctuating promises and reforms. The "social partnership," the typical Austrian method of political conflict resolution is one of the main reasons that only partially positive results have been achieved.[1]

FIGURE 20.1

Import-Export Balance of Sulfur Compounds for Austria
(overall deposition 1991 in 1,000 t sulfur)

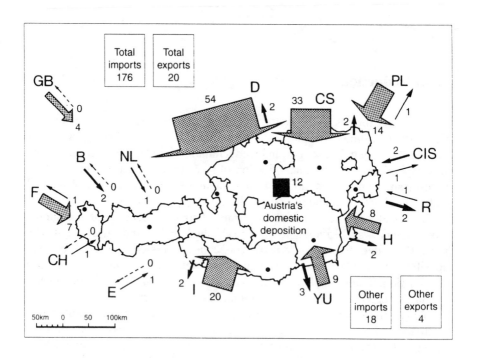

Source: Federal Environmental Agency, Vienna 1993.

1. Comprehensive appraisals of the Austrian system of social-partnership is given by Peter Gerlich et al. (eds.), *Sozialpartnerschaft in der Krise*, Vienna (1985); and Anton Pelinka, *Sozialpartnerschaft und Interessenverbände*, Vienna (1986).

In addition, because of the federal character of the Austrian Constitution, considerable parts of the environmental legislative and executive powers rest with the Austrian provinces: environmental policy in Austria is still a cross-sectional matter (*Querschnittsmaterie* — legislative and executive competences are divided among different federal ministries or partly belong to the provincial parliaments and governments unless expressly included in Articles 10–15 of the Austrian Constitution).[2] Amendments to the Constitution in 1983 and 1988 strengthened the position of the federal government; but the protection of nature and regional planning remained with the provincial governments. This legal split makes it difficult for environmental problems to be managed through political measures.[3]

However, within the European context, the Austrian environmental policy record during the past two decades has been relatively remarkable.[4] During the last two decades, numerous legal measures, including a restriction on the sulfur content of heating oil and diesel fuel and regulations on industrial plants' emissions have been successfully implemented. But Austria's environmental status depends also heavily on the environmental policies of neighboring and other European countries. As a consequence, international cooperation in environmental matters has become of great importance.

2. Historical Development of Environmental Concern

In more advanced industrialized countries and regions like the US, Japan, and Scandinavia, measures for the protection of the environment were already taken during the 1960s and early 1970s, whereas in Austria during this first period such measures were just being considered or at most reaching the planning stage. During this time hardly any environmental awareness in the present sense of the term existed, but the negative impacts of a booming

---

2. For the legal aspects of Austrian environmental politics cf. Bernhard Raschauer, *Umweltschutzrecht*, Vienna/Cologne/Graz (1988).

3. Cf. Hans-Peter Dürr, "Problems of Environmental Cooperation in Europe: A Non-Governmental View," in Markus Jachtenfuchs and Michael Strübel (eds.), *Environmental Policy in Europe*, Baden-Baden (1992), pp. 57–67.

4. Cf. e.g., Martin Jänicke, "Conditions for Environmental Policy Success: An International Comparison," in Jachtenfuchs and Strübel (eds.), op. cit. (footnote 3), p. 82; cf. also the British daily newspaper "The Independent" of December 16, 1993: according to OECD statistics on environmental protection Austria ranges first among 21 OECD countries.

economy and of technical progress (noise, pollution, emission, etc.) were observed by the public.

The postwar reconstruction period of the Austrian economy ended in the late 1960s, and a phase of delayed social reform under the first Social Democratic government started in the early 1970s. Environmental problems became clearly discernible in a number of sectors. They became especially evident in the deterioration of the water quality in the lakes and in the degradation of the forests. Environmental policy was eventually recognized as a field of governmental action to improve living conditions of the population as a whole and was part of an overall reformist strategy of the Social Democratic Party in power. In addition, the global economic crisis reaching Austria in the late 1970s, slowed down the process of taking effective measures for the protection of the environment.

Two major events were of prime importance for the environmental policy of the 1970s: First, as an indirect result of the first environmental conference of the United Nations in Stockholm in 1972 (UN-Conference on Human Environment) some institutional foundations were laid at the national level, the core of which was the setting up of the "Federal Ministry of Health and Environmental Protection." Measures, however, were still taken primarily by other ministries like the Ministry of Agriculture which applied the Forestry Code in 1975 and measures for the improvement of the water quality of lakes and rivers. Measures to decrease the sulfur content in petroleum were taken by the then Ministry of Trade and Industry, in the Industrial Code of 1973, and in the Mining Code. Environmental panel prohibitions within the framework of the 1975 Criminal Law became possible for the very first time. As a consequence of the two oil crises of the 1970s, Austria was able to cut down the increase in energy consumption in the period between 1976 and 1990 to a yearly average of 0.3 percent while achieving an annual average economic growth of 1.8 percent; in the same period, industrial production growth was disengaged from overall economic growth through the abandonment of energy-intensive methods and investment in modern plants. Industrial production increased by approximately 70 percent whereas energy consumption rose by nearly 5.3 percent (Federal Chamber of Commerce, 1991).

Second, the Parliament passed the Nuclear Ban Law in 1978 as a consequence of the negative result of the so-called Zwentendorf-Referendum of November 1978, when a narrow majority voted against the opening of the first nuclear power station in Zwentendorf near Vienna. The anti-Zwentendorf campaign later proved to become the starting point for the formation of environmentalist groups throughout Austria. From the time of the anti-Zwentendorf campaign a clear trend was created toward greater ecological awareness in all parts of the political public, as well as the beginning of a coherent environmentalist movement.[5] From 1980 to 1986, increasingly serious environmental problems became obvious. The local deterioration of air quality in specific areas in Austria, the spread of "new forms" of damage in forests over large areas (located far from the noxious emission sources), and the increasing effects of heavy transit traffic led to a very distinct polarization of the public discussion (e.g., the Hainburg conflict). Several important legislative measures were taken.

In 1980 the *Dampfkessel-Emissionsgesetz* (Steam Generator Emission Law) was passed; this law was in effect until the end of the Small Coalition Government of the Social Democratic Party of Austria (SPÖ) and the Freedom Party (FPÖ), from 1983 to 1986. In this period, the impact of growing pollution from internal and external sources became more and more visible. For example, sulfur emissions brought new forms of damage to forests and nitrogen fertilizers endangered rural land and subsoil water sources. Some 35 acres of arable land were lost daily in this period due to erosion, highway construction, forest roads, building of houses, etc. (*Environmental Report of the Austrian Statistical Agency and the Austrian Federal Environmental Agency*, 1991, p. 167). Political grass-root groups in favour of environmental measures increased pressure at the end of this period, as in most countries of the world, by protests against the common pattern of industrial development, or at least against its effects. For the first time ever, parts of the environmental movement were constituted as a political party and were elected to the local and provincial political bodies before being finally recognized at the parliamentary level in 1986. This transition of the environmental movement to an institutionalized, democratic participant in the Austrian political system marked a turning point of the Austrian political culture. This process forced the established parties to seriously consider ecological issues within their own programs.[6] Ongoing damage to the forests (which was extensively discussed in the mass media), the Hainburg controversy (environmental groups together with parts of the middle and upper strata of society protested against the construction of a hydroelectric power station which would destroy some of the most beautiful parts of the Danube wetland east of Vienna), and the Chernobyl nuclear disaster in April 1986 led to growing public pressure on the government. The Hainburg conflict caused enormous tension also within the two powerful political parties, i.e., the Social Democrats and the Austrian People's Party, between their respective economic sections (the trade unions

---

5. Cf. Herbert Gottweis, "Neue soziale Bewegungen in Österreich," in Herbert Dachs et al. (eds.), *Handbuch des politischen Systems Österreichs*, Vienna (1991), p. 315.

6. Cf. Volkmar Lauber, "Umweltpolitik," in Dachs et al. (eds.), op. cit. (footnote 5), p. 560.

and the union of industrialists) and the "green factions" of these parties. This conflict led to a more autonomous stance in the fields of energy and environmental politics of the parties and to a noticeable weakening of their open identification with the positions of "their" respective interest group.

During the 1980–1986 period a number of legal measures were taken, particularly beginning in 1984. This was especially evident in the enactment of the Clean Air and Water Protection Regulations (including a restriction on the sulfur content of heating oil and diesel fuel, regulations on steam boilers and boiler plants) and the Waste Disposal Law of 1983, the introduction of US emission standards for cars (catalytical converters) in 1985, and above all the incorporation in the federal constitution of the federal government's commitment to protect the environment (Article 10,1 in 1984).

For the first time during this period direct and intrusive measures affecting privacy and property rights were regarded as necessary for the protection of the environment. Environmental taxes were considered for the first time, but not levied. The environmental administration was extended, and the creation of the Environmental Fund in 1983 (financial means for environmentally sound investments) and of the Austrian Federal Environmental Agency (*Umweltbundesamt*) in 1985, which is closely related to the Ministry of Environment, was an important step in support of the ministry with scientific expertise. A number of other institutions (research institutions and funds) were partly restructured to stimulate environmental research, although shifts in funds and projects were not emphasized.[7] Traditional research institutions, such as the *Österreichische Forschungsstiftung Seibersdorf,* the *Forschungsgesellschaft Joanneum*, showed a rising propensity to invest in projects concerned with environmental problems, and new institutions, such as the Austrian Institute for Ecology and the Center for Protection of the Environment and Nature were established. However, considering the comparatively small amount of money which these institutions have had at their disposal it is clear that their role to stimulate environmental research and to increase environmental awareness was limited, and remains so today.

Austria's international cooperation took place within the respective international organizations (e.g., the ECE-LRTAP was signed in 1979 and ratified in 1983); at the bilateral level with the conclusion of environmental treaties (1985 with Hungary); and at the multilateral level (the Danube Declaration in 1985).[8] Austria also had a central role in finalizing the Vienna Convention

---

7.   Cf. ICCR-Project CT-Research, Responsiveness of Scientific and Technological Institutions to Environmental Changes: The Austrian Case, Vienna 1991, p. 17 ff.

8.   The Austrian Environmental Foreign Policy of the 1970s and 1980s is well covered in a doctoral thesis by Klaus Christian Martischnig, *Österreichs umweltpolitische Aktivitäten im bilateralen und multilateralen Bereich: Seine Zusam-*

and — later on — the Montreal Protocol on the protection of the ozone layer and in other multilateral agreements.[9]

During the fourth phase (1987 till now), an ever-growing interest of the Austrian public in ecological issues has developed. This period began with the establishment of a new Great Coalition Government between the SPÖ and ÖVP (with a declared policy of joining the EC), the entrance of the Greens into Parliament for the first time (with six representatives out of 183), and the appointment of an environmentally active woman as Minister of the Environment, Youth, and Family. The staff for environmental affairs was increased and the environmental agenda of the ministry was considerably expanded to include the fields of hazardous waste and atmospheric pollution.

New legislative measures were taken, especially in the field of hazardous waste, chemicals, smog alert, and truck transport on special transit routes during night time. In the electoral campaign of 1990 both powerful parties published new programs, in which environmental issues were of prime importance. The ongoing international discussion about the green house effect and climate change had a considerable impact on their political programs and strategies. The Social Democratic Party underlined the necessity of an "ecologically sound restructuring of industrialized societies," and the People's Party called for the establishment of an "eco-social market economy." Most important was the discussion about new economic instruments to overcome environmental problems through environmental taxes. Taxes could function as a framework for market forces, they are bureaucratically "cheap" and function as incentives for technological and organizational innovation. But the social partners were against taxes especially on energy resources because — as they pointed out — there was the problem of international competitiveness which would have affected the Austrian economy. Although Austria often in its own view wants to be an international protagonist of environmental measures parts of the government and some political factions inside the parties frequently argue against an Austrian "Alleingang" (go-it-alone policy).

At the international level, Austria concluded several bilateral environmental treaties with Central European countries, took over the chair of the environmental working group in the Hexagonale (now Central European

---

menarbeit mit den Nachbarstaaten und die Tätigkeit im internationalen Rahmen, University of Salzburg (1990).

9.   Cf. Winfried Lang, "Negotiations on the Environment," in Viktor Kremenyuk (ed.), International Negotiations. Analysis, Approaches, Issues, San Francisco-Oxford (1991), pp. 343–356.

Initiative — CEI, cf. Chapter 13 of this book) and again played an active role in the elaboration and negotiating processes for the Montreal Protocol.

3. Assessment of Results

3.1 Air Pollution

In previous decades investigations were carried out on forest damage from atmospheric pollution such as sulfur dioxide and hydrogen fluoride in the vicinity of industrial emitters. Massive damage was registered in the nearby forests. However, in the mid-1970s the air-quality standards established for SO_2 provided the impetus for reducing SO_2 and other emissions throughout Austria in a comprehensive manner. Thus since the early 1980s numerous legal measures have been partly successful in achieving a reduction of emissions.

SO_2 emissions were drastically decreased from about 195,000 tons in 1980 to approximately 49,000 tons in 1990 (cf. Table 20.1). Because of long-range transfer of air-polluting substances, however, the sulfur content of rain remains more or less the same. Austria is a heavy net importer of sulfur emissions (cf. also Figure 20.1).

Dust emissions (particulate matter) decreased during the 1980s by almost about 50 percent. Further decreases will be more difficult.

NO_x emissions decreased only less than 10 percent due to reductions of emissions by private cars and heavy industrial polluters. Motorized traffic (especially with trucks and buses) has steadily been increasing. The declared goal of 50 percent of NO_x emissions by the year 2000 will not be achieved if more effective measures are not taken.

VOC emissions have increased by almost one-fourth between 1980 and 1990. During the summer, Austria has the highest concentrations of tropospheric ozone in Western Europe. However, guidelines have been established to help cut emissions by 50 percent by the year 2000.

CFCs in propellants have been banned since 1990. A total phaseout of the use of CFCs is scheduled for 1995.

The per capita output of CO_2 in Austria is approximately 7.2 tons per year, which is the European average. The government has committed itself in the 1990 Energy Report, to a 20 percent reduction by the year 2005 provided sufficient measures are being taken and provided measures are economically feasible. The increased use of nuclear energy as a means of reducing CO_2 emissions is not seen as an acceptable alternative. Considering the global

TABLE 20.1

Balance of the Emissions of Air Pollutants 1980–1990
(values in 1,000 t)

	SO_2	NO_x	VOC	CO	CO_2[a]	Particulate Matter
1980	195	233	366	1.268	58.480	75
1983	116	228	380	1.180	51.914	68
1985	95	229	394	1.205	54.694	55
1987	73	227	407	1.268	55.299	42
1988	61	215	416	1.161	53.026	39
1990	49	209	404	1.095	57.109	-

a CO_2 emission values do not include emissions from wood burning

Source: Calculations by the Federal Environmental Agency (Vienna 1992), incorporating diverse specialist literature.

threat arising from the adverse effects of greenhouse-gas emissions Austria has signed the 1992 climate convention in Rio, which had been negotiated in the context of the UNCED preparatory process.

3.2 Water Resources

1.6 percent of the Austrian territory is covered with water. Austria's overall water requirement is about 2.6 billion m^3 p.a., or 333 m^3 per inhabitant. The industrial water consumption is 1.5 to 1.7 billion m^3/year, that of the agricultural sector is around 0.2 billion m^3/year. For the end of this decade, the following per capita daily consumption volume is envisaged: private consumption 100 l, industry 200 l, and agriculture 40 l.

Over a ten-year period, the contamination of running water in Austria by biologically degradable materials from industry could be lowered from 70 million to 2.7 million population equivalents.

Although Austria's water supply — because of its geographical situation and climate — is (still) satisfactory, the status of subsoil water is endangered due to chlorohydrocarbon and domestic sewage. In spite of this fact, the pollution of Austrian rivers from the industrial sector has been reduced by 85 percent. Similar results were obtained for Austrian lakes, which are once

TABLE 20.2

Balance of Industrial Contamination
of Running Water

Industrial Sector	1979 PE^a (Mio)	1989 PE* (Mio)
foodstuffs and semi-luxury foods	5.0	1.0
chemicals	1.0	0.2
textiles	0.5	0.1
cellulose and paper	9.0	1.2
other	1.5	0.2
Total	17.0 (= 100%)	2.8 (= 15%)

a   population equivalent

Source: National Report of Austria for UNCED, Vienna 1992, p. 7.

again of high quality. The breakthrough in implementing water pollution control was achieved primarily by the creation of public subsidies models.

Hydro-electric power is a major source of power production in Austria, its share in the overall domestic energy production (coal, oil, gas, etc.) has risen to approximately 60 percent. In 1988, its share in the total primary energy consumption lay around 15.2 percent.

3.3   Forests and Landscapes

Approximately 46 percent of the Austrian territory is covered by forests. In the early 1980s like in other European countries forest damage was observed on a large scale. This was mainly connected with effects of air pollution. National data on the state of treetops in Austria's forests have been available only since 1985. In spite of temporary recovery in the late 1980s the percentage of trees with average and considerable damage has remained high, especially in years with dry summers.[10] In 1993 according to ECE crite-

---

10. Cf., among others, the annually published reports of the Austrian Federal Environmental Agency. For an overall view cf. Werner Katzmann and Heinrich Schrom (eds.), *Umweltreport Österreich*, (1st ed.), Vienna (1986) and Marina Fischer-Kowalski (ed.), *Öko-Bilanz Österreich*, Zustand – Entwicklung – Strategien, Vienna (1988).

ria 8.2 percent of trees were damaged. 36.9 percent of trees were slightly defoliated. This cannot be interpreted as damaged but as a warning stage.

Similar tendencies have been observed in the cases of soil, fauna, and flora. In terms of both its composition and health, the soil is threatened by many sources. Among the dangers are: appropriation of land for construction; industry and transport development; entry of noxious materials; and agriculture and forestry mismanagement. The destruction of and changes in the biosphere, caused by the intensification of agriculture and extension of housing, transport, and industrial areas, as well as by the pollution of air and water bodies, have resulted in increasing danger to animals and plant species. Over 4,000 plant species have been placed on the red list of endangered plants, and over 10,000 animal species have been classified as endangered. Considering the transboundary dynamics of the loss of species' variety Austria has signed the convention on bio-diversity at the Rio Conference. So far the convention has not been ratified.

3.4 Transport

Austria is of central importance for the European economy and transport because of its geographical position between two EC states. She is also an important transit country between Eastern and Western Europe and a highly frequented tourist area.[11]

Since the 1970s, transportation over the Alps has grown quickly, indeed more rapidly than the growth of Austria's domestic product. As can be seen in Figure 20.2, growth is almost exclusively from the increase in private cars. The share of the railway decreased from 71 percent of the volume of goods in 1970 to only 31 percent in 1987.

The growth of international transport flows and the limited number of available routes in the Alpine region due to the precipitous topography have resulted in extreme forms of pollution.[12]

---

11. The problems of Austria as a highly frequented European transit country in the north-south and west-east axis are best analyzed in Helmut Koch and Hans Lindenbaum (eds.), *Überrolltes Österreich. Zukunft unter dem Transitverkehr,* Vienna (1991).

12. The special problematique of the western federal countries of Austria can be found in Hubert Sickinger and Richard Hussl (eds.), *Transit-Saga. Bürgerwiderstand am Auspuff Europas,* Vienna-Munich (1993).

3.5 Waste

During the eighties, the waste situation in Austria was characterized by a
shortage of space available for dumping and, simultaneously, by a decreasing
acceptance among the population of new landfills or waste treatment plants.
44 million tons of waste are produced annually. In order to reduce or prevent
waste, the Waste Management Act and a Federal Waste Management Plan
were recently enacted. On the basis of the Waste Management Law, ordi-
nances have been issued to regulate waste prevention through retrieval and
utilization of packaging waste, batteries, accumulators etc., or through separate collection of waste from construction materials as well as biogenic
waste. To guarantee the correct treatment of waste, the import and export of
waste is subject to governmental approval. The Austrian government holds
the view that a problem-oriented waste policy should also take into account
the international dimension. Although there is increasing resistance to make
deposits available on a local or national level, transboundary transfer of
hazardous waste should be limited to the minimum. For this reason the Basel
Convention was ratified in 1993.

FIGURE 20.2

Transit Transport of Goods on Austrian Rail and Roads
(1970–1991)

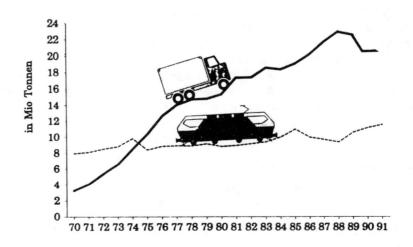

Source: Federal Ministry of Public Economy and Transport, Vienna 1992.

4. Main Characteristics of Austrian Environmental Policy

Most of the Austrian political measures that have had an impact on the environment in the postwar period have been supply-oriented. This can best be seen in the massive investment in road transport infrastructure which contrasts sharply with the very limited investment in rail infrastructure. Thus road transport dominates as the cause agent of most of the destructive emissions. Special environmental problems arise in ecologically sensitive regions such as in central zones of the cities, along transit routes through the Alps as well as in the preservation of protection forests, which constitute one third of the total forest land and therefore play a vital role for Austria.

The main characteristics of the Austrian environmental policy include the following:

A major role for public authorities: most environmental expenditure[13] came from public sources in the 1970s and 1980s. Such a high percentage of public subsidies can be a constraint on further private investment. Today industrial environmental investment is higher than public expenditure.

Implementation deficits: in some fields (like waste deposits) environmental damage is a result of disregard of regulations and norms, although regulations exist.[14]

A minor role in economic policies: so far environmental policy has focused mainly on governmental programs, legislation, and subsidies. Economic instruments, such as emission charges and fines (or energy taxes) are discussed, together with environmental regulations and standards, in order to promote technological improvements and — in the long run — structural economic changes, to lower the costs of environmental protection, and to provide incentives for the conservation of resources.

Weak organization of environmental concerns: a major problem of environmental policy is due to the organizational imbalance between environmental polluters and the public interest in environmentally sound development. The interests of polluters in "soft" measures are more specific and much easier to organize than a diffused public interest in the status of the environment.

---

13. 75 percent of the environmental expenditure stem from governmental sources, cf. Harry Glatz, "Österreichische Umweltpolitik im Überblick," *Politische Bildung* no. 3 (1989), p. 4.

14. Cf. Lauber, op. cit. (footnote 5), pp. 564.

Active international involvement: the resistance of the Austrian population in 1978 to use nuclear energy led to a negative evaluation of this technology. Following an initiative of the Austrian Chancellor, Franz Vranitzky, the Austrian government pursues an active nuclear policy in promoting a nuclear power free zone in Central Europe as a first step toward a global abandonment of the use of nuclear energy.[15] The fundamental changes in Europe could offer new possibilities for regional cooperation, at both the private and political levels.

5. Conclusions

The Austrian case of environmental policy shows no great differences compared with other Western European countries. Like the others it is confronted with a steadily degrading environmental situation, and improvements in emission figures are only partial. No systematic attempts have been made so far to introduce ecologically acceptable technologies and production processes on a larger scale.[16] But the overall record of the Austrian environmental situation is still comparatively good. Austria, a small industrialized country with rather well-established economic and political infrastructures, thus fits well into M. Jänicke's[17] and V. Prittwitz' (cf. Chapter 4 of this book) "capacity approach." Its long-term *economic performance* is surprisingly good.[18] Its technological, material, and institutional possibilities for applying environmental measures are well established. Austria's *innovative capacity* may be not as high as that in comparable countries like Switzerland or Sweden, but its high position on the scale of world-market integration gives strong impulses for innovation. In addition, public innovation funds have

---

15. The conditions in the nuclear power plants in Austria's eastern neighboring countries have been described in "Angst vor dem Osten. Schwierige Nachrüstung von Reaktoren," *Folio of the Neue Zürcher Zeitung* (NZZ), Folio, June 1993, pp. 7–12; Austria's environmental policy toward the former socialist countries of Eastern Europe is discussed in a diploma thesis by Martin Kaspar, *Österreichs umweltaußenpolitische Beziehungen zu Mittel- und Osteuropa,* Vienna (1993).

16. Cf. Jänicke, op. cit. (footnote 4), p. 71.

17. Cf. Martin Jänicke and Harald Mönch, "Ökologischer und wirtschaftlicher Wandel im Industrieländervergleich. Eine exploratorische Studie über Modernisierungskapazitäten," in M.G. Schmidt (ed.), *Staatstätigkeit,* (special issue no. 19 of the Politische Vierteljahresschrift), Opladen (1988), pp. 389–405.

18. Cf. Helmut Kramer and Otmar Höll, "Österreich in der internationalen Entwicklung," in Herbert Dachs et al. (eds.), op. cit., (footnote 5), pp. 50–69.

been established. The *strategic capacity* which refers to the ability to implement comprehensive and long-term objectives and also leads to a high endowment of authorities with well-defined powers in the environmental sector is insufficient. Important environmentally relevant competences are distributed over a number of ministries and regional parliaments; the environmental ministry — with little financial resources and a small staff — still lacks competence and does not have organizational power. Austria's *consensual capacity* is traditionally high. Being a typical small industrial country, the degree of corporatism between the representatives of capital and labor in collaboration with state authorities is high. But the cooperative policy style that in the past had a great impact on the positive Austrian record toward world market integration[19] has so far not been flexible enough to systematically consider environmental interests. In periods of weak economic performance (as at the beginning of the nineties until now) environmental concerns usually play but a minor role in political decisions as well as private investment. So the overall outcome is more or less ambivalent: social partnership has enabled environmentally sound investments as far as they seemed to be economically significant in a short term perspective — in 1990, 2.7 percent of the Austrian GDP were spent on investment in environmental protection, more than half of it came from public sources — but has been a strong obstacle for necessary structural environmental changes in the whole economic fabric.

Considering the extent of environmental damage in Austria, which is, according to estimates[20] at least 6 percent of the Austrian GDP per annum, the public authorities for the past two decades have tried to control environmental damage by legislative regulation and subsidies. Structural changes have not been applied. The motivations and horizons of the public authorities are often constrained by their own interests in power and their close involvement with economic interests.[21] In most of the cases, end-of-the-pipe technologies were installed, although the concept of clean technologies, which is by far the most profitable form of environmental protection (because of their preventive and structural effects), has assumed top priority among scientific and some governmental institutions. The

---

19. Cf. Otmar Höll and Helmut Kramer, "The Process of Internationalization and the Position of Austria. Problems and Current Development Trends of the 'Austrian Model'", in Otmar Höll (ed.), *Small States in Europe and Dependence*, Vienna (1983), pp. 184–219.

20. K.-J. Hartig, "Clean Technologies – Strategien der öffentlichen Wirtschaft," in *Gemeinwirtschaft* 4 (1989), p. 31.

21. Especially in cases where environmental competences are safeguarded by authorities with primarily economic orientation, such as the ministries of economy, finance, and transportation.

industrial sector has been reluctant to adopt a new generation of technology, which is not surprising.

However, many of the Austrian problems are transnational and can only be solved within international cooperation. These problems include acidification of soil, lakes, and forest damage due to air pollution; pollution of rivers and lakes; deterioration of air quality in cities and industrial areas; and problems created by traffic (especially but not only) crossing the Alps. All of these problems are of transboundary nature, and most of them are relevant for Europe as a whole. It still remains unclear whether the European OECD states will consistently follow a path of sustainable development. Nevertheless, one thing is certain within the next decade; Austria — due to its integration ambitions — will develop an environmental policy that is strongly influenced by the EC. International cooperation and agreements have already been concluded but must be extended and their implementation must be more vigorously monitored in the future.

About the Contributors

Christer ÅGREN

Dr., Director of the Swedish NGO-Secretariat on Acid Rain, Göteborg.

Markus AMANN

Dipl.-Ing., Dr., Head, Transboundary Air Pollution Project, International Institute for Applied Systems Analysis (IIASA), Laxenburg.

Maria BERRINI

Architect, Presidente Istituto Ricerche Ambiente Italia, Milano.

Jan C. BONGAERTS

Dr., Director, Institut für Europäische Umweltpolitik, Bonn.

Michael BOTHE

Professor of Public Law, Dr., Faculty of Law, Johann Wolfgang Goethe University, Frankfurt.

Bo R. DÖÖS

Professor, Ph. D., Chairman of the Society on Global Environmental Management, Vienna.

Irene FREUDENSCHUSS

Dr., Minister-Counsellor at the Austrian Mission to the UN, New York.

Gerhard HAFNER

Professor of International Law, Dr., Head of the Division of General International Law, Federal Ministry for Foreign Affairs, Vienna.

Peter HARDI

Dr., Ph.D., Senior Fellow, International Institute for Sustainable Development, Winnipeg, Canada.

Otmar HÖLL

Univ.-Doz., Dr., Austrian Institute for International Affairs, Guest Professor of Political Science, University of Vienna.

Robert HULL

B.A., M.B.A., Adviser to the Director General of the Environment Commission of the European Communities, Brussels.

Tapani KOHONEN

Dr., Counsellor for International Affairs, Head of the International Affairs Division, Ministry of the Environment, Helsinki.

Winfried LANG

Professor of International Law and International Relations, Dr., Ambassador of Austria to EFTA, GATT, the United Nations and their Specialized Agencies in Geneva.

Volkmar LAUBER

Professor of Political Science, Dr., Ph.D., LL.M., University of Salzburg.

Peter Cornelius MAYER-TASCH

Professor of Legal Theory and Political Science, Dr., University of Munich.

Georg POTYKA

Minister, Dr., Head of the Division on International Environment Protection and Bilateral Nuclear Matters, Federal Ministry for Foreign Affairs, Vienna.

Volker v. PRITTWITZ

Univ.-Doz., Dr., Gesellschaft für Politikanalyse, Berlin.

Peter H. SAND

Associate Professor of Law, Dr., LL.M., Legal Adviser, Environmental Affairs, The World Bank, Washington D.C.

Gunnar SJÖSTEDT

Dr., Swedish Institute for International Affairs, Stockholm.

János VARGHA

Dr., President of ISTER, East European Environmental Research, Budapest.

Franz VRANITZKY

Dr., Federal Chancellor of the Republic of Austria.